BEYOND
THE
SAND STORM

FROM BAGHDAD TO PHILADELPHIA

My dear Neighbour Suzan
Great to know you.
I wish you abundant health,
joy & prosperity.
Malka Al Saadi
10/5/19. Free Library of Phil.

Malka Al Saadi

authorHOUSE®

AuthorHouse™
1663 Liberty Drive
Bloomington, IN 47403
www.authorhouse.com
Phone: 1 (800) 839-8640

Published by AuthorHouse 08/30/2016

ISBN: 978-1-5246-1970-1 (sc)
ISBN: 978-1-5246-1968-8 (hc)
ISBN: 978-1-5246-1969-5 (e)

Library of Congress Control Number: 2016911969

Print information available on the last page.

I have no country to fight for; my country is the earth, and I am a citizen of the world.

Eugene V. Debs

Dedication

To those who enriched my life and helped turn it into a delightful mosaic painting: My family, friends, teachers, patients and students.

Acknowledgments

The first spark of this project was brought to life by my sons. Mutaz was the first to suggest writing a memoir and Mohammed encouraged, advised and financed; both worked effortlessly to improve the content throughout the process. I would like to heartily thank Mark I. Wolfson and Donna Cicalese, SSJ for their valuable comments and grammatical corrections in the manuscript.

My daughters Afaf and Abeer and my sister Amal share the credit of reminding me of many interesting incidents. I am grateful to my siblings Najiha, Kawkab, Dawood and Mohammed, cousins Thamira and Ali for their indispensable efforts in providing me with family photos from what was left after looters violated the sanctity of my home. My second cousin Rasa'il and friend Azhar were the doves that carried the "olive branch" from Baghdad to Philadelphia, so I can finally find peace with the remainder of the photos they brought to me. My dear friend Dr. Cecile Ibrahim provided me with comfort in those agonizing nights following the bad news of the house break-in; her soothing words encouraged me to continue with the project. My utmost thanks go to my graceful friend Madeleine Segal Marx for her diligent help in providing worthy suggestions and advice despite her own busy schedule and obligations.

A special appreciation is extended to Tim Graham whose expertise restored the old damaged photos and Jack Brauer for providing the cover photo. I am immensely grateful to Iraqi photographers: Mohammed Al-Dhamat, Ahmed A. Hadi, Yasir Muhsen, Bilal Ameer, Belal Dhafer Saleh, Abdulwahab Khaled, Ali Bader, Ashraf Issa, Mazin Jawad and Iraqi Artists Mahmoud Fahmi and Nadia Osi. Last but not least, my thanks to all the professionals at Author House who participated with dedication to get the book published.

Map of Iraq illustrating main cities – Courtesy of wwww.d-maps.com

Introduction

Columbus Day, October 11th 2010...

We moved to a lovely neighborhood amidst Pennypack Park in the far northeast of Philadelphia, PA, 16 months after we arrived in the U.S.

I was making room for the new furniture to be delivered from "United" at Franklin Mills, when I fell from the stairs leading to the basement and broke my ankle. A few weeks earlier, I had paid a visit to the office of the Educational Commission for Foreign Medical Graduates (ECFMG) in order to process credentialing my medical degree, which would make me eligible to practice medicine in the States. I was thrilled to see a senior officer check out my records confirming the results of the exam I successfully passed in 1967. Knowing that I was going to be wheelchair bound for over three months, I gave up on the entire idea, and opted to confine myself to the walkout basement where I fell. Since setting foot (an un-fractured one) in the states, Mutaz had suggested to me several times to start writing my memoir, but I did not heed his advice until the day I fell. I started thinking, "is all this a coincidence?". Maybe God had other plans for me instead of pursuing the continuation of medical practice while in my 70s, a process that is both time consuming and expensive, and with no guarantees. Maybe this fall was meant to be, but why on Columbus Day? A day marking Christopher Columbus' arrival, and discovery of America? Was this a sign to start my own journey on paper? Over the next few days, my mind was processing thoughts faster than I thought possible. A thousand ideas rushing into my head, competing for attention.

I spent most of my time alone, looking outside the glass door onto the forest. When you're caught alone in such circumstances nature starts talking to you, and indeed the sound was loud and clear. The natural beauty of the forest is breathtaking in Autumn, such a gracious time of the year that is best called “Awesome” with the leaves beautifully changing color like a harbinger rhythmically whispering to us “Christmas is around the corner”. The color change is nothing but the elegant lights decorating the Christmas tree. Ironically, these falling leaves are just like the days of our lives; once they fall they become merely “memories” yet still ingrained in them is a story to tell. The agile migrating birds crowded in the sky make me contemplate for a minute, what makes them leave their “home country” and fly far away to a strange land? Isn’t it in search of a better livelihood for their hatchlings? Isn’t it an inherent right of birds and humans alike? Don’t these birds bring beauty and power, through diversity, to their new land? Does all this ring a bell, as big as the striking Liberty Bell in the heart of Philadelphia, reminding us of the great American Independence and its core values?

It was during this time that I decided to write my book. Unlike my academic articles, this was personal, it was emotional, and I was on a mission to tell my story, despite my broken foot and lashing osteoporosis. At first, I started jotting down my scattered memories sporadically, collecting momentum and ideas with time. I indulged with Mutaz in a mother-son team. In addition to writing my own story, we collaborated in searching, checking, comparing and often translating hundreds of websites, listening to family members telling their own side of the story, re-writing and refining the script over and over. Initially, Mutaz suggested having the book edited by a professional, but I wanted to maintain its originality in an attempt to paint an honest picture, a true reflection from the heart, even though my mother tongue is not English.

I was born in Baghdad, “the City of Peace”, in 1941 and spent my early childhood in a Jewish neighborhood. I finished my primary education in a Christian neighborhood and enjoyed the diversity and harmony of Iraqi culture. At 17, I entered the Iraqi college of medicine, and lived through the heart of the events following the 1958 revolution. In 1976, I had the opportunity to study and practice medicine in the United Kingdom. When I returned to Iraq in 1981, my country was at war with neighboring Iran. Lasting 8 years, it became the longest in modern history. Less than two years after the war ended, Iraq invaded Kuwait and lost the ensuing war against a coalition of 32 countries who fought to liberate Kuwait. Iraq was then subjected to sanctions by the United Nations Security Council that culminated in its occupation in 2003. The unprecedented violence in the aftermath of the war and subsequent sanctions left Iraq at rock-bottom. Like millions, we left our dear ones and fled for our lives, and being more fortunate than most others, we were blessed with a new welcoming home in the City of Brotherly love-Philadelphia. Out of respect for privacy, I have altered the names of some characters mentioned in the book.

DAUGHTER OF IRAQ
1941-1958

A Queen is Born

I was born on 27 February 1941 to a middle-class couple that had been longing for a child for nearly a decade. Their education was modest but they were smart, natural intellectuals, raising six children who all became successful: three medical doctors, a university professor, a chemist and a statistician. I was received with cheerful delight not only by family members and relatives but by neighbors, Muslims and Jews alike. My father was the only son of his parents to survive to adulthood and my aunt Khairiya was their only surviving daughter. Dad's first marriage failed after four years mainly because of childlessness. His second wife, my mother, had to wait another four years to be blessed with a first child. Greetings and gifts varied. Our Jewish neighbors and friends shared the joy by tailoring hand-made embroidery. Simha fashioned hats with satin pink ribbons *(Gawriya),* Farha made a large triangular cloth to wrap a baby's torso and limbs *(the Gimat),* and Gurjiyya tailored a long, white embroidered satin vest that I wore even when I was four years old.

My paternal grandmother named me Malka even before I was born, after her daughter's name. This was my aunt who sadly departed this world before enjoying her 14th birthday. It is an old Arabic name that can be pronounced Malaka, meaning talent or Malika, meaning queen. I was the only one I knew named Malka through all my years of study. I met several Jewish friends in the United States who told me they are familiar with the name, as they had aunts or relatives bearing it. In a happy coincidence, 68 years after being named Malka, I got to see a city pronounced similarly to my name, the mesmerizing city of Malacca in Malaysia, but that's yet another bed-time story to tell. Our household consisted of my parents, my paternal grandmother, and my recently widowed aunt Khairiya with her two sons, Mohammed Saied and Sultan, who all moved from Bab al-Agha to live with us.

Jidoo's Family

Jidoo, Arabic for grandfather, was from a conservative Baghdadi family. He was a construction foreman and business owner, well-known for his expertise in building architectural arches, following in the footsteps of his father. Grandpa Dawood (David) generously did repair work for widows and orphans for free in his spare time. My dad's grandfather Salman Al Mulla, Arabic for religious teacher, was so-called not for having a religious profession but rather for being honest and faithful. He was a devoted follower of Sheik Abdul Kader Al-Gailani (A Sufi cleric from the 11th century). Grandfather was a tall bulky man, with a dark complexion, wide hazel eyes and a strong personality.

My grandmother Najma was petite with a fair complexion, amber eyes and rosy cheeks, and blessed with a pleasant smile despite being toothless. She was from a wealthy family that owned several properties and bazars in east and west Baghdad. Grandmother didn't inherit anything though, because while her father was away making pilgrimage to Mecca, her two brothers turned all their father's assets into endowments for males only. A pilgrimage trip would take months in those days.

Iraqis adore sleeping on rooftops in the summertime. Unlike western-style roofs, Iraqi roofs were flat and surrounded by relatively high walls. Grandfather was a kind husband and a gentle man; he used to carry his wife Najma up and down the stairs to the roof when going to bed. When grandmother sat outside her house, the neighborhood kids would playfully joke with her asking for apples, because of her rosy cheeks. I was 11 years old when she passed away at the age of 90, but I still remember her deep kindness and calm demeanor. Grandmother would argue with my parents when they took me to school, fearing that studying might exhaust me. On the other hand, she would shout at me when I would put on her tiny shoes and run into the yard.

My father was a tall, slim, man with a wheat-colored complexion and almond shaped bright eyes, full of tenderness but also a firm resolve. My mother had a matching complexion; she was short with a curvy figure, a well-defined face, and wide hazel eyes. She had a Baghdad boil (leishmania) on her left cheek, a skin lesion caused by a parasite and spread by a sand fly bite. She used to curl her thick dark hair and apply fragrant oil after her daily bath. Her teeth were always whitened with walnut tree bark (*Deyrum*). As with most arranged marriages, my parents did not meet before the wedding. It was a tradition that the bride's family would sew several long sleeping gowns (*Dishdashas)* for the future husband-to-be. When my mother saw my father's clothes, she was astonished at how tall he was. Another tradition was the arrival of the *hamla*, a delivery of the bride's belongings, including clothes, sheets, ornaments and other collectables, to the husband's house some days before the happy day of the wedding. My father was very pleased to smell the freshness of my mother's perfume in the *hamla* and thanked his mother for her suitable choice of bride.

My father, Salman Dawood Al-Saadi, 1937

My Mother's Family

My mother, Salima Saleh Al-Hakeem, was from a deep-rooted Baghdadi family. Her grandfather owned an herb store in the al-Dahana district of Baghdad, and so he was called Al-Hakeem (healer). He had no blood relation to the well-known Al-Hakeem family of clerics, some of whom are now members in the Iraqi government. Mother was orphaned at a very young age. In World War I her father was drafted into the army, fighting against Hungary, Russia, Britain and France. At that time Iraq was occupied by the Ottoman Empire, which is modern day Turkey. Grandfather Saleh shared the ghastly stories he lived through while at war. One story was about when food was so scarce the soldiers cut their boots into small pieces to make a broth, and another even worse was when there was no water and they drank their own urine. A short while after returning from the war, Saleh became bed-ridden and died, leaving behind my mother Salima, uncle Abid and Aunties Na'eema and Noriya.

It was customary that if a woman became widowed, her brother-in-law would marry her to insure the children were raised within the family. Keeping to this custom, Mom's uncle Naji married my grandmother Najiba. Later on they had three other daughters, Ghaniya, Sadiqa and Sabeeha. Naji lived a very successful life manufacturing water tanks and selling them to the government. He also built a mansion surrounded by orchards in Karrada district. This district later flourished and became one of Baghdad's most up-scale neighborhoods. Everything comes at a price though; as his wealth increased he chose to marry a second wife who bore him more children and this meant more responsibility and more mouths to feed.

Forty Neighbors

The house that witnessed my birth was inherited by grandpa; he rebuilt it in its same Baghdadi style. My father and aunt Khairiya then inherited it, with two thirds for Dad and one third for my aunt, according to Islamic law. The house number was 31/148 in the (*Faraj Allah) Agd Al Yahoud* – the Jews' quarter in central Baghdad. It was like most houses in the forties and fifties, with an open yard in the center surrounded by rooms and other facilities. The ground floor had two elevated rooms (*Tabga*), each of which covered a basement *(Sirdab)* and faced spacious slates (*tarar*) supported by robust wooden pillars (*dalag*). The second floor had two bedrooms, the bigger one with several windows overlooking the central yard, and the second room overlooking the street. The roofs and widows were wooden and the floor was paved with elegant square brick blocks.

A few weeks after my birth, a revolution led by Prime Minister Rashid Ali Al-Gailani against the pro-British Monarchy erupted in Iraq (May Revolution). My mother would hide my crib under her bed during the British air strikes that supported the Monarchy. The war lasted one month, In the aftermath Al-Gailani escaped, Iraq was reoccupied and Prince Abdul-Ilah came back to power. Baghdad was torn with violence, with looting and crime targeting the Jewish community for openly showing support for the monarchy. Needless to say, our neighborhood being a predominantly Jewish area suffered a big share of the chaos. The sad thing was that honoring neighbors was of great value among Iraqis, yet these shameful acts were committed by ruthless thugs. Prophet Muhammad's teachings are to respect, protect and help neighbors. A "neighbor" is not just the one next door but includes all those up to forty houses in all directions - effectively a whole neighborhood.

My father, my Cousin Mohammed Saied, our neighbor Kadhum Rammao and his son Jawad guarded our Jewish neighbors. They were armed and dressed in Arab costumes so no offender dared to approach.

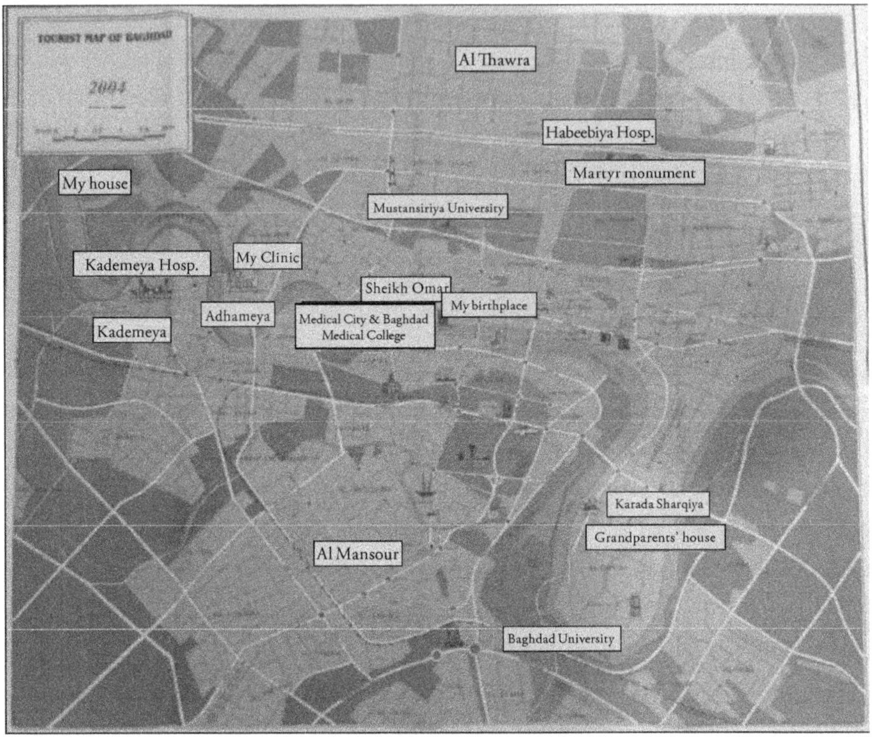

Mapping my Baghdad memories

Do Not Argue with a Bee

My mother got married before celebrating her 20th birthday. This was regarded as a late age for marriage, and both her two-year and five-year younger sisters were married before her. To their credit young girls those days were great housewives and successful mothers, looking after large households, and often with little means. Arabic food is labor-intensive. A typical housewife was expected to home-make almost everything. She would cook, bake bread and pastries, make vinegar, pickles, jam, rose water, tomato paste, dates syrup, dry vegetables and prepare dairy. Sewing, embroidering, cleaning, and attending to her husband's, in-law's and children's needs were an additional chore. Not all girls were lucky to get an education at school in those days. Household appliances were mainly manual until the mid-fifties and laundry was done in a big basin (*Tashit*) using a large block of soap. Pressing clothes was done by a heavy coal-heated iron, wheat bran was used for washing dishes, and the traditional cooking stove was heated with oil, resembling a slow cooker in functionality. A cube-shaped bar of bay oil soap was used for hair washing. This was mainly imported from Aleppo, Syria and was completely natural, giving a heavenly pleasant aroma. Clay *(Khawa)* was used for hair conditioning. Natural clay, called Bentonite, was known by the early Romans for its many health and cosmetic benefits. Lux and Palmolive soap brands were available for hand and body washing. Walnut tree bark (*Deyrum*) was used for teeth whitening and lip coloring. Eyeliners and blushes were home made from herbal mixtures. With all that said, those working bees truly deserved not to be argued with by their spouses, though ironically the culture remained male-dominant.

The way houses were built meant that people were close to one another, and socializing often occurred freely on roof tops. Building was mainly with bricks or mud bricks (sun dried), with timber roofs topped with palm leaf matts or plywood. During the fifties roofs were replaced by iron rods with bricks and eventually by concrete. The wooden windows were also replaced by iron and later by aluminum. Toilets were squat-style with the toilet pan at floor level. By the sixties most houses had western toilets with bidets. Occasionally, a snake would dangle from the wooden ceiling due to the open-space architecture. It was regarded as wrong to harm these snakes as they were called "house snakes" and were left alone.

Charcoal iron – Courtesy of Ali Al Marieh and www.mstaml.com - Arabic Internet Market

"Return of the storks" A painting by Iraqi artist Mahmoud Fahmi (courtesy of artist)

No Camels Just Flying Carpets

As far as I can remember there were all kinds of cars in Iraq. Although privately owned cars were scarce, there were taxis as well as the old wooden buses. Two-story red elegant government-owned buses became available in the late forties. One of my exciting memories is riding in a horse-drawn cart (*Arabaneh*), which we sometimes used to take from our house in central Baghdad to my aunt's in Ewadhiya. It was open, allowing the fresh cold air to sweep along our youthful skin.

One of the most distinctive old water-transport means was the *Quffa*, a round boat made of weaved reeds and pomegranate twigs and coated from both sides with Asphalt. First used by the ancient Akkadians, the design remained the same for thousands of years. it is believed that Moses' mother used a smaller version of it, laying him on the Nile River to escape Pharaoh's royal death sentence. Speaking of boats, it is also believed that Noah's Ark came to rest on Mount Judi in northern Iraq.

The first car to enter Iraq came in October 1908, traveling from Aleppo through the western desert. Iraqis came out to look at it; some were looking underneath the car in an attempt to see the horse that was pulling it, as they were only familiar with horse driven vehicles. The car belonged to a famous Scottish merchant, David Forbes, whose family owned a business of importing and selling licorice from Syria to Europe and the U.S. This vehicle's arrival coincided with the building of a railway between Baghdad and Istanbul, Turkey by the Germans. A few people thought that Forbes' car was the train Iraqis were excitingly waiting for. One of the city's wealthiest people, Hamdi Baban, bought the car and thus was the first Iraqi to own one.

Iraqi Airways was one of the earliest airlines in the Middle East, founded in 1945. The logo of the fleet is of a swallow bird in flying motion; these birds are excellent flyers reaching speeds of 217 miles per hour. Southern Iraqis welcome them to nest in their houses and consider them good omens, as do sailors at sea where their appearance means they are close to shore.

An Indian colleague whom I met in Malaysia in 2008 thought that Iraqis rode camels for transportation until even today, and that girls are not allowed to attend school. Despite the world becoming like a small village where access to all sorts of information is affordable, lots of people still have misconceptions about the Middle East. If you often make generalizations, you might as well believe in flying carpets.

From Cradle to Grave

Sending children to school became mandatory by the late fifties in Iraq, yet the legislation was enforced only after the mid-seventies. Regardless, most parents were keen to see their children get a proper education, especially in

Baghdad and large cities. The culture in Iraq attaches much importance to attaining knowledge, and that it is considered one of the superior deeds in a person's life. One of the most famous sayings of the Prophet in this aspect is: "*Seek knowledge from cradle to grave*". Moreover, the first revelation of the Quran starts with the word "*Read*" – *Surat Alalaq*. Education in Iraq is free for all, including primary schools, secondary schools, universities or higher studies. Elementary schools are usually coed; high schools are exclusively gender-specific, while colleges and universities are mixed, with one exception - Queen Alia College, that was later re-named "College of girls". There were private schools before the 1958 revolution; these were abandoned by law until the nineties, when private institutions were re-established on a fairly wide scale. On the governmental level, Iraq has not witnessed any gender discrimination related to education.

University studies were available only in Baghdad, where there were separate colleges of medicine, dentistry, pharmacy, engineering, science, literature, law and high school teaching. In 1959, Baghdad University was established and incorporated all the existing colleges and added several others.

Farmers in ancient Iraq sanctified Mother Earth as a pregnant woman. Throughout Iraqi history there were queens and popular female figures. In modern Iraq there are countless names of women who excelled in science, art, literature, architecture and business. A few examples include Maria Theresa Asmar, an Assyrian Chaldean author and traveler, born in 1804 in Tel Keppe, Iraq, was the author of "Memoirs of a Babylonian Princess". During the nineteenth and twentieth centuries several others carried the torch of civilization. The first school for girls was established in Iraq in 1908; many women in aristocratic communities created women's organizations and participated in building modern Iraq.

The first female Iraqi doctor was Dr. Anna Suthian who graduated in 1939 from the American University in Beirut. The first female Iraqi lawyer was Sabeeha al Sheikh Dawood who graduated in 1941, followed by Ameena Al Rahhal, who was also the first woman to drive a car in Baghdad, in 1936. Both were graduates of the Iraqi Law school. Naziha Al Dulaimi (1923-2007), a medical doctor, became in 1959 the first female minister in modern Iraqi history and in fact the first of the entire Arab World. Nasik Al Malaika (1922-2007) was an Arabic poet considered by many to be the most influential contemporary Iraqi female poet. Iraqi born architect Zaha Hadid had been one of the most renowned engineers in the world; she received the Sterling Prize in 2010 and 2011. In 2012 she was made a Dame in Britain. Zaineb Salbi, an Iraqi-American and dedicated human rights activist, entrepreneur and media commentator, started in late 2015 to host *Nidaa* (The Call of Women), a talk show similar to the famous "Oprah" show, mainly featuring famous Arabic women. Oprah Winfrey is Zaineb's executive producer for the show and was the first guest to be hosted. Zaineb founded "Women for Women International" at the age of 23 and is the author of "Between two worlds". Being the daughter of Saddam Hussein's private pilot, she had a lot to tell from heart to heart. The list goes on for singers, painters, actors and scientists.

Eat as You Like, Dress as People Like

There is an old Iraqi saying that goes in line with what the British say "style breeds success". In Baghdad and in the big cities, European-style clothing for women and men has been the norm for the majority since the forties. Some men used to wear special headdresses (*Sidara*) as a formal fashion accessory especially in Baghdad and big cities. The (*Yeshmagh)* and (*Iqal)* head dresses were also used by many while some remained bare-headed. Elderly ladies cover their hair with a black silk shawl. A large number of women used to wear a black, full-length outer garment (*Abaya)* in the presence of men that are not husbands or kin they are forbidden to marry (*Mahrams)*. This has been gradually abandoned altogether by most women since the sixties, with the exception of wearing them when visiting holy cities. In fact, women in Iraq traditionally had more freedom than in other countries in the region. However, since the Gulf War their situation has become increasingly worse, the H*ijab* became popular in Iraq only in the nineties after 1991 war. Wearing trousers was not favored by Iraqi ladies and this is still the case in some conservative communities. Christian women in villages around Mosul dress in long gowns of bright colors and a cloak tied over one shoulder; on their heads they wear veils and beads over a small turban with a band of gold coins. Traditionally, Kurdish women, especially the young, wear colorful and heavily embroidered clothing. Older women wear darker colors and more gold accessories because when women get married they would receive a dowry of gold gifts from their grooms, and the amount of gold pieces a woman wore reflected her status amongst other women in the society. Kurdish men wear baggy pants with a plain shirt having full sleeves. Vests are worn over the shirt and the head is covered with a turban. The costume is often completed with a dagger worn at the waist.

Traditional Arabic attire; Left to right Abdul Wahab wearing Yeshmagh & Iqal, Malka, Dr. Alia and Dr. Sameer Haddadin who is wearing sidara- Baghdad wax works museum photography shop in 1997

You May Step on the Bride's Foot

One of my early childhood memories was my uncle Mohammed Saied's marriage. The bride was Karima, my father's cousin. Endogamy was common, and arranged marriages were the norm though not mandated, as the decision has to be mutual between the two families. My uncle prepared a gorgeous bedroom and sitting room. This didn't mean much to the family, as the main concern was how much gold he could put up to secure their daughter's future. In addition to the wedding dress with its accessories, there were party dresses, day and night costumes, Abaya, sleeping gowns, cosmetics and shoes. My mother had the privilege of choosing the seamstress, Marsel, who was our Jewish family tailor, well known for her artistic hands. I remember her residence near al-Ferdous Circle (renamed al-Nahdha later) at King Ghazi Street.

The groom was honored at a dinner party with all male guests at our big house. It was a tradition for the groom's father or father figure to honor the occasion in this way. My mother and all the aunts were cooking the entire day. The party tables were glowing with fancy Iraqi meals like *Dolma* (vegetables stuffed with rice and ground meat), *Kubbat Halab-Allepo's Kubba* (a torpedo-shaped or round fried croquette stuffed with ground mutton), *Kubbat Burgle* (cracked wheat) made by one of the family's Christian friends from Mosul), *Beryani* (seasoned rice and meat), *Qoozy* (whole roasted lamb), and different *Tabsi*s (fried veggies with meatballs). The sweets menu included *Mehallabi* (milk pudding) and *Halawa* (sweat dense confections), besides the favorite *Zalabia* (deep fried flour in pretzel shapes) and *Baklava*.

Left to right: Beryani rice, Kubbet hamudh, Chicken Tabsi, Dolma, Falafel, Kubbet Halab and Lahma b'ajeen

I also witnessed the religious wedding ceremony of my cousin Sultan in the early fifties. The bride, Fatima, was also a relative. It was celebrated at her brother Mohamed's house, which had been recently bought from the Iraqi Jew Dr. Dawood Nesim who had left Iraq for Israel. The invitees were women, as the men were with the groom in an adjacent room. A 5-foot embellished lighted candle decorated the entrance. The bride was sitting on a chair with her feet immersed in water perfumed with rose water, which was made locally by instilling roses in boiling water. She sat facing a large tray in the center of the room containing a plate of henna and Myrtle surrounded by seven other plates, each filled with white-colored edibles like sugar, yogurt, white sweets, white rice, and *Minasama*. The Quran was laid open on the table, open to the page which read: "*And one of His signs is that He created mates for you from yourselves that you may find rest in them and He put between you love and compassion; most surely there are signs in this for people who reflect*" (Surat al Roum 21). The traditions of religious Muslim weddings are a mixture of religious and cultural rituals, and haven't changed much for hundreds of years. The guest who was deemed the happiest in her marriage would rub two cloves of *Nabat* (Rock Candy) on a white handkerchief held over the bride's head, wishing her the same luck and happiness. The marriage forms would only be signed after a well-heard affirmation of acceptance by the groom as well as the bride. The bride is not supposed to say "I do" until having heard the message repeated several times by the *Qadhi* (religious official).This was a sign of her timidity which was expected and appreciated. After that the bride would start kissing all the women one by one while receiving a gift from each - either money or a gold ornament. At the conclusion the guests are sprinkled with rose water before leaving.

The time between the actual marriage and this ceremony would vary from a few days to several months. The night before marriage is celebrated as "Henna Eve" by both parties, each at his or her parents' house. Before leaving, the guests put henna on their palms after the celebrated couple has done so.

The big day celebration takes place at the bride's home with a ladies party full of leisure, dancing and singing. Refreshments or a meal are typically served. The groom comes from his dinner party to take his bride home accompanied by friends and relatives in a cheerful demonstration, lighted with large candles, traditional music and dancing.

One of the voluntary traditions involving only the bride and groom is foot-stepping. It is said that whoever remembers to step first on their spouse's foot on the wedding day would gain dominance in their marriage life. For me and Abdul, we both forgot to step on each other's feet and shared our dominance.

Wedding tray- Courtesy of Drs. Shahad Abdulameer and Layth Abdulrasoul

Welcome Ramadan

The month-long observance of Ramadan is of great significance to Muslims. It commemorates the month when God (*Allah*), through the archangel Gabriel, revealed the first verses of the Quran to Prophet Mohammed on *Lailat al-Qadr* (*the Night of destiny* which is said to be more worthy than 1000 months of worship). A sighting of the new moon signals the beginning of the month according to the lunar calendar. For the entire month Muslims refrain from food and drink between dawn and sunset. Mother used to wake up well before dawn to prepare the pre-fast meal (*suhoor*), usually consisting of rice and lamb meat, fruit juice, followed by tea. After saying our prayers, we would go back to bed. School and work start as usual but end an hour early. In preparing for (*Iftar*), the breaking of the fast at sunset, the typical family table is always full of a variety of delicious foods. The most popular starter is lentil soup, after eating several palm dates. A sighting of the next new moon signals the end of Ramadan and the beginning of the Festival of Breaking the Fast (*Eid al-Fitr*), when people dress in new cloths, pass along holiday blessings to each other and enjoy three days of goodwill and get-togethers.

Before the *Eid* prayers all Muslims have to give away the alms of *Zakat al-Fitr* to those less privileged (approximately 10 US dollars for each family member including newborns). This is separate from Zakat, which is the third pillar in Islam whereby people donate 2.5% of their annual savings to those in need. Ramadan wasn't observed in churches but the spirit of Ramadan is indeed in line with the teachings and blessings of the church, and some Christian friends would fast a number of hours with us in Ramadan or even invite us over for Iftar. Out of respect, the majority of Christians would refrain from eating or drinking in front of us. Some Muslims would occasionally go to a church, offer vows to the Virgin Mary and light candles while saying a little prayer. I so much miss those days.

A blend of authenticity - Zalatimo Baklava from Jordan

Kleitcha– National cookie of Iraq flavored with cardamom and rose water

Trick or Treat

One Ramadan tradition that children have great fun with is "*Majina*", the Iraqi Equivalent of Halloween. Although it has similarities, there is no connection with horror or the origins of Halloween. It is also observed in several Arab Gulf countries under different names like *Qarge'an* in South East Saudi Arabia, Kuwait, Bahrain and Qatar, *Hag Al Layleh* in United Arab Emirates and *Qaranqshaw* in Oman. Every alley bustles with excited children dressed in traditional attire going door-to-door, calling at all neighborhood houses and singing "*Majeena ya Majeena, hilly el-chees wanteena*" meaning open the sack and give us – just as in Halloween, they are given sweets. If the household is too poor to give something or they simply don't open the door the kids would sprinkle drops of water by the house entrance as a sign of wishing them blessings. Traditionally, the kids would sing while playing small drums but nowadays that is less observed. The song goes like this:

"Majina" Oh "Majina"...
Open the sack and give us
Are you giving to us? Or we are giving to you?
We will take you to the house of Mecca (Kaaba)

If the household is late in opening the door for the *Majina* kids, it's presumed that the family is resting on the rooftop so they would sing:

"Oh people of the roofs are you giving us something, or should we leave?"

If the father or father figure opens the door and gives something, the kids will close by singing:

God bless the head of this household
By the Grace of God and his prophet Ishmael

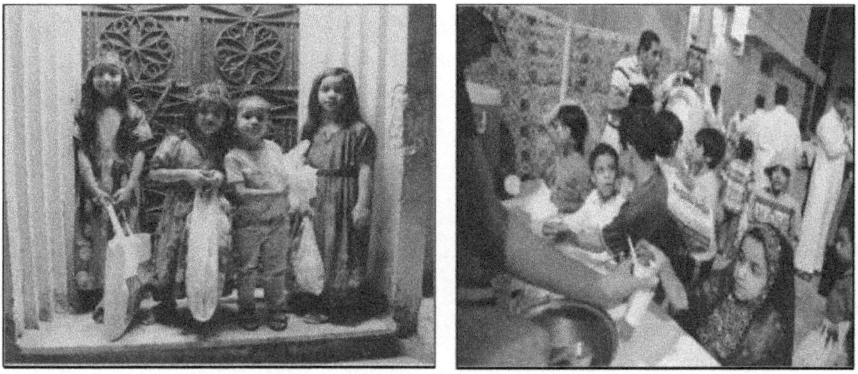

Majina (Qarge'an) in Saudi Arabia- Courtesy of Barakbits.
com- "Good News from the Middle East".

A blessed-cursed Nation

Iraq is a bit larger than California and smaller than Texas. It is located southwest of Asia, northeast of the Arabic peninsula and is bordered by six countries: Turkey to the north, Iran to the east, Jordan to the west, Syria to the northwest and Kuwait and Saudi Arabia to the south. Iraq is floating on a sea of oil, ranking third in oil reserves, only behind Saudi Arabia and Iran. However, oil is merely one of its many treasures. Iraq's history dates back to 5000 BC. Its strategic location in the Middle East was part of the Silk Road, an ancient network of trade and cultural transmission routes through regions of the Asian continent connecting the West and the East. Two abundant rivers, the Tigris and the Euphrates, made it part of the fertile crescent. It also has a diverse climate and topography, as well as rare minerals – it has the seconds largest phosphate reserve in the world after Morocco. All of these are Iraq's curses and blessings. Al-Iraq, in the literature has different meanings: "shore of a great river with grazing land", and "country with deep roots". Mesopotamia, Greek for "land between two rivers", is the land which makes up present-day modern Iraq.

Many great civilizations have prospered in this land, and ultimately turned to dust. Over the centuries Iraqi people have been decimated by countless wars and epidemics; cities have been built, destroyed, and restored again, just to be destroyed again, and rebuilt....

Iraq is second after Israel to be the nation most often mentioned in the Bible, though it is mentioned using several other names, like Babylon, Land of Shinar, and Mesopotamia. Many prophets roamed this land. Between the Tigris and Euphrates rivers, near Qurna in south Iraq, grows a sacred ancient tree called Adam and Eve's Tree; here is the place where God told Adam and Eve *"In sorrow shalt thou eat of it all the days of thy life" (Genesis 3:17).* Abraham was from Ur. Noah (*Nooh*) was from Tel Fa'ra. Jonah (*Younis*) was commanded by God to preach in Nineveh. Job (*Ayoub*) lived 20 years in Iraq. Enoch (*Idrees*) was born in Babylon. Ezra's tomb (*Uzair*) is in *Maysan.* Ezekiel's tomb, (*Thul-Kifl*) is also in Babylon. Additionally, many Muslim sacred mosques are distributed all over Iraq, including Imam Ali's shrine in Najaf, Imams Al-Hussein and Al-Abbas in Karbala, Musa Al-Kadhum and Mohammed Al-Jawad in Kadhimiya, Ali Al-Hadi and Hassan Al-Askari in Samarra, Abu Hanifa in Adhamiya and Abdul-Kadir Al-Gailani in central Baghdad.

Since its beginnings, this land has produced many inventions to benefit humanity. To name a few, the first known form of writing (cuneiform), the wheel and the iron plow were all invented in the land of Iraq. Sumerians excelled in mathematics; they were the first to codify square and cubic roots. The Code of Hammurabi contained laws that covered all levels of human interaction and became the basis of modern law. Neo-Babylonian (Chaldean) scholars postulated the existence of planets and the division of the day into 24 hours, the division of an hour into 60 minutes, and of a sphere and a circle into 360 degrees. The Epic of Gilgamesh is often regarded as the first great work of literature dating from the third dynasty of Ur (2100 BC). The Assyrian king Ashurbanipal created the first library in history with thousands of clay tablets. When Alexander the Great saw its remains he was inspired to create his own library, but died before implementing the idea. King Nebuchadnezzar II in 600 BC built the hanging Gardens of Babylon. Of the many great scholars and scientists who lived in Baghdad was Al-Khwarizmi who wrote several math texts, ten of which have survived. The name "algebra" is derived from the title of his book "*Kitab al-Jabir wa al-Muqabalah.*" When western Europeans received translations of one of his math texts and saw the author's name, they called him "Algorismus" as a Latinized version of his given name. Modern mathematicians and computer programmers still use the term "algorithm."

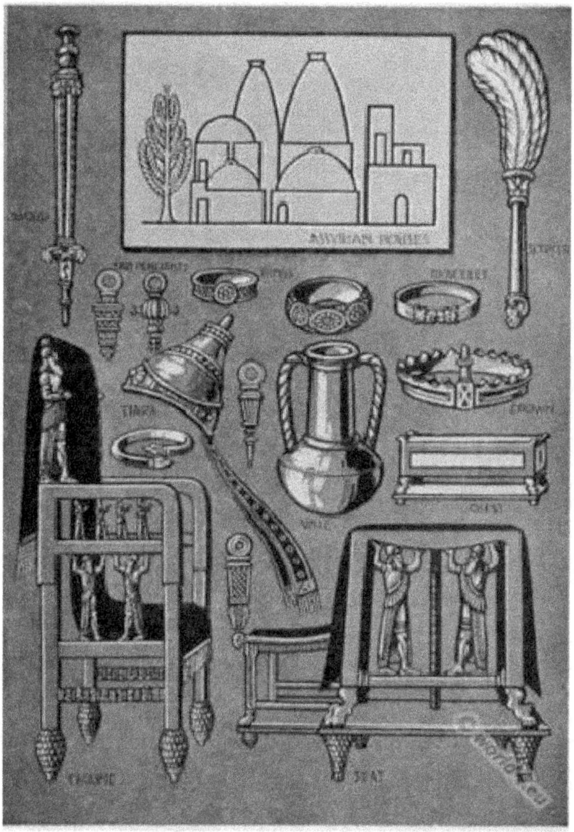

Assyrian furniture, jewelry and weapons- Courtesy of world4eu – costume and fashion history

Ziggurat of Ur 2100 B.C.
in Southern Iraq

Iraq, history and civilization – Courtesy of Ashraf Issa

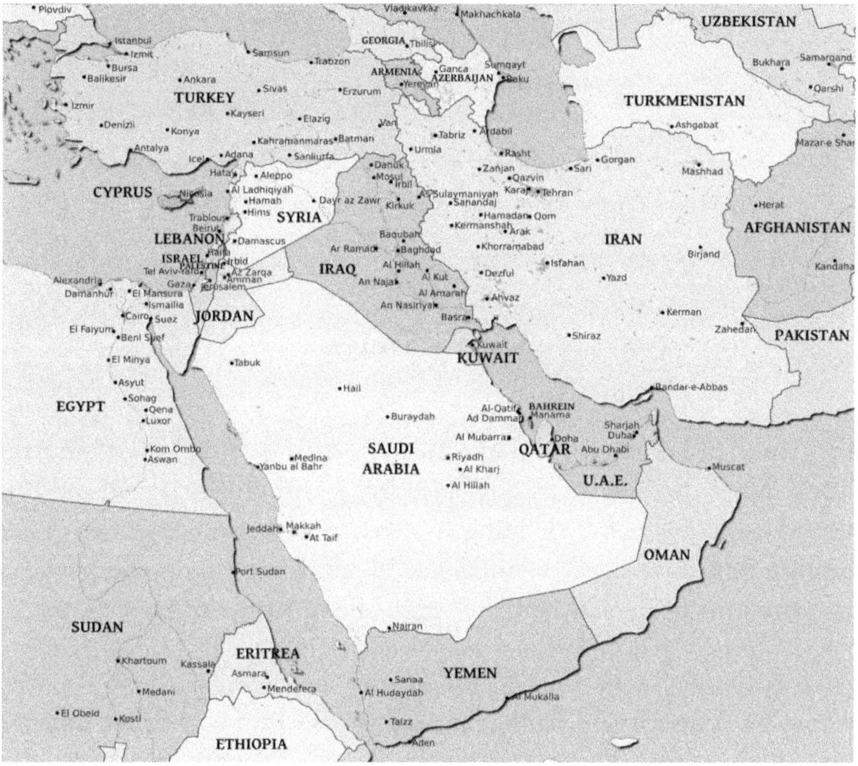

Political map of Middle East

Palm trees in Basrah- Courtesy of "The Blessed Tree" magazine and Dr. Ali Afifi Ali, Author of: "Date palms of Iraq in voyagers' books"

Lion's Share

The Ottoman Empire ruled Iraq with an iron fist from 1534 to 1917. After World War I the Empire was defeated by the Allies who signed the 1916 Sykes-Picot Agreement, dividing its territories between themselves and creating respective zones of influence. Great Britain won the power of mandate over all Iraq at the Conference of San Remo in April 1920.

Faisal I, the son of Hussein-Sharif *Mecca* was chosen as the future king of Iraq by Winston Churchill, the then British Prime Minister, and was crowned on August 23, 1921. When Iraq came under the British Mandate on April 25, 1920, Iraqi nationalists were not satisfied with the Anglo-Iraqi Treaty and they demanded independence. In June, 1930 a new treaty (The British Mandate of Mesopotamia) was signed by Prime Minister Nouri Al-Sa'eid, which was effective for 25 years. Before granting independence to Iraq, the 1930 treaty gave power to the British to establish military bases overseeing their interests in Iraq - one in *Shi'aba* (*Basra*) and the second in *Habaniya* (*Anbar*).

The League of Nations admitted Iraq on October 3, 1932. With this the British mandate officially ceased but not British influence. King Faisal I died mysteriously on September 1, 1933 in a Swiss hospital. His son Ghazi I assumed the throne and reigned for six years. Although educated in England he held a deep hatred for the British and the feeling was mutual. King Ghazi had sympathies toward the Germans, and also articulated that Kuwait is part of Iraq. He died in a suspicious car accident on April 3, 1939. His son Faisal II was too young to take over so his uncle Prince Abdul-Ilah became regent.

In January 1941 there was political unrest in Iraq and a civil war was imminent.

Regent Abdul-Ilah was informed of a plan for his detention and managed to escape. In April 1941 Prime Minister Rashid Ali led a successful coup against the monarchy and established a new government which was not recognized by Britain. Consultations between British leaders resulted in a decision to bring troops from India to Iraq, and the British moved in on Baghdad on May 27. Rashid Ali was defeated and fled to Germany with other members of his government and the regent was reinstated.

The Notorious Farhud

When Prince Abdul-Ilah came back to Baghdad from his exile on June 1, 1941, a festive crowd of Jews crossed over the west bank of Tigris River welcoming him and celebrating the occasion. They were attacked by some military and paramilitary individuals and were soon joined by civilians. Anti-Jewish riots soon spread throughout Baghdad, especially on the east bank of Tigris, where most of the Jews lived. By nightfall, a major, shameful pogrom was underway. The rampage of murder and plunder in the Jewish neighborhoods and business districts continued until the afternoon of the following day, when the regent finally gave orders for the police to fire on the rioters, and he brought Kurdish Peshmerga in to maintain order. In the Farhud, 179 innocent Jews were killed, 242 children were orphaned and 586 businesses were looted. The total property loss was estimated by the Jewish community's own committee to be around 680,000 pounds sterling.

The Farhud resulted in a split between the young Jews and their traditional leadership. The new generation turned in two different directions: one joined the Communists and the other joined the Zionists. Both were underground movements. Two of the young Jews reached the top ranks of the Communist Party and were hanged in 1949. The General Assembly voted in favor of a partition of Palestine on November 29, 1947 increasing tension between Arabs and Jews in Iraq. The authorities then started to oppress the Jews. The most important effect which shook the Jewish community to the core was the hanging of Shafiq Adas, one of the wealthiest Jews in the country, right outside his house in Basra on September 23, 1948

By the Rivers of Babylon

The Diaspora of Iraq was one of the most ancient of the Jewish people. Samaria, the capital of their northern kingdom fell to the Assyrians in 555 BCE and the Kingdom of Israel came to an end. The Kingdom of Judah in the south, including Jerusalem, survived the Assyrian threat and lasted another hundred and fifty years until it fell to the Babylonians. Jews were taken as captives to Babylon after the destruction of their first temple where they integrated into the land of their captivity and took on an important role in economic and cultural development.

Official Iraqi statistics, based on the 1947 census, put the total number of Iraqi Jews at 118,000 or 2.6% of the total population of 4.5 million. During the years 1948-51, over 100,000 Jews immigrated to Israel, with several thousand others leaving to other countries; only 6,000 Jews remained in Iraq after the mass immigration. Back in 1869, when Midhat Pasha carried out the Vilayat System, he appointed a prominent Jewish leader, Menahem Daniel as a council member of Baghdad. Daniel was also elected to parliament and this became a precedent which was followed later by the election of Sassoon Eskell to parliament. In 1832 Midrash Talmud Torah was founded in Baghdad, which continued its activity until the mass immigration in the mid-twentieth century. In 1840 a religious academy, Yeshivat Bat Zilkha, was founded. By the 1920's numerous schools had been established, mostly by Jewish philanthropists which were maintained by both the Jewish community and by regular contributions from the Iraqi government. Jewish students began attending universities in Iraq and abroad after World War I. Government schools were open to Jews as well as to other religious and ethnic minorities in the 1930s when Iraq became independent. There was no restriction to the number of Jewish students in government schools and colleges. A considerable number of prominent Jewish writers and poets emerged, whose works in Arabic were both well-known and well regarded. Among them were the poet and historian Meir Basri and the poet Anwar Sha'ul. Jewish journalists contributed to the Iraqi press and occasionally wrote for the Arab press outside Iraq. Salima Murad, an Iraqi Jewish singer was nicknamed "Pasha", a title only given to high-ranking government officers as a form of high appreciation. She was married to one of the most popular Iraqi singers in the Arab world, Nadhum Al Ghazali who was Muslim.

Iraqi Jews excelled in the medical field; three of the well-known doctors still remembered by Iraqis are Drs. Dawood Kubbai, a general practitioner and pediatrician, Gorgy Rabee, a physician with a high British degree and Jack Abboodi, a professor, neurologist and psychiatrist. They all graduated from the Iraqi Royal College of Medicine. Dr. Kubbai, a 1938, graduate worked in Amarah -- some 200 miles south east of Baghdad. He was loved by the people there as a philanthropist as well as a doctor. He treated the poor free of charge, and even paid their pharmacy bill if needed. When he moved to Baghdad, weekly trips from Amarah to Baghdad were arranged for his patients who refused to see other doctors. He was jailed in 1969 and fled the country after being freed to continue his career in London. Dr. G. Rabee continued his practice in Iraq until the sixties when he left to Israel and was honored by being given the key of the City of Jerusalem for his medical services there. Both Kubbai and Rabee were the attending doctors for several members of my family. Dr. J. Abboodi was the best in his specialty and to him goes the credit of building a special hospital to treat mental illnesses.

King Faisal I had good personal relations with individual members of the Jewish elite through his twelve-year reign. He appointed Sir Sassoon Eskell as his first finance minister, who insisted on the British Oil companies to pay the price of Iraqi oil with gold instead of any other currency. There were four Jewish representatives in the Iraqi parliament; the number increased to six in 1946. In the senate Menahem Saleh Daniel represented the Jews, and after him his son Ezra Daniel. After July 1958, during the rule of Abdul Karim Qasim, the Jews enjoyed full rights of equality and freedom just as other minorities did. During Abdul Salam's rule and the following Ba'ath era, the Jews suffered oppression and harassment. In 1969 Al-Baker ordered the hanging of several young men who were Muslims, Christians and Jews, on the verdict of being spies to Israel, in al-Tahrir Square in central Baghdad. After the incident most of the remaining Jews left Iraq.

"Rivers of Babylon", a song performed by Boney M. in 1978. The song is based on the Biblical Psalm 137:1-4, a hymn expressing the lamentations of the Jewish people in exile following the Babylonian conquest of Jerusalem. The namesake rivers are the Euphrates and Tigris; it goes like this:

"By the rivers of Babylon, there we sat down, yea, we wept, when we remembered Zion...

They carried us away in captivity requiring of us a song... Now how shall we sing the Lord's song in a strange land?

Let the words of my mouth and the meditation of my heart, be acceptable in thy sight here tonight"...

Courtesy of Charles G. Gosselink quoting Oliver Butler, author of "Iraq Photographic Studies"

John the Baptist

Mandeans (also called Sabeans) are a little known sect even though their prophet, Yahiya, played an important role in the early history of Christianity. Yahiya, or Youhana, is none other than John the Baptist, who baptized Jesus in the river Jordan. There are 150,000 Mandeans today, of whom 15,000 lived in Iraq until the recent troubles in the country after the 2003 invasion. Baghdad's Mandean temple (*Mandy*) is located in the stylish neighborhood of Qadisiya, not far from the Tigris. At the top of the temple gate, stands the Mandean's distinguished cross (*Darfash*) made of two myrtle twigs, covered with what is believed to be John's garments.

Most of the Mandeans who lived in southern Iraq ended up in Baghdad.

The Mandeans are led by a "sheikh." The sheikh officiates every Sunday, surrounded by his assistants. In the courtyard, grooms and brides waiting their turn adjust their ritual dress (Rastas) for the ceremony. After applying water and sesame oil to the young couple's foreheads, the sheikh puts a sprig of myrtle in their hair as a symbol of the soul's immortality. He offers the groom a bowl of holy bread and a bowl of water, while the bride waits in a nearby room. Women of the community will have tested her virginity; soon her husband-to-be joins her along with their two families. The couple is seated back to back and the priest touches the heads of the couple and lightly brings them together. The ceremony ends in the waters of Tigris, where all the participants submerge their bodies in water as a form of purification. Mandeans do not eat pork, and their respect for life forbids them from eating most female animals. Besides fish which is their favorite food, they can also eat chicken and mutton, only after having thoroughly washed the animal before slaughtering it. The Priesthood is handed down from father to son. The Mandean calendar begins in April, Yahiya's birth month. The year is divided into twelve months of four weeks each. The main religious holiday is Panja in April; it lasts five days during which families stay at home to celebrate with each other. Aside from their religious life, the Mandeans are completely integrated in the Iraqi society.

Over the centuries, the Mandeans have mastered the craft of goldsmithing, and many of them work in this traditional vocation as artisans. They have also produced professors, artists, doctors, engineers and poets. Lamia' Abbas Amara and Abdul Razzaq Abdul Wahid are talented poets loved by all Iraqis. A well-known Sabean scientist was Abdul Jabbar Abdullah (1911–1969) an Iraqi wave theory physicist, dynamic meteorologist, and President Emeritus of Baghdad University during the late fifties and early sixties. He was one of four students to be taught by the famous Albert Einstein. In order to humiliate him, the Baathists fully shaved the renowned scientist's head, put a leash around his neck and tied it next to a bunch of scabby dogs. They also broke the "Parker" pen that was given to him by Albert Einstein. making him burst in tears. Dr. Abdulla earned his Doctor of Science degree from the Massachusetts Institute of Technology in 1946, before being appointed head of the Iraqi Teacher Association and then chairman of the Department of Physics of the College of Education in Baghdad. In 1952, he became a visiting research professor in meteorology at New York University, and in 1965 he joined the National Center for Atmospheric Research as a scientific visiting scholar. He later held professorial and research posts at the University of Colorado in Boulder, and the State University of New York in Albany. One of our Sabean friends who welcomed us in Philadelphia is Dr. Tahseen Al-Saleem and his family, an Anatomic and Clinical Pathologist affiliated with Temple University, whose son-in-law, Dr. Firas Al-Saidi was one of my medical students in Baghdad.

Mandean wedding rituals, Sabean cross (Darfash) on left

Christian Iraq

St. Thomas, the doubting apostle, brought Christianity to ancient Mesopotamia in 33 AD. He was one of the 12 apostles of Jesus Christ and was informally called *doubting Thomas* because he doubted Jesus' resurrection when first told, (in the Gospel of John), followed later by his confession of faith, "My Lord and my God", on seeing Jesus' wounded body. History indicates that Thomas came from the Syrian city Edessa (present day Urfa in Turkey), accompanied by two more Christians, Mar Addai and Mar Mark (Mar in Aramaic means Lord) to establish the Assyrian Church of the East. The church gained strength and spread from the Assyrian city of Erbil in northern Iraq to neighboring countries including Egypt, Greece and North Africa. Later it spread to China, India and Europe. Early Mesopotamian Christianity was Semitic linguistically; Aramaic was spoken in Syria and Palestine as well as in the Assyrian and Chaldean Empires.

The story of Sheikh (Mar) Matti is quite interesting. The Assyrian King of north Mesopotamia, Sennacherib (not to be confused with King Sennacherib who lived from 704-681 BC), was infuriated to learn that his son Behnam along with his daughter Sara and 40 friends of Prince Behnam went to see Sheikh Matti seeking a cure for Sara's leprosy, a disease that no one could cure in those days. When Sara was cured, they all accepted Christianity and were baptized by the Sheik. After returning home, the king beheaded them, after which he left his palace wandering in the fields screaming as loud as he could that he failed to keep the kingdom under his influence and control. The queen was mourning the loss of her children, until Behnam appeared in her dream asking her to bring Mar Matti to heal his father. The queen begged the king to agree and he eventually heeded her. After being healed by Mar Matti's prayers the king asked him to be baptized along with his friends. He also asked his people to accept Christianity as the official religion of the country. Before that incident, Mar Matti and many monks were hiding from the king in caves carved in the mountains just outside of Mosul. One can still see these caves all across the face of the mountains. When the Arabs defeated the Persians and invaded Mesopotamia (part of which is modern Iraq), in the seventh century; they were warmly welcomed by Nestorian Christians who had already built a prosperous civilization in Mesopotamia. The Nestorian Christians continued to participate effectively in the building and development of modern Iraq. Islam recognizes Judaism and Christianity as religions of God; both Moses and Jesus are considered to be Prophets to Muslims in addition to Mohammed, Abraham, Isaac, Jacob and others. There is one complete *Sura* (chapter of 98 verses) in the Quran named Mariam (Mary), and Jesus's name is quoted 25 times.

The first female Iraqi doctor, Anna Suthian, and the first female graduate from the Iraqi medical school, Malak Ghannam, were Christians. There are countless renowned Iraqi Christian professionals. Examples include Hormuz Rassam, a native Assyrian who discovered the clay tablets that contain the Epic of Gilgamesh, Caloust Gulbenkian, an Armenian businessman and Philanthropist well-known for his many contributions toward establishing major projects in Iraq, Azad Bonni, professor of neurology at Harvard medical school, the beloved singers Seta Hagobian and Afifa Iskandar, Razzouq Ghannam, the famous journalist, the football player and coach Ammo Baba, and last but not the least the well-known Iraqi politician Tariq Aziz who was the deputy Prime Minister and close advisor to Saddam Hussein from 1979 to 2003. The 1987 census in Iraq counted 1.4 million Christians, 8% of total population. They lived mainly in Baghdad, Mosul, Basra, Erbil, and Kirkuk. Christians began to leave in the 1990s when the UN sanctions on the Saddam Hussain regime began to bite into their lifestyles. Statistics are now hard to come by, but it is thought that as few as 300,000 Christian Iraqis remained in the country.

Mar Matti Monastery in Mosul – Courtesy of Ishtar TV

"Afta" the Midwife

My parents did not wait long before welcoming their second daughter Amal, who was born in 1942, followed by Layla in 1943. My brother Dawood, the long-awaited son, was born in 1945.

Dawood's birth was the first memorable event from my early childhood. At the age of four I was allowed to stay in my mother's room while she was in labor, attended by the midwife Afta. Family members were hoping the newcomer would be a boy. Iraqis call the midwife "Jidda" (meaning grandma) as a symbol of love and respect. The birth was greeted with celebratory *Halahil* (Ululations). All present were embracing each other with joy. My response was to bring my savings box and empty all the contents onto Afta's lap. She accepted it and gave me a big hug.

Midwives are paid generously, and are honored with dinner parties on days 1, 7 and 40 after delivering a baby, and are invited to all family events. Jidda Afta was a dear relative of my father, a well-respected figure in the neighborhood and a "grandma" of all the family's children.

To express his devotion and satisfaction of being blessed with a son, Dad promised a religious sacrifice. We paid a visit to Imam Ali's Shrine in Najaf, accompanied by Jidda Afta and some relatives, each carrying a lighted candle. In a couple of touchy moments, Dawood was stripped of all his golden jewelry and pure silk clothes. Everything was donated toward the shrine's maintenance and services. The ceremony took place in the mosque and was concluded by slaughtering a sheep in the outer yard; the meat was distributed to the poor. Dawood got circumcised when he was seven days old, a Jewish circumciser *(Ze'irty)* whose sole profession revolved around performing circumcisions, was called in to our house where he did a perfect job in no time. The family celebrated modestly, even though many Iraqis celebrate this event with a big party including dinner and traditional dancing.

Sitting from left: cousins Amal, Thamira & my sister Amal. Standing from left: cousins Nouri & Fu'ad, Malka and Aunt Sabiha – 1946. Courtesy of Thamira Mohammed Ameen

Stinkweed Dance

Traditional medicine was popular in those days. Home-based care included massage and different manipulations for several conditions. If a baby keeps crying for no apparent reason, they say it is "*Mebrug*" (flopped-back head), and an experienced elder lady will manipulate its limbs into certain positions using olive oil as a lubricant. Then she wraps the child tightly in a cloth, keeping the arms at the sides and the legs straight. When we had a swelling or bruise after a fall, mother used to massage the area with hot oil and put "*Fteraya*" (lump of hot dough) on the area and wrap it. When aspirin would not help Dad's headaches, Mother would massage his neck and forehead, and then cover his head with a square large cotton scarf, tying a ribbon around the head. This was followed by gentle tension on the cloth all around. Unexplained abdominal pain was also relieved the same way by massaging the abdomen in circular movements followed by exerting negative pressure on the umbilicus using a special small glass. Tattoo and cautery were other methods for treating chronic pain in some rural areas. It was quite common to see patients with chronic abdominal pain have several scars on their abdomen from previous burn treatments. When I was around ten, my thyroid became slightly enlarged. I was taken to Jidda Afta as a first measure, and she applied burnt grease on my neck and brought a needle in order to prick the site. Noting how scared I was my aunt took me back home, and the next day I was at Dr. Hasan Al-Hasani's clinic to have treatment for my thyroid.

There were herbal stores selling remedies for different medical conditions. Of those, I remember Chamomile from which an herbal infusion was made to treat colds, allergies, muscle spasms, dyspepsia and menstrual disorders. Babies with gas cramps were given Gripe water. Eucalyptus leaves were used in steam inhalations for respiratory problems by clearing the bronchial tree. *Meramiya,* (sage) continues to be used for gastro-intestinal disorders, night sweats and menopausal symptoms, to improve memory and as an antiseptic mouth wash. The only herbal medicine I had seen used by my family was *warid mawi* (herbal borage tea) Mother used to give it to us when we had fever and to adults when they are dejected or nervous. Although herbs are natural remedies, their potential dangers have to be kept in mind, such as overdose, impurities and interaction with ordinary medications the person is taking. Back in the late 90's I was called by neighbors urgently to help a young man who had developed a reaction to an overdose of *Jozat altaib* (nutmeg). After taking what he thought was a very small amount (a tablespoon), he was in a deep sleep and hardly responding.

People used to widely believe in the evil eye and hence had developed practices to counter it. One way was by burning *harmal* (stinkweed) in a fire and then requiring all family members to jump over it, taking turns starting with the most vulnerable to the evil eye. While burning, the plant is known to produce a strong fetid smell which was believed to expel the evil. As children we experienced this with Dad who would sometimes come back from work feeling down and tell mom, "Um Dawood, let's burn some harmal". Another interesting belief was a form of color therapy. When a child was sick with measles they used to dress them in red or even cover them with red cloth; hoping the high energy in the color would protect the sensitive skin from harmful sunlight.

The Big House with Shanasheel

In 1945, Father bought my aunt's share in the family house. He decided to rent it out to Jewish families and move to an upscale neighborhood. We rented a big house in Hitaween owned by a Baghdadi merchant. Our neighbors were mostly well-known conservative families. There were several shops scattered in the area, some schools and a mosque. Our residence was midway between the two commercial areas of Dahana and Sadriya. It was of eastern style with many large ornamental windows (Shanasheel) overviewing the road. We had a nice big basement and four spacious bedrooms. The two walk-in closets hardly ever lacked roasted nuts, dried fruits and pastry. Fresh fruits were purchased daily to be kept in the basement and banana clusters were hung from its ceiling. Iraqi fruits, especially apples, plums, oranges and sweet lemons, have special flavors not matched by any others that I have tasted. There were many sweets stores in Dahana, selling *baklava, zalabia* and *halqum*. *Halawa Khidr Elias* is made especially for Christians to share after their three day Bau'tha fasting, which historically commemorates the repentance of the Ninevites at the hands of Prophet Jonah, according to the Bible. *Min a' sima* (from heaven) is made from *tranjebeen*, a sweet tree sap in northern Iraq believed to be originally sent by God for the Jews during their 40 years wandering in the desert It is also mentioned in the Quran.

Mother was a first-class housewife. The house was clean and tidy all the time, the embroidered sheets were perfectly pressed and utilities well maintained. No one was allowed to put on clothes that were not ironed, including underwear and handkerchiefs, our shoes were always shining, and a daily bath was the rule. Both my parents were strict with our discipline We had to go to bed early and wake up early, wash hands before and after meals, start our meal with praising the name of Allah and thank Him after finishing, respect our elders, and be kind to the youngsters. The wise elders used to say, "discipline is more precious than a son."

Our bread was homemade. A lady used to come to our house to bake it after mother had prepared the dough. One time the lady didn't show up and the dough was going to be spoiled. Mother decided to do it herself and ended up with small thick bread discs that we declined to eat. But dad encouraged her and after that, a baker she was. A few weeks later we all enjoyed delicious thin bread from Mother's hands. We did not have the traditional built-in baking facility. Instead our baking vessel *(tannour)* was kept inside a metal barrel with wheels, and Mother would move the barrel into the yard for baking and take it back to the kitchen after it was done. Breakfast was the most interesting meal for us, consisting of sesame-covered pastry called "window of lovers" (*shubbak al- habayib)*, as it resembled a window in shape We used to have it with tea milk. Eggs were usually served half-boiled. During weekends we had cream (*qaymer)* with honey or jam. Another favorite was broad beans with soaked bread, flavored in lemon juice with dried *(butnij)* betony -- a relative of the mint family. On top of the dish were added fried eggs, or *hareesa,* which is made by cooking whole wheat grains with meat until it forms a thick soup. One of my favorite dairy products was r*oba* – a yogurt made by villagers in round wooden boxes to sell in the city. They would carry it on their heads while walking and singing, "*roba hilwa roba*"- yogurt sweet yogurt.

When we moved to a new house, my aunt Khairiya and her family bought a house in Ewadhiya and settled there. We spent the weekends with them and had the chance to make good friendships with their neighboring children. It was a lovely prosperous neighborhood, and the roads were wooded with eucalyptus and oleander and there was a nice round public park nearby. At our aunt's house, the usual dinner on Fridays was grilled fish, made by aunt Khairiya, and bread baked by her daughter in-law Karima. Many Iraqis cook extra food on daily basis in order to feed unexpected guests, who show up without prior notice. In our household, that was not necessary since Mother would present a full table in no time.

Processions Mourning Imam Hussein (Prophet Mohammed's grandson) on the tenth of Muharrum each year used to pass by our house. Many family members and friends would gather to view the convoys from the *Shanasheel* windows overlooking the road. During these gatherings I got to know many women relatives whom I had heard of but had never met.. Two or more of them came few years later asking for my hand for their sons. Mothers used to look for brides for their sons at different ladies' gatherings.

Shanasheel in Basrah – Courtesy of Bilal Ameer

(Roba) Yoghurt peddler – A painting by Iraqi artist Nadia Osi (Courtesy of artist)

First Day of the Rest of My Life

When I was six, aunt Sadiqa took me to al-Dahana Primary School for Girls. The assistant principal (sit Sa'adya) was impressed with my appearance and after talking to my aunt she remembered her as a colleague in school. To me it was a big honor to be registered in that school. Mother was overwhelmed by the good news, she distributed *khubz al-Abbas,* a wrap of parsley, basil, and other green leaves in fresh Pita bread, to friends and neighbors. Iraqis express their devoted sacrifices in a variety of interesting ways khubz al-Abbas is the simplest and cheapest, others include *Shai al-Abbas,* a ladies' party with refreshments or a meal, and *mewled al-Nebi,* also a ladies' party celebrated with religious songs glorifying Allah and praising Prophet Mohamed. Other sacrifices include slaughtering a sheep and distributing meat to the needy.

My first day of school was overwhelming. I had never held a pen and paper in my hand before When the teacher asked us to write the letter alif (ا), mine spanned the whole length of the paper. After a few days I was one of the best and continued to be the best during all my school years. Al- Dahana primary school was a popular public school in Agd al-Nasara (Christian's quarter). The Central Rahibat (Nuns) School was right next to ours. It was a private school owned and run by the church. I always admired its well-behaved students and liked their olive green uniform with a white starched collar. My school principal (*sit Naiema*) was a capable administrator with a character marked by firmness and tact. The school was clean and well looked after and the dark-colored wooden windows were frequently polished and the glass was seamlessly clean. Public schools were free but we had to buy our own books and stationery, and also had to pay one Iraqi dinar a year to finance the sportswear supplies. Our uniform consisted of a navy blue dress with a white starched collar, and a red ribbon in our hair. The morning assembly was a respected daily routine during which we sang the national anthem under the supervision of the principal and all the teachers. The first 15 minutes in the class were devoted to checking our cleanliness beginning with the nails (had to be clipped short, clean and not polished), hair, underwear and shoes. My second year teacher, a blond haired, calm lady, used to keep her *abaya* (a black silk outer vest) in my desk drawer, an honor that many envied me for. The fourth year teacher used to talk to us about the war in Korea which was going on at the time, warning us about the scourge of wars. Our attitude towards teachers was one of respect and sanctification; we used to memorize the poem of Maruf al Rusafi "stand up for the teacher, graciously venerate him, the teacher is as sacred as a messenger".

The few classmates whom I still remember are: Evon Madhi, a well-behaved, well-dressed Jewish girl who left to Israel in the second year, the two sisters A. and H. Anber, who became gynecologists later on, Inaam Al Atraqchi, the blond moon-faced girl with curly golden hair, and my best friend, Bushra Al Sinjaqly, who had lovely ginger hair and a white face. She too became a doctor and specialized in pathology.

Thursday's assembly was devoted to saluting the flag. I was lucky to get the honor of raising the flag several times each school year. Social events included an annual school party where students presented plays, songs, dances and other activities We also had volleyball and table tennis teams who participated in competitions with other schools.

Palace of Flowers

Before the conclusion of the first school year, demonstrations erupted against the government in 1948. We were in school and unaware of what was going on. Teachers gathered the classes, one room for each grade and read us moral stories with some riddles and jokes. Of those I still remember "The Bundle of Sticks", demonstrating how strength is in unity, and the "Lying Shepard" showing that deliverance is in honesty. We enjoyed an ice cream treat brought to us from the recently opened Palestine Express Gallery. Every now and then one of us was called out to leave the school with a family member. When my turn came I met my father who looked worried and rushed me home. I learned years later that many were killed by the police and more were jailed in the demonstrations. The government fell and a new cabinet came to power.

Amal began school in 1948-1949 and Layla went to school the next year. Two years later Dawood attended al-Fatih al-Jadid, a newly opened coed school. We used to walk some 15 minutes to school together passing through streets that are too narrow for cars, stopping by to buy snacks or stationary. Our most favorite was pickled mango sandwiches from Qeryaqoz, the Christian grocery owner.

I started studying English in the fifth year. Our teacher, sit Farida, was a small-built lady with a pleasant face and wide eyes, and her voice was soft and musical. One of the pupils addressed her with a nickname: "Hello

Ferooda" while passing by the teacher's room. The pupil was dismissed from school for seven days and the punishment was announced on the Thursday assembly. My six-year primary school term ended with the final general exams. I scored a full grade of 100. I was twelve at the time although my looks and actions seemed older; I started to wear an Abaya and learned to tailor dresses for myself and my sisters. Dad bought me a *Singer* sewing machine, I excelled in using it and began to copy the styles displayed at high end stores. My youngest sister Kawkab was born around that time. I gave Mother a hand in caring for her as well as sewing all her clothes.

On December 21, 1950 Queen Alia of Iraq died of a malignant growth in her lower abdomen at the age of 39. She spent her last days in the Royal Palace, *(Qasr al-Zuhoor),* the Palace of Flowers. Her physicians were Dr. Dixon, a British physician, and Professor Kamal Al-Samara'e, who were both staying in the palace during her last days. Her only son, King Faisal II, was 14 and already orphaned, as his father King Ghazi I died in 1939. People were sad for her premature death and sympathized with her son. Hundreds of thousands took to the streets to attend the official funeral that started from the Royal Palace in Harthiya to the Royal Cemetery in Adhamiya. The Palace was altogether abandoned and its flowers faded away, mourning the departure of their queen.

Seasons of Sorrow

The Spring of 1950 witnessed the Tigris river flood, affecting not only inhabitants of flooded areas, but our once financially stable family. The water swept through areas of Baghdad including the Baghdad-Kirkuk railway and al-Karrada al-Sharqiya, the neighborhood where my mother's family lived. My father hired a truck and brought our relatives with some of their belongings to live with us for a while. As children we were jumping in joy to have more family members, especially kids, at our house. The tragic thing was that my father lost his business in the aftermath of the flood. Dad was a middle-man grain dealer; selling his merchandise on credit to small traders, and he too bought on credit. Those traders in the affected areas lost their businesses and homes and so were unable to pay back debts. Dad paid his debts but had nothing left afterwards, so he closed his business and was unable to recover it ever again.

From that time on our life changed. Father did not have a full-time well-paying career, so he struggled to provide a decent living. To add to the hardship, our house which had been rented to Jewish families became vacant when the tenants left for Israel. We found ourselves unable to pay the high rent for the big house we were occupying, so we had to move back to our old house which we owned. There, my sister Layla got sick, and after a struggle with illness and several stays in the hospital she passed away before completing her eighth spring. She had been the most beautiful flower of the bunch. Several months later we were deeply saddened by the passing of our dearest grandma Najma. By that time, we already had two new family members, my sister Najiha who was born in 1948 and Mohammed in 1950. I still remember the day Layla left us When I was on my way home from school a child in the neighborhood told me that my dear Layla had died. I ran home pulling out the red ribbon from my hair with tears washing my face. At home I saw my sister's body lying with her beddings on the floor facing the *Qiblah* (in Mecca), surrounded by sympathizing relatives and friends. At least two of the neighbors brought tea trays each full with boiled eggs, fresh bread, tea, and a hot drink of herbal borage tea (*warid mawi),* which has a mild analgesic and tranquilizing effect. After completing the relevant paperwork, Father came in accompanied by friends and relatives to take the dear body to her final resting place in al-Mantiga near Kadhimiya. Amal and I ran for two blocks after the funeral crying "farewell Layla". One of our Jewish neighbors embraced us with hugs and took us back home. Weeks before my sister's death we used to buy fancy sweets for her from our pocket money, knowing that although she liked them, she was far too ill to enjoy them. Later the school year came to an end. Layla was said to have had very good marks. In memory of my beloved sister Layla, I will list some of the meanings of her name, a few of which are: the ecstasy of wine, moonless night, and a girl born at night. In Hebrew it means angel of the night.

The Earth is Revolving

After five years of renting out our family house, it was in bad shape. My mother put exceptional effort into beautifying it. While cleaning the basement she was bitten by a snake, which was followed by a miscarriage, necessitating hospitalization and blood transfusion. During my mother's stay in the hospital, our youngest aunt Sabeeha was called upon to take care of us. As she was only a few years older than me, I would call her by her given name, but during this time she was tempting me with sweets just to call her "aunt" to prove her authority over the rest of us. After that incident, the home repairs were finished, and the old room and the underlying basement were modernized. Wooden windows were replaced by iron ones, the roof was redone, the brick floor was changed and so was the bathroom.

Although we bathed daily at home, mother used to take us to a public bath on Fridays and we spent most of the day there. We enjoyed that ritual a lot, taking with us all sorts of fruits in a special *tasat hammam*, a globe-shaped silvery metal decorated box. Our clothes were wrapped in an ornamented silk-lined cloth. We each had a luxurious white embroidered quilted napkin to sit on while putting on our clothes. We would also take scrubbing sponges (made of Luffa plant fibers) and pumice (volcanic rock) to exfoliate the dead skin of the soles. The bath we went to was called *Hammam al-Sayid*. It had a large outer hall equipped with many wooden terraces. The inner hall had dozens of alabaster basins supplied with hot and cold water, one basin for each family. There were many private cabins too. The floor was heated, and the whole atmosphere was saturated with perfumes of soap mixed with the aroma of citrus fruits. The masseuses' services included reception and massage, as well as helping with toweling and changing clothes. The bath for men was in the same block and had the same name.

Mother spent her time primarily at home and only went out to visit close relatives or to join the family in paying a visit to holy shrines. We were always with them on these visits. Father did all the shopping, which was brought home by *Faisal*, the young worker at his family's grocery store.

When Dad lost his business, he gave up this task and it became the duty of Amal and me to do the job. Mother would give us half a dinar to buy our daily groceries from the nearby market. We learned to pick the best products and to bargain. As for other requirements like clothing, Mother and one of her sisters would join us to go to the commercial districts of *Souk Daniel* (Daniel's Market) or to *Shari'a al-Nahar* (River Street), the latter of which was famous for the best apparel for women. Dad engaged in a full time job after more than a year with his relative Hussein Nassir, who owned a huge fruit market (*alwa*), leaving home at sunrise only to come back at sunset. Our financial status did stabilize but never fully recovered.

At that time (1950-1951) only a few Jewish families remained in the neighborhood. When our next door neighbor Gurjiyya, was celebrating Sukkoth, Amal and I were invited to share her celebration. The place was well decorated; palm fronds were nesting in the central yard with all sorts of fruits, mainly dried, looking amazingly natural. Sukkoth (the feast of Tabernacles) is a biblical holiday celebrated on the 15th day of the month of Tishri (late September to late October). Sukkoth, plural of sukkah, is a walled structure covered with flora such as tree branches. It is intended to recall the type of fragile dwellings in which the Israelites dwelt in the wilderness after the Exodus from Egypt. Throughout the holiday the sukkah becomes the primary living area of one's home. It is a vacation period during which activities that interfere with relaxation and enjoyment are not permitted, such as laundering, mending clothes, and engaging in labor-intensive activities. In 2015 as I was having a walk in my neighborhood in Philadelphia, my neighbor Myna called me and my son to show us the sukkah in her backyard It was a small wooden structure with a table in the middle, but nothing like the ones I saw in Iraq.

Within one year all the Jewish families in our neighborhood had left for Israel. Some had sold their homes either to Muslim neighbors or to strangers who came from other areas of Baghdad. Many of the new dwellers were Mandeans (Sabeans) from the south of Iraq. They carried many of the Muslim traditions and culture. Some Jewish neighbors did not have the chance to sell their properties; they were frozen by the government and rented to the public. I remember at least three Synagogues in the vicinity -- one was converted to a primary school and the others became markets for selling clothes.

Embrace the Hareesa

The flood of 1950 ruined the house owned by mother's family. A new structure was built to include two units, one was a modern house which was rented to help them financially and the other was an open style house (*mushtamal*) consisting of three rooms, facilities, a large garden plus two paved yards.

The family was accustomed to cooking Hareesa (a soup of wheat grains with meat requiring hours of hard work) during *Ashoora* and distributing it to the needy and to acquaintances. There were three giant copper pots atop a bonfire in the large yard - the cooks were professionals aided by male family members. All my aunts and their families stayed overnight at grandma's house for the occasion, and we would spend the night with other children of the family, chatting and playing. In the early morning, we ate hareesa and helped in distributing it. Mother's family had an enormous garden with three palm trees, two pomegranate trees and several citrus trees, all fruit bearing. The simplest way to describe those fruits was to imagine each fruit as a bottle of juice hanging on the tree, packed with unforgettable flavors just waiting for us to pick it and quench our thirst. The rose shrub was by far the most graceful amongst all the ornamental plants. Not only did its blooming colors give delight to the eye but its aroma was our source of homemade rose water. Aunt Sadiqa was artistic in sewing and embroidery, but nevertheless she did not consider making it a form of livelihood. She sewed for herself and daughter only. Amal and I were lucky to have the occasional dress made by her.

Ashoora Hareesa cooking in Baghdad

Ashoora cooking in Houston, Texas (Courtesy of Shahad Moheddin)

Long Live the King

Faisal II was the only son of King Ghazi I, the second king of Iraq, and his wife Queen Alia. King Ghazi died in a suspicious car accident on April 4, 1939. Some Iraqis accused the British consul for plotting the death, while others accused Nouri al-Sa'eid, the then Iraqi Prime Minister. I was told by family members that demonstrators went to the streets against the perfidious ministry shouting: *"If Faisal was old enough he would have taken his revenge."* Faisal reigned from April 4, 1939 until he was killed with other family members during the 1958 revolution.

As a child, Faisal studied at the Royal Palace with other Iraqi children. As a teenager he attended Harrow School in the United Kingdom with his cousin King Hussein of Jordan. Faisal attained his majority on May 2, 1953, an event celebrated all over the country. I witnessed a ceremonial march with thousands of people standing by the roadside, all the way through al- Rashid Street up to Bab al-Mu'adhum, then to Adhamiya, where the Royal cemetery is located. We were standing near the children's hospital (*Himayat al-Atfal*). The King was standing in an open royal cart accompanied by King Hussein, waving to the crowds with a bright smile illuminating his face. Commencing his rule with little experience, he initially relied for political advice on his uncle Crown Prince Abdul Ilah, and General Nouri Al-Sa'eid, a veteran politician who had already served several terms as Prime Minister.

In 1952 the Iraqi government reached an agreement with the Iraqi Petroleum Company (IPC) to share profits on a 50/50 basis along with other benefits. This agreement was the framework for the dramatic development of the oil industry and a six fold increase in government revenues. At the outset, 70% of the oil revenues were set aside for infrastructure development. A Development Board was instituted and completed many major projects as well as initiating or planning many others. One of the major projects that was completed was al-Tharthar project, which included a dam on the Tigris River, to prevent flooding and to create a reservoir. Another was al-Habaniya project, which served the same purpose on the Euphrates River. Other major projects included: Queen Alia Bridge, al-Aeimma

Bridge, Dokan and Derbendikhan Dams. Cornerstones were laid for the Iraqi National Museum, the Royal Court and the parliament building, the Central Power Station, and residential complexes in west Baghdad. The Dairy Products Factory and Baghdad Broadcast Station in Abu Ghraib were opened, along with scores of other mass projects.

Hastening Faisal's demise was the decision taken by his regent, Prince Abdul Ilah, allowing Great Britain to retain a role in Iraqi affairs through the Anglo-Iraqi treaty of 1948 and later the Baghdad Pact in the mid-fifties, which allied Iraq, Turkey, Iran, Pakistan and the United Kingdom against the Soviet Union. Massive protests were staged against each of these alliances, resulting in the deaths of hundreds of demonstrators and an increasing the deterioration of loyalty to the Iraqi Crown.

The toppling of Egypt's monarch, King Farooq, in 1952 provided an impetus for a similar undertaking in Iraq. Faisal's political situation completely deteriorated in 1956 with uprisings in the cities of Najaf and Hay. Meanwhile the war between Egypt and Israel in response to Nassir's nationalization of Suez Canal only exacerbated popular opposition to the Baghdad Pact and thus to Faisal's regime.

In 1958 Syria joined Nasser's Egypt to form the United Arab Republic, which inspired the Hashemite Kingdoms of Iraq and Jordan to establish a similar alliance two weeks later. This alliance formally became The Arab Federation of Iraq and Jordan and Faisal became its head of state. Soon a revolution led by Iraqi army officers erupted on July 14th 1958. It was triggered when King Hussein, fearing that an anti-western revolt in Lebanon might spread to Jordan, Requested Iraqi assistance. Instead of moving to Jordan, Colonel Arif led a battalion into Baghdad and immediately proclaimed a new republic. The King and royal family were brutally murdered, followed by Prime Minister Nouri al Sa'eid and his son. Alas, Iraq lost a humane, distinguished, and ambitious young king.

King Faisal II and Prince Abdul Ilah at Pasha Ayan's house in Basra in mid 1950's

Courtesy of Ahmed Pasha Ayan

Bringing My "A" Game

From among the many secondary schools in Baghdad, I chose al-Mansur, not because it was the best, but because it was less than 30 minutes walking distance from home, situated in *al-Sinek*, a few hundred meters from al-Rashid Street in central Baghdad. At that time, secondary school studies spanned five years - three years as middle school, and two years as high school – where one could specialize in one of the branches of science or in literature. At the end of the third and fifth years there were national general examinations.

During the first few weeks I experienced difficulties in English lessons, but soon I got over it, and began competing for the highest marks There were three competitors for first-in-class, Fawziya Sadiq, Rajiha Al-Niamey and me. In the end, we alternated being the winners.

Students who got an average of 85% in all subjects were exempted from the final year exams. For single-subject exemption one had to get 90%. Fifth and third-year final general examinations were a must for all students, whatever their marks. I was exempted in Arabic, mathematics, and either chemistry or physics in years 1, 2 and 4.

Our school arranged several exhibitions for students' art work and Handicrafts. One I still remember in detail was an exhibition held at the Hall of Fine Arts opposite the Royal Court in Kesra, an area in north Baghdad, which was inaugurated by the minister of education. Some of Amal's and my work was exhibited.

We enjoyed our walks from school to home with our friends, window shopping at Orozdi back, Naim Naamu, Wartan Martin and Coronet book shops, Zebluk, and Hafid al Qadhi gallery, and passing by Studio Arshak, several movie theatres and the Brazilian Coffee Shop. Occasionally, my friend Amal Al-Saudi and I bought some small things from Orozdi just to listen to the music Shish-Kebab by Ralph Marterie, played at our request.

Left to right, Thamira, Malka & Amal reading together at our old house in 1957

Teachers & school mates at the handcraft exhibition - 1957

Embroiled skirt on left is my work!

Golden Tooth

During the summer holiday in 1955 Amal and I spent a week in the hospitality of our cousin Sultan and his wife Fatima. They had recently moved to Najaf where he was appointed as a manager at al Rafidain Bank there. As we were shopping in the crowded Najaf market Amal noticed a goldsmith, who made tooth templates. She asked Fatima for one. As Fatima did not have children of her own and was fond of us, she agreed. Immediately Amal had her golden tooth template fitted, and when Fatima urged me to have one too, so I did. When we went back home Dad was angry at what we did. After a few months Amal's template fell off, but mine was firmly stuck to my tooth, and a dentist had to remove it with difficulty in 1958.

Baghdad Television Broadcasting commenced on May 2, 1956. It was the first station in the Middle East. King Faisal II sponsored the opening ceremony which was broadcast live. Many Iraqi singers participated in a concert, the most popular of which were: Hdhairi Abu Aziz, Afifa Iskandar and Nadhum al-Ghazali. Sabeeha Al-Mudaris was the first female broadcaster to have her face shown on TV.

My maternal grandma passed away in 1957. She was our beloved active grandma whose life centered on her six daughters and son with their families. We were lucky to have uncle Abed live with us after losing his mother. Uncle Abed was well-educated and a perfectionist. He brought a lot of books for us to read, which widened our education and he conducted poetry competitions for us as well as common knowledge riddles. I remember him as a modern-style Iraqi; his career in journalism gave him a chance to refine his political skills. At one time he was accused of being a communist but was eventually acquitted because of insufficient evidence. Uncle married his first cousin Sajida a few months after moving to our house, they stayed with us for about a year, during which time both of my parents were generous and supportive to them.

In the spring of 1956 I participated in a school trip to Samarra. I had to make an exceptional effort to convince my dad to give me permission to go because we had to spend one night there. Samarra is some 67 miles north of Baghdad on the west bank of the Tigris River. It is one of the four holy cities of Iraq and considered the largest ancient city known in the whole world. Its majestic ruins extend about 6 miles horizontally and 21 vertically, and was built by the Abbasid Caliph al-Mutasim in 836 AD to replace Baghdad as the capital. It was later abandoned by Caliph al-Mutamad, preferring to go back to Baghdad. The city's artistic, literary, and scientific splendors have remained a legend in Arab history. It is well known for the Al-Askareyyan Shrine, and the Great Mosque built by al-Mutawakkil. The mosque minaret, the famous spiral al-Malwiyya, rises to a height of 170 feet, and was influenced by the earlier Mesopotamia ziggurats. We went up the steps of the spiral to the top. Next we paid a visit to the shrines, prayed, and then went sightseeing in the city and concluded our tour by shopping.

In 1957 our school participated in a televised scientific competition program, against al-Rashid Secondary School for Girls. The school administration chose five beautiful blond girls as contestants and another group as stand-bys. I belonged to the second group. When the competing teams were unable to answer a mathematics question, we were asked to give an answer. I gave the correct answer but sadly it was not counted as a point for our team. The videographer zoomed in at my face which was filling the screen The family and friends who watched the program were so happy and proud that it didn't matter who was the winner.

I studied for the final year national examinations with my friends Rajiha, Nawal, Fathiya and Amal. I shared the highest marks in our school with Fawziya Sadiq; we both entered the College of Medicine at Baghdad University. Amal and Fathiya entered the College of Science, and became successful secondary school teachers. Rajiha finished higher studies in chemistry to become a university professor and Nawal chose a banking career. One of my classmates did not get the proper marks to enter the medical college and she decided to repeat the whole year of studies. She passed the tests the next year, and was able to enter the medical college. She became a successful doctor.

Left to right Nawal, Rajiha, Fathiya and Malka at a school picnic 1958

Malwiyya minaret, Samara

The Magnificent Seven

My five siblings and I formed the colorful fabric of our household. As a child, I was known as being quiet, obedient, and organized, but also picky. Being a 5- year old; I did not like the hairstyle my mother made for me. She used to pull a tiny portion of my hair into a pigtail in a bun. Instead, I would convince her to ask our 20 year old Jewish neighbor to style my hair the way she did her own, tying it into a ball-shaped bun. The same went for attire, accessories and even book wallets.

Amal, which means Hope, my one-year-younger soul mate, was easy going, brave and cheerful. An incident that won us all a punishment from Dad, was her participation in the wedding party of our neighbor Rabboa'. In her early teens, she went with tens of lady guests in a bus transporting all invitees to the groom's house for dinner, without asking permission. That angered my father so much that he told my mother to take all the girls and leave the house. For the first and last time in our life we had to spend that night at aunt Ghaniya's house, who lived next door. At 17, Amal studied medicine abroad on a full scholarship, followed by a Master's degree then a PhD. She is now a beloved wife and a successful mother of three university graduates, Tina, Ahmed, and Farah. She and her husband Farooq visited us in Philadelphia in 2013 and we spent most of the night recounting the good old days. As usual, cheerful Amal was joking and confessed that when we were young children she used to be jealous and often plot against me. Amal was asked to get milk from a neighborhood peddler, who would milk the cow and sell fresh raw milk. She would add a small amount of water to make up for the container's unfilled portion in order to appear smarter than me, and I would be blamed by Mother for allowing the milk-lady to cheat me.

Dawood (David) was four years younger than me. Being the first-born son gave him many privileges, and he used to accompany my father on all his trips and outings. Even his food was special as he didn't like most Iraqi dishes (his preferred dish was grilled kebob from a nearby restaurant). Since childhood Dawood was a book worm and spent all his pocket money on books, which he prized to the extent that no one was allowed to read them without his permission. He stacked them neatly in the book case and was able to recognize immediately if they were slightly moved in his absence. That hobby definitely paid off; besides being a smart physician he has published 6 books unrelated to medicine in the United Arab Emirates. His eldest daughter Ayser became a civil engineer, the other two, Sahar and Ban, are medical doctors.

Najiha, meaning Successful, was born two years after Dawood. Dad was at first disappointed because he hoped for a second son, but after talking to his sweet mother, she scolded him and asked that he should kiss his wife's and daughter's foreheads and be thankful to God for their safety. That he did and kept his promise to love them forever. Najiha looks physically very much like me, to the extent that even neighbors greet her as "Dr. Malka" when visiting me in England. I can sum up her personality through the spelling of her name. "N" for being such a nice person, "A" for the fun activities she always comes up with at gatherings, "J" for the joyful spirit she spreads, "I" for being immaculate and "H" for all the heroic stances she took in her life. One example of Najiha's heroic adventures was when she applied for a governmental scholarship to finish her studies abroad. Although equipped with high marks, no contact was made, so she escalated the situation directly by filing a complaint with the presidential office. A few days later she receives a phone call and the person on the line was no other than Saddam Hussein himself! Back then he was the Vice President of Iraq. After a short discussion, Saddam Said: "You know there are certain conditions in order to be considered" Her reply: "I certainly do but my grades are quite high and my English is perfect". Najiha got her Master's degree in rural development from Reading University, UK followed by a PhD, and worked as a teaching professor at Baghdad University for 34 years. Her only daughter Zaineb followed in her footsteps, not in calling any presidents or vice presidents, but in doing her post-graduate studies at the same exact university.

Dad had his dream fulfilled two years later by having the second son Mohammed, who was a smart expert in public relations from early childhood. In spite of having a Bachelor's degree in Chemistry, his practical thinking made him choose a business career. He makes friends wherever he goes and is capable of helping and solving their problems with a passion. He raised six children: Ahmed, Zeena, Lina, Suleiman, Dawood and Bushra. All have earned university degrees.

The youngest sister Kawkab, meaning Planet, was in my company most of the time, as I used to share caring for her with Mother. She is a perfectionist in her career, in her relationships with others, as well as at home. Her house is always tidy and her children are well-behaved and always well-dressed as if they were going to a formal party. Having a Bachelor's degree in statistics, she worked for over 27 years in the Oil Ministry and then retired voluntarily because she couldn't cope with the new chaos and corruption in Iraq after 2003. Her eldest daughter Rusul is now an environmental engineer, and the youngest, Rolla, is a dentist.

In our family as in most Iraqi households, tradition requires that the head of the family has the full respect, while being provided with all comfort at his home. Accordingly, we used to get our evening meal early, after taking the daily bath, then go to bed before Dad returned from work. Whenever one of us had been naughty during the day, that one would be called and disciplined, in moderation. One day we were threatened to be denied school because two of us didn't get the expected full marks. Mother began to collect our books pretending that Dad was going to start burning them. In a quick motion I pulled the book I needed for the next day examination and ran to hide under my bed to read. When I came out my parents were laughing and all was good.

Mother had health issues by the late sixties, and she suffered repeated chest infections due to alternating exposure to heat and cold while baking our bread outdoors and then coming into the cool indoors. We all begged her to quit that habit, but she wouldn't listen, sacrificing her health just to provide Dad with the soft home-made bread that he is able to chew with his dentures. One day we took advantage of her absence from home, and made an agreement with Dad to break the clay backing oven. This was our only coalition with Dad against Mother, who historically was always the peace negotiator between us and him.

The Magnificent Seven is a 1960 American western film, portraying a group of seven gunfighters hired to protect a small agricultural village in Mexico from a group of marauding bandits and their leader (Wallach). In 2013, the film was selected for preservation in the United States National Film Registry by the Library of Congress as being "culturally, historically, or aesthetically significant". People can be magnificent only by helping other people, "A true believer loves for people what he loves for himself". I don't mean to brag about my family, but during the years I saw how each and every one of us helped out people in their own way. I'm proud of my siblings and their achievements. I also counted my deceased 8- year old sister Layla because I believe that had she lived she would have lead a magnificent life. Even so, she continues to live through our legacies and achievements.

Finally, for all the movie buffs out there, a remake film is currently filming and is scheduled to be released on September 23, 2016.

My Parents with siblings Najiha, Mohammed and Kawkab in their backyard -1962

FAMILY AND CAREER 1958-1976

College of Medicine and Baghdad University

The Iraqi Royal College of Medicine was established in 1927. It was one of the first medical schools in the Middle East, with a curriculum matching that of the Royal College of Edinburg. The first dean and founder was Sir Harry Chapman Sindernson (pasha), a British physician who was also the personal physician of the Iraqi royal family. He graduated from the University of Edinburg in 1914. In the army, he was assigned to Iraq as an army doctor, and then was seconded for the British administration as Deputy Director of Medical Civil Services in 1919 and 1920. Sir Sindernson was one of the most influential figures in recent Iraqi medical and political history. During his service until retirement in 1946 he achieved exceptionally high standards and brought fame and prestige to the new medical college. The new building for the college was established in 1930 next to Al Majeedi Hospital on the east bank of the Tigris River. The name of the college was changed to "Iraqi College of Medicine" after the July 1958 revolution.

In 1927-1928 twenty students were accepted to the Iraqi Medical College: eight Jews, seven Muslims and five Christians. The graduates of this first class were 5 Jews, four Muslims and three Christians. Jewish and Christian students usually had the financial means to attend private schools whereas Muslim students typically attended the few available public schools. Malak Ghannam, who was the first female to enter the college, did so in 1933, joining the seventh class. She was followed by Habeeba Baithun the next year; both were Christians. The first female Muslim entered in the tenth class and was my pharmacology teacher, Saniha Amen Zeki.

Baghdad University was established in 1962, and all existing colleges became affiliated to it. The second medical school established in Iraq was Mosul Medical College and was opened officially in 1959. The University of Mosul was established in 1967.

Basra University was affiliated to Baghdad University from its founding, however it became an independent organization in 1964. At present it includes 14 colleges, including a college of medicine. Today every province in Iraq has at least one public university that has a medical college, in addition to several private universities, but none of them has a medical college. In Baghdad alone there are four colleges of medicine.

Royal College of Medicine 1948 class, Sir Harry Sanderson in the middle, Cecile and a number of my professors are among the class - Courtesy of Dr. Cecile Ibrahim

Dreaming and Making Reality

Early in the morning of July 14, 1958 while we were still sleeping on the roof top during the hot summer, we were awakened by the loud sounds of a radio broadcasting the success of a revolution against the monarchy. This date marked a big change in Iraq's history when for the first time Iraq became a republic. Our beloved king and all the royal family were brutally killed. The other high government officials were either killed or jailed and subjected to trials. My feelings were a mixture of grief, panic, and anxiety. It was a traumatic experience for a 17-year-old girl who was naive but patriotic. Having earned very good grades, I thought I was on track to achieve my childhood dream of serving my people by fighting disease, but in that moment I had my doubts. My country sank into a vicious circle of chaos, violence and wars, not only for days or weeks, but for decades to come.

We started applying to individual colleges since Baghdad University was not officially established at the time. It goes without saying that my first choice was The Royal College of Medicine. The second and only other choice was Queen Alia College for Girls since my father was not willing for me to join a coed college besides medical school, which he respected a lot. While I was waiting to be called for an interview I learned, by chance, that the interviews were conducted a day earlier, the names were announced on the broadcast local news, which I missed. I went to the college the next day and was directed to see Professor Ali Kamal (a well-known psychiatrist), who was conducting his tour in the hospital. I greeted him and apologized for being late, but he was kind and welcoming. The one question he asked was: "How much is the sum of 1+7"? When I answered 8, he thanked me and wished me good luck, the interview was over. I was accepted to the college, and my name was among the top quarter.

The first day in college was not an easy experience. After a long commute, I located the lecture room with difficulty. It was huge with three rows of long wooden terraces and full of students. To my relief the number of females was close to that of males. Professor Rosbeck had just started lecturing. The subject was chemistry, usually one of my favorites. I hardly understood anything this time, as he was too quick and I was not familiar with his accent (I think he was Dutch). After an hour the lecture came to an end and I had a few minutes to learn the names of the students sitting beside me. I was soon interrupted by the start of the next lecture, which was physics by Professor Terint, a British, small-built, active middle-aged professor. He immediately jumped and sat on top of the long table in front of him. I found the subject interesting and absorbed most of it.

My cousin Sultan bought me the books, stationery, a white laboratory coat and a dissection set. The composition books were especially made for The Royal College of Medicine with leather covers marked in gold writing. We used to buy medical books from McKenzie bookshop at al-Rashid Street.

Our syllabus included chemistry, physics and biology. Professor Boswell, the biology Professor, who was also European, was serious and taciturn though very efficient. The 2-hour lectures were succeeded by 3-hour practical training after a lunch break. In the physics lab, we performed experiments in teams of two or three. The teams were chosen by the department and had to be gender mixed. As we all came from gender segregated schools, we were embarrassed to talk to or sit next to colleagues from the opposite sex. By the time we had graduated, five or six of my colleagues were married or engaged to classmates and several others did the same after graduation. We used to spend the 3-hour break studying in groups. Usually girls sat together in the lecture hall or on benches in the garden and studied together and one by one we would read out what we gathered from the lecture, while the listeners corrected mistakes and added what was missing. The best students were those who came from Baghdad College, Rahibat, and Central schools, because they were proficient in English and in medical terminology.

Most students were involved in politics, some being pro-government and others anti-government. The Communists, Kurds, National Democrats and some Independents were supporting Qasim's cabinet while the Ba'athists, Arab Nationalists and some Independents were against him. Occasionally arguments between students would get heated and lead to a confrontation. Both sides were calling the Independents "hesitant," and were trying to win them over by helping with studies, giving them textbooks or providing student accommodation. I have always been neutral in politics and didn't belong to any party. Thus, I had good relations with all, and most of my friends were Independents. Despite all the difficulties, I passed the examinations on the first trial and was promoted to the second year.

During that year I participated in a student carnival, feeling proud to put on a doctor's coat and hang a stethoscope around my neck. When the march was over, it was dark and I did not like using public transport, so I went to my aunt's house near the college where my dad was waiting to take me home. Next morning Dad said there was no need for the "*abaya*" because everyone had seen me without it. I was content but asked that Amal would be allowed to stop using her *abaya* too. My parents agreed and since that day we became unveiled.

High Heels Dilemma

By the second year I got used to the college environment and studying in English. Our syllabus consisted of physiology, biochemistry, anatomy, histology and embryology, the last two were taught by foreign professors while the other subjects were covered by Iraqis. Upon finishing that year, all students were promoted to the third year to complete the same subjects with the same teachers. The third year final examinations were tough; as they included all of the material we studied in two years. I passed on the first trial, though some smart students couldn't make it even after a second trial two months later, and they had to repeat the whole third year.

One of my bitter memories in 1960 was an incident which took place on what turned out to be, as I learned later, the day of The First Conference of The National Union of Iraqi Students. I was on my way to attend a physiology lecture by Professor Sadiq Al Hilali, and was surprised by the big crowd in the college main garden, which consisted mostly of strangers. I did not stop to see what was going on. When the lecture was over, my entire class was held by the police, who told us to get into a truck. My friend R. K. who was nearby pulled me to a sidewalk leading to the teaching hospital, but before we could break away from the crowd, a policeman hit each of us with a whip and pushed us up into the truck, which was full of male and female students. We were taken to the Ministry of Defense. At that moment I noticed that I had lost one of my shoes, and as I was wearing my first pair of high heels, I became lame and was tired of standing because I couldn't find a seat. We waited for more than an hour to be met by a high-ranking military officer who addressed us quietly and praised the medical career, concluding his talk by giving us advice to excel at our studies and leave politics to others. In fact, most of us didn't care about politics, and the ones who did had already escaped the site while we were in the lecture room. At last we were allowed to leave. I asked a friend who lives near my house to share a taxi with me. When I got home, I cried bitterly because of the humiliation we were subjected to, though I didn't know that the worst was yet to come.

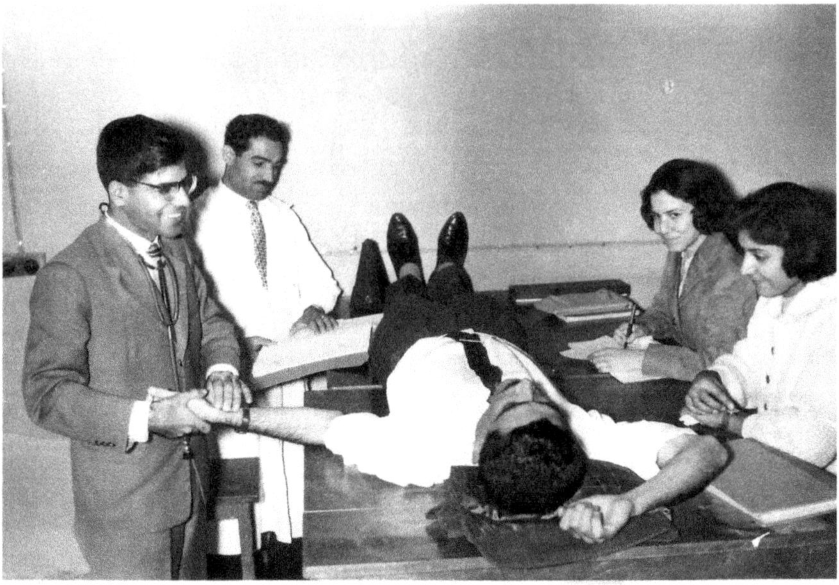

In Physiology lab examining a co-student -1959

Year 4 at college was more interesting; with hands on clinical training in medical subjects, in addition to the major subjects of pathology, pharmacology, bacteriology and microbiology. In that year, I got good grades in all but pharmacology. I retook the test after the 2-month summer holiday and passed it and was promoted to year 5 with my classmates. During the time I was studying at the university, many happy family events took place. The most exciting to me were moving to a new house and my sister's studies abroad.

Our family had moved to al-Sulaikh. Dad chose to buy a lot in that quiet area, preferring it over al Mansur, which was the prestigious area. He said it was to keep away from important government institutions. Although the house was built by an experienced contractor, I got to make changes in the layout, choose the floor and window designs as well as the finishing. The place was surrounded by huge orchards and green fields and it was the first to be built in an agricultural neighborhood. Even electricity and water supply were not available, we had to have ours extended from a remote source. A few months later, two of our relatives built their houses next to ours followed by many others.

Amal graduated from high school with excellent grades, though she did not wish to pursue medical studies. Her first choice was the College of Science, but where she ended up was an amazing coincidence. We heard of scholarships abroad, and one of them was for studying nuclear medicine. We got word only one day before the official interviews, and quickly decided to go directly to the office of the Minister of Industry. He was the head of The Atomic Energy Commission, the agency that was sponsoring the scholarships. Amal's late application was accepted and she was invited for an interview the next day and I accompanied her. All the other applicants except one were boys. Amal was accepted and given a full scholarship to study nuclear medicine in Moscow. Now we had to face the daunting task of convincing Father to allow his 17- year-old daughter go abroad. Many open-minded relatives tried hard to persuade him, and after several long discussions Dad finally accepted the idea. She commenced her studies immediately and had to study medicine first and then the specialty. She wrote to us weekly in detail with plenty of photos. Her roommate Natasha from Kiev was studying ballet and shared photos too. At the end of each school year, Amal spent the two-month summer holiday with us. In Early 1962, Amal wrote that an Iraqi colleague's parents were going to visit us to ask her hand for their son. At first Dad was furious and decided to pull her out of the program, saying that he sent her to study not to marry. Once he met with the family he miraculously changed his mind and gave his blessings to her. The next summer holiday Amal and Farooq came to Baghdad, got married in a family gathering and left to finish their studies.

Almost There

The fifth year covered a wide range of subjects including forensics, community medicine plus all medical and surgical subspecialties. Violence during this year culminated in the fall of Abdul Karim Qasim and the beginning of Ba'athist era. Few weeks before the mid-year Exams, students all over Iraq went on strike and were soon followed by taxi drivers and public service workers. Students were divided; the group who supported the government opposed the strike, while those against it called for the strike. Being neutral didn't discourage both sides from pressuring me. I was eager to finish my studies, but worried about what would happen if I took the exam. I decided to take the forensics and community medicine exams and ignore the other subjects, as those two were major subjects for year five only. The college appeared almost empty and there were clashes between students from both sides. On my way out of the exam room, I saw my colleague A. Z. injured. Her shirt was torn as her fiancé was being beaten. Walking few steps further I was shocked to see a senior colleague M. S. staggering and bleeding from a wound in his chest. Sometime later I learned that he did not make it. In less than two weeks a successful coup ousted Qasim on February 8, 1963, with thousands of casualties. Some of our colleagues vanished and we never heard what happened to them.

The sixth year training started immediately after the end of year five. Besides training and shadowing in the four main medical branches we were required to conduct a project in community medicine. Ours was surveying the health status in a small underprivileged Christian community near Baghdad College. We went beyond the survey by treating the sick, giving medications as well as providing health education.

We were trained in general surgery in wards 12 and 13, as we did in year four with Professors Aziz Shukri, Tahrir al-Gailani and Khalid Naji who met with us every morning to give valuable instructions. He had a sign on the wall above his desk that read: "*Do Not Trust Anybody Even Your Father*" His advice was to not depend on information volunteered by others. Our training in internal medicine was in ward 1 with Professors Farhan Baqir and Mahdi Murtadha Their abundant knowledge and dedication ingrained in me the passion for medicine. The third branch in our training was obstetrics & gynecology with Professors Kamal Al-Samara'e, Lami'a Al-Badri, K. Kubba, Margret Shukri and Anna Suthian, which was held in Wards 11 and 10. These were always crowded with complicated obstetric emergencies as well as normal labors. We would walk from the main hospital to our training in pediatrics at the Children's Hospital, discussing medical cases with colleagues on our way. The sixth year medical students were paid 20 Iraqi Dinars monthly; quite a sum considering the total monthly income for a graduate of medicine was 41 Dinars including the allowances.

My aunt Khairiya passed away two days before the end of the final Exams, after suffering from lung cancer. Her loss broke my heart, but it encouraged me to work even harder and my grades for that subject were among the highest.

The graduation ceremony for Baghdad University took place at *Sahat al-Ka'shafa,* the Scout's Square. We all stood up and took Hippocrates's oath. Our feelings were a mixture of pride, happiness, relief and determination. We were now real doctors ready to take our full responsibility toward our patients, families and humanity.

Graduation ceremony at Ka'shafa square in souring July 1964

The Iraqi Medical College, my sixth year class 1964

Valley of the Shadow of Death

After the 1958 revolution, Brigadier Abdul Karim Qasim became the Prime Minister and Colonel Abdul Salam Arif was his Deputy. The new constitution proclaimed Iraq a republic, and established a Sovereignty Council to fulfill the ceremonial functions of the head of state. Arif was an admirer of the Egyptian President Abdul Nassir, was against communism, and was a supporter of the al Ba'ath party. Qasim was an independent nationalist and against Imperialism and he was not a communist. Soon the relation between the two leaders soured. Arif promoted a strong relationship with Nassir, for the purpose of joining the United Arab Republic (Egypt and Syria), while Qasim preferred to distance himself from Nassir.

Internally, Qasim initiated the Agricultural Reform Law which gave privileges to working farmers, built 35,000 housing units in Baghdad, and founded al-Thawra City in East Baghdad for poor families who had been dwelling in mud houses (serifa). He was interested in women's equality, and in a radical modification of the Personal Status Law. This law regulated family relationships by restricting polygamy, determining the minimum age for marriage, and protectiong women from arbitrary divorce. The most revolutionary decision was Article 74, which made women and men equals in receiving inheritance. He appointed the first female minister in Iraq, Dr. Naziha Al-Dulaimi to the Ministry of Municipalities in 1959. During his reign *"al Hureya"*, the liberty monument, was built by sculptor Jawad Saleem and engineer Rifa'at Al Chadirchi at al Tahrir (liberation) square in the middle of Baghdad. The monument is 30 feet high and contains 14 pieces of cast bronze from which the artist wanted to interlace past and present events in Iraq's history. There are Sumerian, Babylonian and Assyrian inscriptions throughout the monument. The most attractive feature is located in the center of the piece and shows the image of a soldier breaking the prison bars, which speaks of strength and determination.

Iraq took two bold steps in the oil industry. The first was the foundation of OPEC in 1960 through the meetings in Baghdad with representatives from Iraq, Iran, Kuwait, Saudia Arabia and Venezuela. They formed a global oil organization consisting of five members and later growing to include eleven members. Then in 1961, Iraq issued Law Number 80 which stripped the Iraqi Oil Company of 99.5% of the areas which it had not yet invested in, thus restricting its work to areas already developed. These steps lead to a significant increase in oil revenues for Iraq, and at the same time the establishment of the National Iraqi Oil Company was announced.

Qasim tried to balance the demands of military commanders supporting Arab unity with the demands of the communists in control of the Iraqi street. In fact, he had a wavering toward the communists, depending on the political circumstances of the moment. In March 1959, a group of officers led an insurgency in Mosul. The leader was Abdul Wahab Al-Shawaf. The coup did not succeed because it was preceded by the Peace Partisan, which was supported by the communists who broke through city streets. Clashes between them and government rebels led to near civil war. A few months later a massacre took place in Kirkuk, also initiated by communists, claiming the lives of tens of Turkmens, especially the affluent. Qasim eventually diminished his relationship with the communists and reduced their earnings. After those two incidents the Ba'athists made a plan to get rid of him through an assassination attempt. He was wounded but escaped death.

The political situation in Iraq continued to deteriorate as several opposition movements emerged, including the Kurdish one in the north. The Ba'athists and Nasserites called for a strike that contributed to Qasim's downfall. After the 1963 coup Qasim was besieged in his office at the ministry of defense in Bab al Mu'adhum. He was subjected to a short trial and killed at the headquarters of the Baghdad Broadcasting station and his corpse was displayed on TV. Qasim's supporters participated in big demonstrations at the Bab al Mu'adhum neighborhood. They were crushed by the new regime. 5000 were killed and many more were imprisoned. Arif became President and Al-Bakir headed a Ba'athist cabinet. This was yet again a short lived arrangement. Within 8 months Arif shoved out the Ba'athists and replaced them with Nasserites. In 1966, Arif died in an airplane crash and his brother Abdul Rahman Arif succeeded him until 1968, when the Ba'athists took control for the second time, retaining power until the occupation of Iraq in 2003.

Al Hureya (Liberty) monument – Courtesy of Ahmed A. Hadi

Number 13

In order to be able to practice medicine after graduation, the first step is to register for the Iraqi Medical Association, and then get appointed at a public hospital to train as a house officer. When we graduated in 1964, the Ministry of Health implemented the Medical Placement Law for the first time. It involved training for 12 months, three in each of the main branches: internal medicine, surgery, obstetrics & gynecology, followed by three months in pediatrics or another preferred specialty (the requirement was later changed to completing a total of 24 months). After finishing this internship one needed to spend another year in a public health institution in a remote area. Finally, training as a senior house officer is a requirement for doctors wanting to specialize in a particular branch before pursuing higher studies.

All medical graduates were given government jobs within a few weeks. The ones with higher graduation scores were assigned to the best teaching hospitals. My rank was 13 in a class of over 100 graduates, being the ninth among female graduates. Male graduates had to join the army reserve for 18 months before starting their hospital posts.

I commenced my internship at Dar al-Salam Hospital (later renamed al-Ilwiya Hospital). The hospital was, and still is, the biggest hospital specializing in obstetrics and gynecology in Iraq. All the medical staff were females except for the manager, Dr. Anwar Qaimaqchi, who was a gynecologist himself, and the anesthesiologist Dr. Ahmed Jelmiran. The hospital serves most of the capital Baghdad and surrounding areas.

Getting my first job was exceptionally exciting to the whole family. I was going to leave my family house for the first time, and share a room with colleagues. That also meant unpredictable times for sleep, meals not cooked by my mother, standing in line to get to the bathroom, and sleeping amid noises and lights controlled by others. The night before starting my first day, I was tossing and turning, but still I woke up early to get ready. After a hearty breakfast, Dad called a taxi and accompanied me to the hospital entrance handing me my luggage - his eyes were saying: "I wish

I could take it to your room." The hospital manager, Dr. Qaimaqchi's welcoming attitude and gentleness assured me that I was going to survive. He introduced me to Dr. Suhad Shawqi, the chief resident, and asked her to show me all the hospital facilities.

My roommate was Dr. Hana' Al Aloosi who was admired by all. Junior doctors met for meals or tea in our room, even though it was by no means bigger than the others. To my delight I found that my colleague Aliyya Al-Ani had already begun working at the hospital, and then after a few days we were joined by Amal Al-Azzawi. The three of us made a dedicated team with a lasting friendship. We all enjoyed hands-on experience and were eager to participate in all clinical activities, to the extent that on our one day off per week we would ask each other to call when an interesting surgical intervention was taking place so that we could attend.

In my student years, I had no interest in obstetrics and gynecology (OBG). On the contrary, my preference was internal medicine. Surprisingly, by the end of three months training at Dar al-Salam Hospital, I became very interested in OBG. Through my encounters, I got to experience firsthand what it means to be part of bringing a new life to this world, while simultaneously maintaining the mother's life and wellbeing. It is the most rewarding experience unmatched by any other in life. Suhad taught me the proper way to perform episiotomy, to use obstetric forceps, and manage complicated obstetric cases. The nursing staff were over-worked, sometimes taking out their frustration on us, the interns, since we were the most vulnerable people in that environment.

One night I was called to manage a pregnant patient complaining of moderate vaginal bleeding and mild abdominal cramps. She had no idea how many months she was pregnant. On physical examining her, I found that she was pale but otherwise stable, and the uterine size corresponded to 28 weeks gestation but no detectable fetal parts or heart (ultrasound was not available those days). After the necessary preparations, I decided to stay with the patient to perform frequent observations myself. When the pain and bleeding got worse, I called the chief resident who examined her in the operating theater and found the uterus filled with a hydatidiform mole; which was evacuated gently and the patient subsequently did very well. Histopathology confirmed the diagnosis showing no malignant change, and a follow up was arranged. Hydatidiform moles result from fertilization of an ovum with defective DNA, resulting in swollen placental villi. Multiplication of the trophoblastic cells (cells lining placental villi) form multiple small cysts resembling a bunch of grapes. Two to three percent of hydatidiform moles undergo malignant changes, so clinical and laboratory follow-up are necessary. Additionally, the patient must avoid new pregnancy for 6-12 months.

In another incident, I had just started dinner when I was called to manage a woman who had just delivered, but the midwife could not get the afterbirth (placenta) out. I left immediately and hastened downstairs to the labor room. The scene was scary. A huge purple mass was at the vulva, which was the uterus inverted inside out, with the placenta still attached to its exposed inner wall. There was significant blood loss. The patient was in severe pain, pale from low blood pressure and had a rapid pulse. I started resuscitation and called the chief resident, who arrived within few minutes. After proper analgesia, the mass was replaced with difficulty by gentle and steady pressure Then the placenta was separated and removed manually, while uterine contractions were secured with intravenous medication, and antibiotics were given to prevent infection. Uterine inversion is a rare complication of vaginal delivery, resulting from mismanagement of placental delivery by pulling on the umbilical cord and/or exerting abdominal pressure to push out the placenta. The complication occurs especially if the uterus is not contracted properly. This was the case in our patient; the midwife asked a physically strong assistant to push the uterus down with extra force.

By the end of the third month we departed Dar al-Salam, each to a different hospital. Even so, our friendship got stronger. I was assigned to al Sheik Omar hospital and then to the newly established al Tifl al Arabi (Arabic Child) hospital. On one of my night's duties I met my relative Karima in the emergency room accompanying her 6-month old, Ammar, who was in need of oxygen therapy because of chest infection (bronchiolitis). It was as much a relief for her as it was a pleasure for me to be able to help, and the baby left hospital the next day in good condition. I already had some hands-on experience in pediatrics, but nothing like the heavy work load of Dar al-Salam.

The third training period was at al-Shaab Hospital in the surgical department which occupied a separate two-story building. The top floor was dedicated for treating school teachers and the ground floor had two wings, one for general surgery headed by Dr. Ali Al-Naqib, the other for cardio-thoracic surgery headed by Dr. Adnan Sarsam. My duties included pre-operative and post-operative care for varied surgical cases, assisting in the surgical theater, and performing minor surgeries. I witnessed heart surgery for the first time, and although I had to stand on a low stool to see what was going on and be able to assist, the feeling of handling the beating heart was amazing. My resident colleagues were willing to teach and supervise. Hadi taught me suturing the opened abdominal wall in layers and supervised me in performing appendectomy. Saleh insisted that I had to learn how to do the proper surgical knot and that I train on a door handle, and Farooq supervised me performing minor surgical procedures.

The next step towards finishing the internship was to practice general medicine, which I did while still at al-Shaab Hospital. My supervisor, Dr. Bahjet Al Nasiri was loved by his patients. He did not only treat them, he taught, criticized, and guided them, and gave them moral as well as financial support if needed. Dr. Mustafa Saleem, then a senior house officer, was a role model for me. One evening we received a 7-year-old child who was running a high temperature for weeks and was severely anemic. She had a distended abdomen from an enlarged liver and spleen. Dr. Saleem immediately tested a sample of her blood and discovered that she had a greatly increased number of immature white blood cells. He diagnosed her condition as leukemia, but nothing was said to the family until the diagnosis was confirmed by the central laboratory next day.

Al-Shaab was an old general hospital of a unique open design with some 150 beds. I was fortunate to have my old friends Aliyya and Amal appointed to the same facility. The work load was nothing like OBG in Dar al-Salam. At Al-Shaab we had time to enjoy tea in the garden, listen to Um Kulthoum monthly concerts and watch daily episodes of the Egyptian series "Bint al- Hitta." Which was popular on TV those days.

Tikrit It Is

I was sent to finish my second year of practice in Tikrit (Saddam Hussein's birthplace) before it became a province. Once my supervisor, Dr. Bahjet, learned about the assignment, he called his family in Tikrit to take care of me. Arabs in general, and especially in rural areas, are known for hospitality and generosity. In fact, it is regarded an honor to host strangers and show generosity. My parents decided to accompany me on my first visit, exploring the place that would be my home for a whole year. On the outskirts of Tikrit we were welcomed by two groups of notables, each waiting in a coffee shop on the highway One was led by Bahjet's brother-in-law and extended family and the other was headed by his nephew. We went with the elder (Hajj Khattab) and were surprised with a big party. They had slaughtered a sheep and had prepared a big feast. After dinner we were introduced to the hospital staff and welcomed by Dr. Nadhir Al-Saddawi who showed us the hospital facilities and my future residence, which was a room with attached facilities inside the hospital building. The hospital was basic, consisting of two wards, each of which had 16 beds for each gender. The small operating theater was opposite my room and the smaller labor room was next to it. On the other side was Dr. Nadhir's office and on the far end was the dentist's office. The pharmacy was run by a single technician. We had one nurse, two medical assistants, and three genitors. We were all one big family. My parents were relieved on our way back, knowing that I would be in good hands. The next day I gathered my room furniture, cooking utensils and other necessities to be sent to Tikrit, making sure my sewing machine was loaded onto the truck so I could practice my favorite hobby in my spare time. Dad accompanied me on my move to Tikrit, and returned back on the same day.

Sometimes I had to manage cases by myself when my colleague was away. We were two doctors in the town managing different medical disciplines. My colleague was interested in surgery and performed many procedures under local anesthesia. I learned a lot through assisting him in surgery, and also from long discussions we had on various medical topics. We were both preparing for the ECFMG examination and hoping to work in the States at some point. We both took the examination in 1967 and passed.

Despite the limited facilities, I was fortunate to get a chance to manage interesting cases. A young healthy-looking woman consulted me for a headache that had persisted for several weeks. Upon detailed questioning, I found that she had repeated vomiting and that her vision had changed recently. I suspected a brain tumor, which was proven by an X-ray. She was referred to Dr. Sa'ad Al-Witry, the well-known neurosurgeon. He made the same diagnosis and performed a successful surgery for her. She visited me to thank me upon her return from Baghdad. Another interesting case was an elderly man who had severe shortness of breath that started suddenly after excessive coughing. On examining him, I found that he was cyanosed and had shortness of breath, he had a rapid pulse, the trachea was deviated to one side, and one lung was collapsed with no detectable breathing sounds. I diagnosed the case as pneumothorax (a collection of air between the pleural layers surrounding the lung). He was in need of urgent treatment, but we lacked the facilities. I fashioned a device that induces negative pressure from sterile tubes (from an IV administration set) and a partly-filled common saline bottle to aspirate the air collected in the pleural cavity, which was causing the lung collapse. This treatment worked, and it was so rewarding to see him quickly recovered and asking for food.

One night I was the only doctor available. I heard a loud argument between two well-known locals. The event took place in the hospital front yard and escalated quickly to a fight with knives. I was so scared that I blocked my room door with the sewing machine. A few minutes later, the nurse was knocking on my door, asking for me to come out to treat the injured individuals. I only opened the door after being assured that I wouldn't be left alone and that the male medical assistant would be present the whole time. Apart from such limited incidents, people were friendly and respectful to doctors.

In 1965 Tikrit was rather more of a village than a town and had limited services. I used to go to Baghdad every other weekend. The other weekends, staying in Tikrit, I received invitations to dinner or a picnic. In the eighties and beyond Tikrit became a modern city with sophisticated hospitals attached to a university, and staffed by specialists with high degrees.

A Step to OBG

When the 12-month assignment in Tikrit was over, I had the option to choose which branch of medicine to be trained in as a senior house officer, before proceeding to postgraduate studies. I chose OBG training at al-Jamhoori Teaching Hospital (affiliated with the Iraqi Medical College). I was called to meet the Deputy Minister of Health in his office, where I met professor Lamia'a Al Badri, the Chairwoman of the OBG department. I was offered the job in spite of a lot of competition, thanks to my graduation scores. The service in that hospital was one of the best in the Middle East. As for the resident staff, my classmate Zahida Al-Saadi was my partner as a Senior House Officer. We were both supervised by the Chief Resident, Suhad, whom I met previously at Dar al-Salam Hospital. I had one day off per week, which only started after working hours and ended at 8 am the next morning. Zahida and I both had to be available on weekends and holidays. I had the pleasure of assisting Professor Kamal Al-Samara'e in a major reconstructive surgery, creating a vagina (Baldwin operation) for a young lady who was born with a genital abnormality. I was impressed by the precision, attention to details, and the refined manner in his performance. Prof. Samara'e had performed 15 such surgeries with only two failures. Baldwin, the doctor for whom the operation was named, had two failures in his 14 cases. This kind of surgery has been replaced by simpler procedures nowadays.

My other senior attending was Professor Kais Kubba, known for his expertise in managing malignancies. Patients with cervical carcinoma were referred to him from all over Iraq. He used to operate on them every Saturday with Zahida and I alternating in assisting him. Even at that time (1966), Prof. Kubba had been against the blind use of prophylactic antibiotics, not only because they might not target the causative organism, but mainly for fear of creating resistant organisms.

One early morning I encountered a newly admitted patient in critical condition. She had missed one menstrual period and came in complaining of several hours of generalized abdominal pain with severe weakness. She was pale, sweating, and had a rapid pulse with low blood pressure Her abdomen was tender with abdominal muscle guarding. A pelvic examination revealed extreme tenderness. The diagnosis of a ruptured ectopic pregnancy was evident. As I started immediate resuscitation, I noticed Prof. Kubba by my side. He asked if we could get an anesthesiologist to come immediately because time was critical. The on-call doctors had already left and the day staff had yet to come in, so I offered to anesthetize the patient, as I was getting training in anesthesia like all the other residents in surgical departments. In the operating room, I gave the patient diluted Pentothal and before giving the short-acting muscle relaxant, the operation was over and my teacher was closing the abdomen. Aside from being an excellent surgeon, Prof. Kubba was known for his speed. There was a shortage of anesthesiologists in Iraq in those days, so the medical officials decided to train all residents in surgical specialty programs in anesthesia. Zahida and I were alternating days covering anesthetic duties in addition to OBG. When I did obstetrics she gave anesthesia, and vice versa.

In early 1967 Prof. Kubba acquired Iraq's first ultrasound device and kept it in his office. It was so big in size that it occupied most of the space. He instructed me and Zahida on its use whenever we had time. I learned later that Professor Ian Donald, the Scottish inventor of ultrasound, had visited Iraq a year earlier on the invitation of Prof. Al-Samara'e, and had presented his great invention. When the inventor went back home, he was accompanied by a junior Iraqi doctor, Osama Abdulla, who graduated from The Iraqi Medical College in 1962. Abdulla continued to work with Ian Donald and became a well-known figure in obstetric ultrasound. He is credited with inventing a method for placental localization. I met Abdulla in Baghdad shortly before the 2003 war, when he visited Iraq with a group of Iraqi British doctors, including Ali Kubba, Talha Al-Shawaf, Nazar Amso and Mohammed Al-Samara'e. They offered valuable lectures and workshops. Abdulla had just recovered from a liver cancer surgery at the time.

The first time I performed a cesarean section unsupervised, was three months after joining the OBG department, during which time I had assisted in about 50 cesarean sections and performed several supervised ones. A young woman come in with significant painless vaginal bleeding. She was at term, the fetal presenting part was high, the fetal heartbeat was normal, her blood pressure was within normal range, but she had a rapid pulse. I diagnosed the condition as Placenta Previa (low lying placenta). We started her on intravenous fluid. Her blood-type was determined and two pints of blood were cross matched. I could not reach the chief resident, who was living outside the hospital, so I had to act quickly as there was no way to stop the bleeding. I called the on-call anesthesiologist, Dr. Abdul Sattar Al Ani, who was a senior resident in general surgery. The operation and recovery were uneventful. I was lucky not to encounter bleeding from the placental site after delivery, which had to be watched because of the lack of proper contraction in the lower uterine segment. This is an essential factor in controlling blood loss after delivery.

Regrettably, Iraqi health services had a shortage of college-graduate nurses, despite the fact that Iraq was the first Middle Eastern country to establish a 4-year bachelor's degree in nursing program during the middle sixties. Most of the first graduating class of the college were appointed in anesthetic jobs and the rest occupied administrative positions at the ministry of health offices. Graduates rarely became involved in nursing careers. Some continued studies for higher degrees and began teaching at the college or other nursing institutes, and a few become head nurses without having had hands-on experience. Generally, practicing nurses were from underprivileged backgrounds with simple education. Their job required that they sometimes stay overnight in hospitals to take care of patients, which was not seen favorably in a male-dominant culture. Thus, the entire profession was frowned upon, ignoring its nobility in providing the physical, emotional, psychological and social care for the patients. In an attempt to promote the profession, Abdul Karim Qasim nicknamed nurses as the "angels of mercy". I also remember the late minister of health, Dr. Riyadh Ibrahim Al Haj Hussein, who used to praise the nursing profession as even above medical doctors. A nurse in the Arab world is addressed as "Sister", which is a word taken from the British healthcare system.

Our workload was too heavy for two senior house officers in a busy OBG unit receiving emergencies around the clock, not only from Baghdad but also cases that were referred there from all over Iraq. Responsibilities extended beyond that as we had to provide medications for new admissions outside working hours and keep records for receiving and dispensing, not to mention the safe storage and documentation for dispensing narcotics. Aside from that, we had difficulty in getting blood for patients in need. Many of whom required urgent transfusions, such as those with miscarriages, bleeding in late pregnancy or after delivery, those with ruptured ectopic pregnancy and the ones with ruptured uteruses. Blood bank facilities were not available at that time. There were a few men whom we called "donors" who offered to sell their blood for money. They would hang out in the surrounding streets. We had to draw their blood after a quick blood-type and cross match check. Obviously virology screening was not known back then.

An Army of Lovers

Professor al-Badri was not only the head of the OBG department, she was also the Dean of the Nursing College and President of the "Union of Arab Women University Graduates". The union accomplished several educational and social activities in the Arab world at that time. In Baghdad, the movie "The Sound of Music" was played at the prestigious al-Khayyam Theater in 1967. I was invited to go, along with colleagues Zahida, Lami'a and Adiba. The event was attended by highly educated Iraqis, both male and female. During that year we also attended a concert by the Iraqi singer Al-Qubanchi, who is well known for singing Iraqi *Maqam*, a singing style unique to Iraq that touches the souls of people for all occasions happy or sad.

My first trip outside Iraq came in April 1967, when I was part of a delegation attending a union conference in Cairo, Egypt. Professor Anna Suthian and my colleague Zahida were my roommates at al-Melia Palace, a hotel that was part of the Palace of King Mohammed Ali, King Fuad's predecessor.

Besides attending meetings and workshops, we visited the splendid Egyptian National Museum, spending several hours in the huge two story building filled with artifacts dating from prehistoric through the Roman periods. It houses the largest collection of Pharaonic antiquities.

Two special rooms contain a number of mummies of their kings and other royal family. We also saw an extensive collection of papyrus, as well as Greek, Roman, Islamic and Egyptian coins.

During most of the tours, I was accompanied by Zahida. She took me to visit an Egyptian friend, whose sitting room furniture caught my eye. It was a French solid-wood antique set, upholstered with light pink velvet with matching curtains and accessories. Egyptians are famously known for their great style in furniture, internal decorations, and clothing, which is clearly visible also in their media productions. Our host quickly squeezed fresh oranges for us, and then drove us to the zoo. The zoo walkways were paved with colored stones arranged in a lovely artistic design. We concluded the visit by having refreshments at "*Gizirt al-Shai*" Island of Tea.

An interesting outing was the visit to the Giza Pyramids. The ancient pyramid-shaped masonry structures with square bases were truly out of this world. The biggest of the three pyramids, known as the Great Pyramid of Khufu, was built over a twenty year period and rising to a height of 451 feet. Around 2,300,000 limestone blocks were used for constructing it, each weighing an average of 2.5 tons. It is the only one of the Seven Wonders of the Ancient World still in existence. That evening, we paid a second visit to the pyramids to enjoy a "Light and Sound" show and listen to their story. The pyramids were all built to the west of the Nile, which is thought to be associated with the land of the dead, with tombs of the country's pharaohs and their consorts during the old and middle kingdom periods. They were built when Egypt had the most radiant and most powerful civilization in the ancient world.

The other landmarks of Cairo not to be missed included a dinner at the Rotating Restaurant in Cairo Tower, and a day-long visit to "Khan al Khalili," a traditional market where one can find popular Egyptian merchandise, such as jewelry and handmade souvenirs. There I bought gifts for all family members and a precious amber rosary for my father, which he kept with many others for his whole life. Mother gave it to me after his passing and it was still sitting in my jewelry box when I left Iraq. We concluded that day by paying a visit to the nearby Holy Masjid of

Sayyidna Al Hussein, grandson of Prophet Mohammed, where the Imam's head is buried on the grounds of the mosque.

During the nights we attended Egyptian plays and one of Umm Kulthoum's monthly concerts. We were enthralled by her fascinating voice and distinct character. Um Kulthoum was an international Egyptian singer, song writer, and actress from the 1920s to the 1970s. She was given the honorary title of *Kawkab al Sharq* (Star of the East, in Arabic). At a young age she showed exceptional singing talent. In 1944, King Farouk I of Egypt decorated her with the highest level of orders, *nishan el kamal*, a decoration reserved exclusively for members of the royal family and politicians. Her monthly concerts took place on the first Thursday of every month and were renowned for their ability to clear the streets of some of the world's most populous cities, as people rushed home to tune in. Her songs dealt mostly with the universal themes of love, longing, and loss. They are nothing short of an epic in scale, with durations measured in hours rather than minutes. A typical Umm Kulthoum concert consisted of the performance of two or three songs over a period of two to three hours. The "Star of the East" died February 3, 1975, at age 76. Her funeral procession became a national event, with around 4 million grief-stricken Egyptians lining the streets to catch a glimpse as her cortege. She was referred to as "The Lady" by Charles de Gaulle and is regarded as the "Incomparable Voice" by Maria Callas. Even today, she has retained a near-mythical status among young Egyptians. She is also notably popular in Israel among both Arabs and Jews of Arab background alike.

Legendary Nightingale of Maqam

Iraqi music, especially *Maqam,* encompasses music of a number of musical genres and ethnic groups, including Arabic, Kurdish, Assyrian, Aramaic, Armenian, Hebrew, Turkish, and Persian. It has the trait of being sad yet beautiful music that Iraqis resort to in recounting their emotions.

Maqam, which literally means place or location, refers to certain defined sophisticated melodic forms. It is the most noble, well known, and respected from of Mesopotamian singing in the entire Arab world. Dating back at least 400 years, it has 50 to 70 different types, each with their own mood and characteristics. The singer, supported by instrumentalists (*Chalghi*), has to follow certain rules and patters but can also creatively improvise. For example, they can lengthen or shorten their performance.. Texts are often derived from classical Arabic poetry. Generally, Arabs are fond of poetry and flowery speech, an attribute often obvious and easily spotted in any conversation. But for Mesopotamians in particular, it runs in their blood, stretching back to the glory of epics like Gilgamesh. It is said that poetry is the art of all Iraqis and in order to be a true poet, you have to be Iraqi. The most common musical instrument is the *Oud* (lute). Other instruments include the Qanun, Santur, Ney and Tabla. In Iraq and Egypt singers were mostly Muslims, Jews and Christians.

The legendary Mohammed Al Qubanchi (1900-1989) was a superstar of *Maqam*. His family were traders for generations and his name derives from Guban, which means "the person who weighs goods on a scale". Being good with numbers as well as singing, he would work as a merchant in the daytime and practice his passion for singing as night fell.

Since his early childhood he would accompany his father to work and to concerts alike. He adored music very much. One day, when his father sent him to buy lard to cook for an unexpected guest. On his way to the store he heard Maqam singing coming from a distant neighbor's house. Mohammed sat under the neighbor's window so that he could listen to the people singing inside, and forgot all about the guest at his house. After 30 minutes or so he remembered the reason why he had left home in the first place, but was reluctant to go back as he feared his dad's anger for embarrassing him in front of the guest. The neighbor came out and saw Mohammed, and after realizing what had happened, the kind neighbor took Qubanchi back home so he could intercede if necessary. But the father welcomed both with a smile, explaining that when Mohammed was late they borrowed some lard from their next-door neighbor.

Qubanchi did not only study and practice Maqam, but also traveled near and far, mostly to the high mountains up north, to trace the origins of famous songs. Moreover, he mastered Arabic grammar so well that he never uttered an incorrect sentence. He always had an infectious smile, yet was full of poise while performing as a singer.

In 1925 a delegation from the British Gramophone company arrived to Baghdad to record the elite local singers. Qubanchi's share of the records surpassed all the other singers combined. He excelled in his performance despite having never formally studied music in an academic institution. Qubanchi was an advocate of modernization. When traveling to Berlin, Germany to record in 1928, he directed the musicians to wear modern attire. He never left behind the values of his profession of fairly weighing goods and thus never accepted work that he didn't believe in as a singer. He was the first Iraqi singer to have a recorded production. In 1932 he attended the famous Arabic music congress in Cairo. Once again he instructed the entire ensemble to wear western style attire. Before concluding the congress, each musical band was given a period of 10 minutes to perform its best piece in front of King Fuad of Egypt. The king was delighted with Iraq's performance and instructed the band to continue past the 10 minutes. Qubanchi performed a full 90 minutes before the king and his guests, moving from one Maqam to another. He took his audience up to the "seventh sky". The audience, completely reaching a state of ecstasy, forgot about the rules of not making any sound in the presence of the king. They enthusiastically applauded Qubanchi, with no regrets. On the same visit to Cairo, Qubanchi met some of the elite Egyptian entertainers like Ahmed Shawqi, dubbed "The Prince of Poetry", the famous singer Umm Kulthoum, and the poetry writer Ahmed Rami. While Rami and Qubanchi were walking together on one of the Nile river bridges, Mohammed asked, "do you think Umm Kulthoum ever fell in love?" Rami answered, "How can anyone with eyes and a heart not fall in love?" To which Mohammed yelled in excitement, "How elegant! Please go on Rami". The poet replied, "I'll keep going on, only if you promise me that later you will sing what I say in Maqam". Mohammed promised, and Rami went on improvising his amazing words. By that time, people were gathered on the bridge watching the two giants and applauding them. They all got free tickets to some exciting inspirational moments.

It is noteworthy that six out of seven of Qubanchi's accompanying musicians were Jewish Iraqis, including the brothers Saleh and Dawood Al Kuwaiti. Apart from being masters of the Oud and violin, they were the principle composers, for decades, of songs in Iraq that remained popular. In fact, the nightclubs of Baghdad almost exclusively featured Jewish musicians. One of the reasons for that was the existence of a prominent school in the late 1920's for blind Jewish children, founded by the great *Qanun* player Youssef Za'aror. Many of the student musicians came from that same school, eventually forming the Arabic Music Ensemble.

Qubanchi won lots of international awards, one of which was from the United Nations Educational Scientific and Cultural Organization (UNESCO) in 1980 for being deemed the best singer in Asia. He wanted to build a house for his family, but eventually opted instead to build something for the public. He built a mosque at his own expense, near his residence in Baghdad. He was the first person to call for prayers, *Azan* in that mosque and was buried in that same place when his life came to an end. Qubanchi was indeed the master of Maqam, an honest merchant, a lovable person with high social skills, and a philanthropist with a true desire to help others.

Traditional Arabic musical instruments- Courtesy of Amal and Farooq

Missed Royal Cup of Tea

By the end of 1967, after finishing my residency, I was appointed to al-Nasiriya General Hospital as an OBG practitioner. Up to that time, I was the only OBG practitioner who had a residency training background. Everyone was impressed with my performance and I gained the confidence of the Health Authority, as well as the province governors who started to consult me exclusively in caring for their families.

In one incident, I was consulted by a woman in her mid-forties complaining of increasingly heavy menstrual loss which was caused by uterine fibroids. I corrected her gross anemia and prepared her for hysterectomy (operation to take out the uterus). The chairman of the Health Authority, a surgeon himself, ordered that the operation had to be performed under his supervision. Still young and inexperienced, I was upset and I expressed my dissatisfaction with his decision. He was so wise to tell me that his purpose was only to protect me if anything went wrong.

In a very rare case, I encountered a woman who came in from a very remote village, several days after rupturing her uterus. She was extremely ill and was running a high temperature with generalized abdominal pain. Her abdomen was tender and the fetal parts were felt easily under the skin. On detailed questioning, she admitted that she had experienced strong labor pains for long hours a few days earlier. The pains had ceased suddenly and she had immediately collapsed. She and the blankets in which she was wrapped were far from clean. The nursing staff couldn't tolerate the smell so I had to clean her by myself. She received antibiotics and anti-tetanus serum before the surgery. I opened the abdomen, removed fetal parts, and performed a hysterectomy. She did very well, but I had to treat her for incidental pulmonary tuberculosis. Uterine rupture is often a complication of neglected difficult labor, though sometimes it results from the misuse of medications to augment labor, especially by untrained midwives, or occurs in patients with uterine scars, mainly those of repeated Cesarean sections. It is an absolute emergency, and patients usually show up with shock and signs of internal bleeding. This necessitates immediate resuscitation, which has to go hand in hand with procedures to stop the bleeding.

In another case, a patient was referred to me for a gynecological opinion by a general surgeon holding a high degree. The patient's main complaint was that she had blood in her urine. A pelvic examination revealed a mass in the anterior vaginal wall, and my provisional diagnosis was that she had a bladder tumor. The surgeon insisted that the tumor was uterine, and he operated on her, only to discover that the tumor was, in fact, in the bladder. It was such a triumph for me that residents kept talking about it for days. One cannot emphasize the importance of a detailed history and a proper physical examination, no matter how sophisticated the available technical facilities are.

My second chance to travel outside Iraq was in early 1968. This trip was also arranged by the Union of Arab Women University Graduates. Most of the participants were medical doctors, including some of my teachers, along with many other intellectuals. The trip was to Tehran, the capital of Iran, during the reign of the Shah. In those days Tehran was known as the "Paris of the East". We were hosted at a students' residence, yet it was like a 4-star hotel. On the second day after our arrival we were invited for tea at the Shah's mother-in-law's castle. Unfortunately I couldn't attend because I was delayed by traffic from a shopping trip. Despite missing the royal cup of tea, I still got my gift, which was a box of Iranian *sahoon* (almond brittle-a translucent candy studded with toasted almond) wrapped elegantly and sent with my friends. Shopping in Tehran was quite exiting. Most goods were locally manufactured and the prices were tempting. Of all the shopping I did, I remember the stereo album of Elvis Presley's children's songs that I kept for my children and grandchildren to enjoy, and still enjoy today.

At night we attended a concert by Googoosh, an Iranian singer and actress known for her contributions to Iranian Pop music since the fifties.

A visit to the "Museum of The Treasury of National Jewelry" was amazing. It houses the World's most precious gems and jewelry. The most exciting was The Empress's Crown which was placed by Mohammed Riza Shah on the head of his wife Empress Farah, immediately after he had put the Pahlavi Crown on his own head, during his coronation in 1967. That was a precedent, as none of the previous Kings' wives had ever been made a queen They were only princesses.

We had a chance to visit Esfahan, the third largest city in Iran, located 211 miles south of Tehran. It is famous for its Islamic architecture, especially mosques, in addition to the manufacture of delicate carpets. On the way back we visited Qum, the smallest Iranian city regarded as a holy city, where the shrine of Fatima, the daughter of Imam Musa Al Kadhum is located. We had to share chadors borrowed from women in the vicinity, to cover ourselves so that we would be allowed inside the mosque.

Serendipity

A few months after joining al-Nasiriya Hospital, I met Abdul Wahab Al- Mudaris (Abdul), my future husband. He was a young, ambitious, handsome and elegant dentist. Unlike the majority of Iraqis, Abdul looked European with his white complexion. His sincere blue eyes were as deep and distracting as the blue ocean. We met in early 1968 while at work in Nasiriya (225 miles south east of Baghdad) He was the dentist and the director of the Eastern Health Center where my colleague Raja'a and I were assigned to see patients twice a week. Abdul decided to ask for my hand after several weeks, but out of respect for tradition, he asked another colleague to test the waters and take my father's contact information to approach him directly. It took me a few weeks to answer, not only because I didn't know him well, but because my dream was to finish post-graduate studies abroad before anything else. As expected, my family called from Baghdad saying that he had visited them and that they wanted me to come back home. Not surprisingly, they already did a background check on him and his entire tribe! This coincided with the Euphrates River flood blocking the railway from Nasiriya to Baghdad, so I had to go first to Basra by bus, and then take the train to Baghdad. Within several months, on June 28, 1968, we got married. We didn't need a lot of preparation, apart from bedroom furniture, since we were going to live with his mother. We had a small party at my parents' house attended by family and friends, and followed by a five-day stay at the Baghdad Hotel, the most prestigious at the time. On our way back to Nasiriya, we stopped in Basra and were greeted at the railway station by Abdul's cousin Ahmad Zeki Al-Mudaris, head of his big family. Then we spent two nights with his second cousin Aisha Al-Ni'ma, who invited us to a nice family gathering and offered her jewelry box for us to choose whatever piece I liked. With no way out, Abdul chose a precious diamond watch for me.

Abdul was from a well-known Baghdadi family. One of his great-grandfathers, Abdulla Al-Rabatki, was a religious scholar in Rabatka, Mosul. Wahab's father, Abdul Kader, had a business in Basra with his brother Mohammed Saleh. Besides being in trade, Abdul Kader was a preacher at al- Zubair Mosque. The rest of the family stayed in Baghdad and many of them were scholars at Asafiya Mosque. My mother-in-law, Afifa Al-Hashimi, also came from a religious Baghdadi family in Bab al-Sheikh, where her brother Mahmud Al-Hashimi was director of endowments. She loved me as a daughter and I called her Mother, with great love and respect. Abdul was the youngest of three brothers. The other two were Abdul Wadoud and Abdul Karim. Their father died when Wahab was around 3, Karim was 7 and Wadoud 15. Wadoud took responsibility for the family while still at school and worked at the Land Registry Office. Karim attained his law degree and worked at the Arab League until 1976, when he established the Arab British Chamber of Commerce in London, and served as its Secretary General until his retirement in 2003. The two elder brothers were caring, loving and generous to their younger sibling. I was more than lucky to be part of their family. Abdul was a family man, his main concern being our comfort and my success at work and with studies. It is to him, in addition to my parents, that I owe whatever success I have achieved in life. From the beginning he promised to let me finish my post-graduate studies and he kept his promise.

Abdul & Malka engagement photo taken by "Babel", the photographer of the Iraqi Royal family and later of Saddam's - 1968

Here We Come Varna

Our hectic work schedule and family responsibilities didn't allow us to enjoy any decent time off, and from the time we got engaged Abdul had told me about a conference event abroad. We thought that once we are married we could arrange a quick getaway while not being completely “away“ from our work atmosphere. Our two dentist friends who joined us were also newlyweds. In September 1968, I accompanied Abdul to the Dental World Conference in Varna, Bulgaria- a port city and seaside resort on the Black Sea. It is famous for the oldest golden treasure in the world, discovered in its necropolis, and consisting of artifacts dating back to over 4000 BC. Our cozy hotel was on top of a mountain overlooking the sea in the appealing “Golden Sands” beach resort. We dined mostly at a small restaurant at sea level. The exercise we got from going up and down the mountains could not be matched by any gym workout. The only drawback was the language barrier, as few locals spoke English. Once we tried hard to get fish for dinner, but the waiters didn’t understand our request, and after drawing it on a piece of paper, we ended up with a raw fish on the plate.

The conference organizers had assigned an interpreter to help in communications, but only inside the hotel premises. She was a young, blond, attractive woman. One early afternoon, after heading out of the restaurant, Abdul noticed we forgot the wooden-bottle souvenirs we had bought. At the same time, the interpreter was walking in our direction. Abdul asked if I want to go back to get the souvenirs, which I did. When I came back he was talking with the interpreter. Upset, I walked right by them without saying a word. Abdul asked, “where are you going, my queen?” but I didn’t care to answer and went up the stairs as fast and as furiously as I could. Abdul came quickly to check on me, and I told him I was leaving by myself and that he intentionally asked me to go back to the restaurant just so he could talk to the blond woman, and it wasn’t the first time he had a chat with her. A few hours later, I felt ill and poor Abdul had no other choice but to talk to the interpreter again to ask for a doctor. We had been married for only a few months and Abdul was very detail-oriented and social. The reason he had been talking to the interpreter was that he was planning our sightseeing of Sofia. If anything Abdul was always a faithful and sincere man, but at that time I didn’t fully know him.

We had a chance to visit Sofia, the capital and second oldest city in Europe. We visited several museums, the church of St Sophia, and the gold-domed

Alexander Nevsky Orthodox Cathedral that has a capacity of 5000 people. There we forgot our umbrellas just outside the door, only to find them in the same place the next day. We took a short visit to the monument of the Unknown Soldier just next to the churches. It was amazing how disciplined the guard was. Like a bunch of kids, we went back and forth in front of one of the well-dressed guards to check if he would blink. Eventually he gave us a welcoming smile – while probably thinking how silly we acted. Sofia had paved roads with elegant yellow bricks that shine like gold after a heavy rain. Bulgaria is the oldest country in the European continent that hasn't changed its name since it was first founded in 681 AD, and the only Eastern European country that had kept much of its Jewish population from the gas chambers during the Holocaust. The famous founder of Facebook, Mark Zuckerberg, has a Bulgarian ancestry and he is named after his Bulgarian grandfather, Marko, who emigrated from Bulgaria in 1940. Zuckerberg once said, "By giving people the power to share, we're making the world more transparent", and indeed, Bulgaria is a unique discovery to share.

It's a Boy

On September 28, 1969, we were blessed to have our first son, Mohammed, at Ibn Sina Hospital, under the care of my teacher Prof. Kubba. I felt very relieved that the suffering of giving birth was over. When I touched that tiny beautiful miracle of flesh and blood, I felt the joy of possessing all the treasures of the world. Before me was a beautiful face with wide brown eyes, well-formed eyebrows and lots of long hair. His face was shining with beauty. That happiness did not last long. I started to worry about whether I would be at all capable of caring for this precious little thing and also performing my sacred duties to my patients, not to mention to Abdul and other family members to whom I always felt committed. My newborn and I had to leave my parents' house in Baghdad for Nasiriya just three weeks after delivery, because the maternity leave was over and I had to resume work. Total maternity leave was only 42 days, to cover both pre- and post-delivery periods. Besides practicing at the public hospital, I had my own clinic. Still my son was well cared for, even in those days when disposable diapers were not available. This was the case as long as his grandma and I were looking after him. When Mohammed was four months old, my mother-in-law visited Egypt for a few months. At that time, a nanny was looking after him in my absence. My son developed a prolonged fever, diarrhea, and vomiting, and was not responding to the treatment from Dr. Ghani Al-Tahhan, a very experienced pediatrician. We had to admit him to the Children's Hospital in Baghdad to correct his dehydration and treat an infection. When he recovered, my mother insisted on keeping him in Baghdad under her care. It was not an easy decision. We had to put up with this situation for many long months, until we finally reunited in Baghdad in late 1971. Around that time, with the help of two colleagues working in the States, I was offered a job at a hospital in Cleveland, Ohio, but I was unable to leave Iraq. Besides family obligations, I was committed to work for the Iraqi Ministry of Health for ten years after graduating, or pay a big sum of money which I couldn't afford.

My brother Dawood graduated from the Medical College in 1968, and became an intern at Nasiriya Hospital. During his OBG training, he was under my supervision. Just after completing his internship, he got married to Ina'am Al-Wahab, a relative from Karbala. The story of his marriage is quite interesting. During one of his weekends off, he went home to Baghdad, only to come back with an engagement ring shining on his finger Noting how surprised I was, he told me that he went with my parents to visit extended family in Karbala with the intention of seeing that family's daughter. The deal was that if he liked the girl, he would rotate the watch on his wrist to the other side as a sign of his approval to my parents to ask for her hand. He liked the girl, and surprisingly her father's response was immediate. Without wasting any time, they all went to the jewelry market and both rings were bought on the spot.

In 1970 we participated in a conference of the Iraqi Medical Association held in Basra. Again Wahab's generous cousin Aisha Al Ni'ma hosted us in her gorgeous villa. We had the opportunity to visit Kuwait on a 1-day trip. Abdul took me on a self-guided tour as he had visited Kuwait several times before, staying with his brother's family for a few weeks each time.

We went to Salmiya, Al Jahra, and Souq Al Mubarkeya. The weather was too hot so we couldn't go far, but shopping was tempting and we did not waste the opportunity. The Iraqi and Kuwaiti Dinars were of nearly equal value, the two being the strongest currencies in the Middle East.

We welcomed our second child Afaf (Afoo) in 1971. Abdul was so pleased that he cried with joy. He was hoping for a daughter and used to say that their house always missed the feminine touches of young girls, as his siblings were all boys. I was even happier with my little angel and bought pink embroidered dresses with matching ribbons, tiny decorated shoes, and several nice dolls. We needed to have our son to be back with us and with his sister, and my mother reluctantly allowed us to take him for a while.

Left to right Drs. Rasoul, Dawood my brother, Sajida, Khalida, Malka, and nurses- Nasiriya hospital 1971

Eden Again

The beauty of Iraq lay in its lovely diversity, not just in its people but in its geography too, from the mountains and forests in the north, the desert in the west, and the river valleys in the center, to the marshes in the south. The area of marshes consists of 4,500 sq. miles that are seasonally flooded. There are 7,700 sq. miles of various bodies of water, with floating areas of golden reed houses, forming a magical world that is hardly available anywhere else in such capacity.

The Norwegian explorer and archaeologist Thor Heyerdahl was among several explorers who showed an interest in the Iraqi marshes. Heyerdahl wrote about the Marsh Arabs in his book "*The Tigris Expedition: In Search of Our Beginnings*" (1978). He wrote, "*The water was crystal clear; the aqua herbs cover the bottom. I saw fish and rosy wreaths floating on the surface. We moved silently from the green turf and slid between towering rows of reefs and aqua plants. When we were covered with the aqua plants we were shut off from the green doors, we felt that we left the hustle and bustle of the modern world; I felt as if traveling back in time, not to brutality and danger but to a civilization, a completely different civilization than ours at present, wonderful in its simplicity and non-compliance.*" Heyerdahl was interested in finding out if originally there had been contact between the three "mother" civilizations in Mesopotamia, Egypt and the Indus valley. In 1977 Heyerdahl built his largest reed vessel, some 59 feet long, where the Euphrates and Tigris Rivers met, and he named it Vessel Tigris. Tigris sailed 4,225 miles. First the expedition members sailed down Shatt-al-Arab in Iraq to the Persian Gulf and out into the Indian Ocean, and then via Muscat in Oman to the Indus Valley in Pakistan, before finally leaving Asia and sailing across the Indian Ocean to Africa. The five-month journey ended in Djibouti at the mouth of the Red Sea. Surrounded by wars on all sides, the expedition members decided in April 1978 to burn the vessel, and they sent an unanimous appeal to the U.N. asking it to stop delivery of arms to developing countries in the region of the world where the foundations of our civilization were laid.

In 2014, the story was produced in an Iraqi soap opera named *Safinat Sumar* - Ship of Sumer. It was filmed mainly in the marshes of Maysan southern province and acted by locals and a few Syrian artists. In mimicking the original story and as an outcry of protest towards violence and wars, the ship was burnt by the end of the filming. Watching the ship burn into ashes was described by the ship's crew as very sad, especially since they had lots of associated memories and had physically helped in building it with the locals, a process that took 45 days of hard teamwork.

"EDEN AGAIN" is a project sponsored by the Iraq Foundation in 2003 that works on the restoration of the southern marshes.

Marshes of Southern Iraq- Courtesy of Mohammed Al-Dhamat

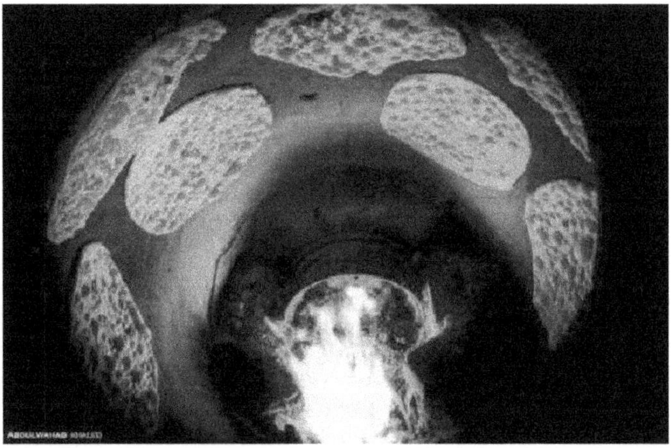

Iraqi flat bread being baked in a clay oven-Courtesy of AbdulWahab Khaled

A marshland woman preparing the clay oven for baking-
Courtesy of Mohammed Al-Dhamat

Acting crew of Safinat Sumar with the ship- Courtesy of Mohammed Al- Dhamat

Building the ship by marshland locals and crew-Courtesy of Mohammed Al-Dhamat

Postgraduate Studies in Baghdad

Baghdad University Medical College offered 12-month studies for High Diplomas in various medical specialties; I started the OBG course in September 1971. At the beginning, Abdul stayed in Nasiriya while I moved to Baghdad, taking Afaf with me. Mohammed was already in Baghdad with my parents. We rented an apartment in Adhamiya and my father had to spend the nights with us. Afoo was enrolled in a nearby childcare center, and a few months later Wahab was transferred to Baghdad and the family was reunited again.

We studied at the Medical City which had been established not long before as a modern hospital with all sophisticated facilities. The OBG department occupied the fourth floor and was equipped with first-class surgical theaters, labor rooms and a newborn care unit. There were two lecture rooms, a cytology lab and two side labs. Several research projects were going on along-side them with grand rounds, clinical-pathological meetings, perinatal mortality meetings, workshops and conferences. During our diploma studies, several world-renowned experts visited Iraq, presenting their knowledge and expertise. Among them were Professor Savage from Britain who lectured about infertility management and artificial insemination. The Dutch scientist Gimsel, who revolutionized infertility treatment by introducing pituitary gonadotropins, lectured us and managed patients over a period of several weeks. We were lucky to learn about up-to-date advances in the field of OBG and observe them performing different procedures.

At the end of the 12-month course, we completed our written, oral, and clinical examinations. The clinical performance was evaluated by a British co-examiner, Prof. Melkin. I was told by Prof. Kubba, that he was impressed with my performance, and that he recommended further studies for me in the UK.

The Last Supper

During my stay at the Medical City, My colleagues and I were shocked to see the severe afflictions of patients admitted to medical wards with mercury poisoning; after ingesting wheat seeds treated with mercury products. The red-colored seeds were meant for planting and not for ingestion. The tragedy set a record in regards to number of casualties; the reported number of deaths exceeded 6,500. The poison mainly affected the nervous system, causing blindness, impairments to motor capabilities, and sometimes even death. Mercury was largely used in agriculture as a fungicide. The tragedy began when there was an over two-month delay in getting the imported seeds, and the time for planting was over. Farmers did not have enough to feed their children and their livestock due to the scarcity of the crop that season. When the red color was washed out with water, the farmers were reassured, so they fed the livestock with the washed seeds, ignoring the instructions with strict warnings. When no harm was observed to those animals after several weeks, they were confident that consuming the seeds and feeding them to their children was okay. They did not realize that the poison was accumulating and its effects would take months to become evident. The poor farmers went on consuming the poison for months before noticing the grave effects. The afflictions became evident in early 1972. The cases were puzzling, but some Iraqi doctors diagnosed them correctly. At the same time, authorities called experts from abroad to manage the cases. The remaining seeds were confiscated, and severe punishment was imposed on whoever was found "guilty" of keeping and storing the seeds. Despite the harshness of the sanctions, some farmers retained the seeds and buried them in their farmland, which lead to contaminated water supplies and further dangers to life. After that tragedy, the World Health Organization and the Food and Agriculture Organization enforced their instructions for packing, trading, and use of these products They added new guidelines to safeguard against such incidents, including labeling the products in the local language, putting understandable danger stamps, and possibly adding a bitter taste to the seeds.

Round and Round We Go

After finishing our diploma studies, we had to work in provinces outside Baghdad for three years. My name was missing from the new assignment lists. I later learned that by the request of Nasiriya officials, the minister of health made the decision to assign me to the city even before graduation. We had no intention of going back to Nasiriya after spending four years far from our family and also suffering from poor weather conditions that affected our children's health. The only other choice given to me by the minister was Anah, a small rural town in the far North West. It was lacking facilities, but it was said to have a nice and moderate climate even better than Baghdad. We took the assignment and had to drive eight hours, mostly through desert, to get there. The city consisted of one long street that runs parallel to the Euphrates River on one side and hills on the other. The houses were on the river banks or scattered on the hills. Farms and orchards were watered from the river by wooden watermills (*Nawae'er*). Families were self-sufficient; each had its own small garden, poultry farm, and special baking oven (*tanoor*). Some even had livestock, since there was not a single market.

Although Anah hospital was larger than the one in Tikrit, it lacked a proper operating theater and anesthesia facilities. Professionally I was back to square one. During the whole year in Anah, I didn't perform a single Cesarean section, much less any major gynecological surgeries as I had performed in Nasiriya while training for my higher degree. We did not even think of establishing a private clinic, because we were occupied with our added responsibilities at home. In Nasiriya we always had at least one nanny for the children; the locals there were willing to do any job for a living. In Anah one couldn't dream of that, as the inhabitants there regarded working in somebody else's home demeaning. At the same time, no one would agree to be deployed from Baghdad to Anah, not only because it was too far from Baghdad, but also because of total lack of any kind of entertainment. Even television broadcasting was out of range.

We were offered a big house on the Cornice with a huge yard full of fruit trees. The Ministry of Health provided housing to doctors in remote areas for a low rent. Our house was a gathering place for the few doctors working in the area as we enjoyed good relations with all of them. The only outlets we all had from work were either family gatherings, river trips or visiting tourist places during weekends. Our main source of food supplies and other shopping needs were from Baghdad once a month - with a full car load. Emergency shopping was from Rawa, the neighboring town across the river. It was a lot of fun going to Rawa with our car on a ferry; sometimes we spent the whole day there with local friends.

Our third child, Mutaz (Matt) was born in 1973 at Ibn Sina Hospital. I thought having three small children, along with me and my husband, would be too much of a burden on my parents, so we decided to go back home to Anah just a week after delivery. There we faced an unexpected incident. A well-known person knocked on our door carrying his sick grandson and asking me to treat him. We apologized politely and pointed out in an indirect way that the pediatrician next to their house was available and another doctor was not far from them. I was on maternity leave looking after three children and on top of that, I was not a pediatrician. The man was furious and left angry, and the next morning we found large rocks covering the roof of our new car in the open garage.

During the next few weeks the Health Authorities implemented the "Health Insurance Law" which called for 3-hour evening health services at the public health institutions with nominal wages for the health professionals and auxiliary staff. All private clinics and pharmacies were closed. This did not affect us financially as we didn't have private clinics but it made our life even more difficult. Our children were already forced to spend the day with us in hospital surroundings. With the new arrangement, they had to spend the evenings too. I submitted a petition for transfer to Baghdad, which was rejected. As a last resort, I wrote a letter of resignation, which prompted the minister to call us for an interview. At the meeting I told the minister about our problems including the car incident. He was understanding and promised to transfer us. He wouldn't allow us to transfer to Baghdad, so we chose Hilla, Babylon. A few days later I received a call from his personal secretary announcing the good news.

Looking back, the Anah assignment was a new experience. The place was a charming vacation countryside, and we made lasting friendships with other families and visited places we had not heard of before. Sadly, Anah was flooded after the construction of a dam in the nineties and a new modern town was built in Anbar as a replacement for its inhabitants. Still, most of them were not satisfied, as little remained of the untouched natural beauty of the original town with its wonderful watermills irrigating the farms and its fruit orchards on the river side.

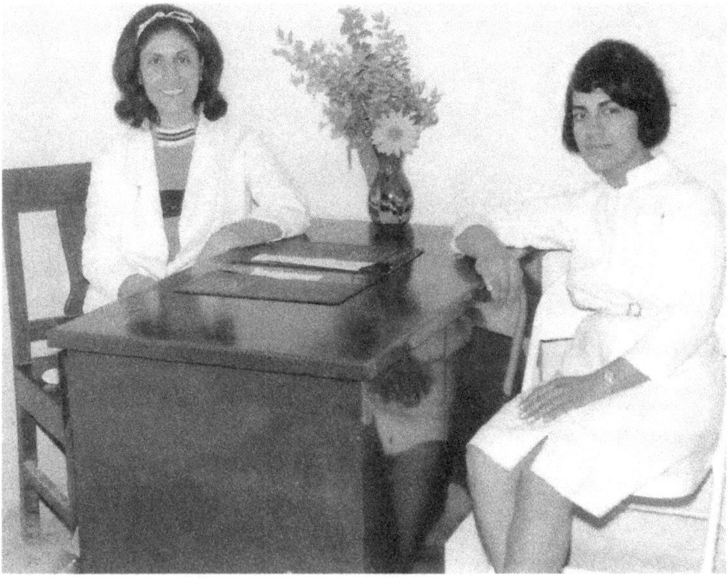

In Anah hospital 1973

Waterwheel in Ajmeya village near Anah and Rawah

Hatchet Man

In 1973, a series of terrifying crimes took place in Baghdad and spread to several parts of Iraq. The unique connection was the crime weapon, a big ax known as "*tubar*," normally used by butchers to cut meat and bone. There was no connection between victims' background, religion, wealth, or profession. Crimes took place in different locations and times, leading to widespread horror all over Iraq. Party members as well as the general public took security duties around the clock. A 24-hour curfew was implemented and Saddam touched on the events in a televised speech, though some believed that those incidents were fabricated by the government to distract people from existing problems, and help find those opposed to his rule. In September 1974, the killer was captured. He admitted that his wife, two brothers and nephew were all accessories; his confession was broadcasted and he was executed after the trial. Rumors continued that he was a government agent who carried out certain tasks until his role expired.

What Happens in Vegas Stays in Vegas

From Anah we went directly to Hilla without stopping in Baghdad, driving our white Renault 6. Our furniture was sent by truck. My heart was dancing with joy; Hilla (slightly larger than Rhode Island) is only 62 miles from Baghdad with a modern highway connecting them. I regarded Hilla as the second best place for us after Baghdad. Although Mosul and Basra are more popular, each of those cities is over 248 miles from Baghdad, and we were fed up from being away from family. The hospital was a modern six-story building, having specialists with high degrees from the UK, in addition to having big operating theaters and a well-equipped labor room with efficient staff. I couldn't wait to start work and practice my passion in OBG.

Hilla locals are generally well to do. A branch of the colorful river *Furat*-Euphrates runs exactly through the middle of the town and is surrounded by date palm trees. The perfect irrigation from the river resulted in abundant fruits and other crops. Hilla is mostly famous for Qaymer al Seddeh (Cream of the Dam), which took its name from the location of the Hindeya Barrage. The city was once a major center of Islamic scholarship and education and is not far from the sacred cities of Karbala and Najaf. The tomb of the Jewish prophet Al Kifl (Ezekiel) is reputed to be located in a nearby village. Hilla is also adjacent to the ancient city of Babylon. The Hanging Gardens of Babylon were one of the Seven Wonders of the Ancient World. With plants cultivated above ground level, the roots of the trees were embedded in an upper terrace built with baked brick and asphalt. There were fortresses and temples in the gardens that contained huge statues of solid gold.

With the help of a friend, we had rented a nice corner house on a main road. While we were busy putting our furniture in place, my father surprised us at the door step. He had never visited while we were in Anah; in fact he had been unhappy that we chose Anah over Nasiriya, regarding it a mistake to prefer a rural town over a large city with much financial and professional superiority.

We were greeted by the general director of the Health Authority, who had been Abdul's best friend for years, and started work the next day -- I at Hilla General Hospital and Abdul at the Dental Center in the old hospital building. There were five gynecologists already in the department, and two of them were old friends of mine. The OBG department occupied the ground floor along with the pharmacy and the administrative offices, while the major surgical theaters and intensive care unit occupied the first floor. Although I was very much excited to get started, I was slightly intimidated that I might have lost my touch after such a long time away from it. My confidence was restored after performing the first cesarean in Hilla uneventfully.

In 1974 we were blessed with our fourth child, Abeer, a doll with a moon face, long eye lashes and straight black hair. My friends used to call her Potato Patties. We slaughtered two sheep instead of one to celebrate her birth, distributing one third of the meat to the underprivileged, another third to acquaintances, and the rest for the family. My 42-day maternity leave was spent in Hilla. To our relief, we were able to find day-care for our children. It was a small family-run facility owned by Um Nassir, a sweet lady originally from the Christian town of Tilkaif, in north of Iraq. Her husband had a van to drive the children, and with two helpers the place was neat and cozy. The children even enjoyed home-cooked meals there.

I always remember with joy Um Maha, our chief nurse in charge of the labor room. She had four daughters, all delivered by Cesarean section. The family had been longing for a baby boy. I performed the fifth Cesarean, while the waiting area was occupied by anxious hospital staff, as all were close friends of Um Maha and her husband, the chief assistant anesthesiologist. Once they found out the newborn was a boy, the crowd outside started celebrating. We had lasting friendships with colleagues in Baghdad, Nasiriya and Anah, but we had so much in common with our Hilla friends that we all kept strong ties with them up through the present time. Several months had passed and we were still unable to find a place suitable for our clinics. My friend Dr. Widad Al-Hasoun, a local from Hilla, asked her husband Ameer, an engineer, for help. He soon found a place and helped in setting up all the requirements.

We also had frequent short vacations to the Habaniya Resort in Anbar which was the Las Vegas of the nation -- a perfect place for weddings, family getaways and college student beach parties. Built by the French in the late 70s, this tourist village had it all: a wide beach on Lake Habaniya, a disco, restaurants, ballrooms, and an amusement park. It also had honeymoon bungalows and large swimming pools, connected with each other by elegant short arched-shaped bridges colored with distinctive light green, yellow and blue floor tiles. All of this was situated amid hundreds of acres of palm trees and carefully groomed lawns, a six-story hotel with 265 rooms, and 500 condo units. During one of our vacations in Habaniya in the mid-eighties with our friends the Al Bairmanis, our 13 year old Afaf spotted an incredibly elegant, shining red Porsche while taking a walk by the vast beach. It was parked by the roadside, and she said to us while pointing, "when I grow up, I want you to buy me a car exactly like this one". The entire family turned toward the vehicle only to see the notorious Uday Saddam Hussein smiling. We held our breath as we silently walked away. We never spoke about that moment within our family until Uday's death in 2003.

One of our adventures was a spontaneous trip to the Kurdish north of Iraq with Dr. Khidr Al Bairmani, his wife Dr. Salwa Al Nouri and their children, who were of comparable ages to ours. Our first destination was Erbil, where we arrived at night. Finding that all the hotels were already booked, Salwa suggested trying the Medical Association headquarters. She and Abdul, the best speakers in the group, went into the office and came back with wide smiles announcing that we got a night's shelter in the place. Officers there volunteered to bring bedding from their homes. We had a wonderful dinner of the well-known "*Kebab Erbil*", watched TV, and then we all slept atop mattresses on the floor of the reception hall. In the morning we thanked them and proceeded to Shaqlawa, the nice well-known resort where accommodation was readily available.

Late in 1975 we had to move, as the house we had rented had been sold and the new owner wanted to settle in. We bought our own smaller house after borrowing from the Real Estate Public Bank with a very low interest rate.

Ishtar gate – Babylon

Madame Tussaud

We were invited by Abdul's brother to visit London. In those days Abdul Karim was an employee of the Arab League and was working on the establishment of the Arab-British Chamber of Commerce, which he eventually served as its Secretary General. At Heathrow Airport he greeted us with his elegant Egyptian wife Sawsan and their daughter Eman. He drove us to their apartment at Bays Water Road opposite the Hyde Park and we enjoyed two weeks in their company.

Eman took us for a free tour to the British Museum, one of the world's largest and most important museums of human history and culture. It has 7 million objects from all continents. It boasts vast Egyptian, Etruscan, Greek, Roman, European, and Middle East galleries.

The visit to the Waxworks Museum "Madame Tussaud" was our first to a wax museum, and we were amazed to see Sculptures of the world's royalty, presidents, famous figures, and artists which look real and were so excitingly presented. The ones I still remember, apart from royalty and presidents were: the Sleeping Beauty and how she was breathing, Charlie Chaplin, Marilyn Monroe in "Bus Stop", Mahatma Gandhi, Alfred Hitchcock, Madame Tussaud, Elvis Presley and Chamber of Horror. Next to the Wax Museum was the London Planetarium where we enjoyed an exciting show about astronomy that took us out into space.

We had a day trip to Brighton, which is south of London, and spent another day strawberry picking. At night, we watched a show "Talk of the Town" and had dinner at the Playboy Club. At the end of the second week we accompanied Abdul's niece Sawsan to her home in Sheffield. From there we had several picnics including one to Scarborough, where we enjoyed the rides in its amusement park. Our children didn't accompany us on this vacation. They stayed with my parents and had fun of another kind -- they attended my brother Mohammed's marriage ceremony.

U.K.- KUT- BAGHDAD
1976- 2003

Swinging City, Swinging Dreams

In early 1976, approval was given to carry out Part I of the exam for membership in the British Royal College of Obstetricians and Gynecologists (MRCOG) in Baghdad. Baghdad University arranged a preparatory three-month course for eligible doctors willing to pursue the program, and was held at the Medical City by Iraqi and foreign scholars. I enrolled in the course, taking two of my children to my parents' house and leaving the others in Hilla with Abdul and the nanny. The courses covered were basic sciences, and because the lectures were meant for postgraduate students, they did not cover general knowledge topics that the audience should have been familiar with. On several occasions, I found I was unable to follow along since I had graduated 12 years earlier and still did not have all the required books. As a result, I decided to drop out of the course and study at home on my own. Not only was I successful in my endeavor, but, I ranked 3rd among 11 successful candidates. Wafa'a al-Nasiri was second and I forget the name of the first. The Minister of Health congratulated us during a meeting at his office and presented each of us with a beautiful Parker 51 pen, along with approval for a two-year leave to study in the United Kingdom to finish the requirements and take the final examination. More excited than I, Abdul quickly made arrangements for our departure. He sold our car, stored the furniture at my parent's house and rented out our house. We left for London in October 1976.

We had so much to discover about London! We learned that London was nicknamed the "Swinging City" because it played an important role in the Cultural Revolution during the mid-1960s. We found that because of the increasing air pollution over the centuries, it also was given another nickname: "The Smoke." To me it was indeed the city of fresh dreams swinging before my eyes.

From Heathrow Airport my brother-in-law Abdul Karim took us to his apartment in Bays Water Road. His wife and daughters were on vacation in Egypt at the time. We stayed with him for two weeks while trying to find a suitable apartment. Finally, we moved into a clean, well-maintained one at Shepherd's Bush, not a prestigious area but well within our budget.

Our two eldest children went to school, but the others were under school age. Part of the requirements to sit for Part II of the MRCOG exam, besides passing Part I, was to practice OBG in recognized hospitals in the U.K. for 18 months, submit a log book of 20 cases in whose management I participated, and complete two research projects. In order to practice medicine in the U.K., one has to be registered with the British Medical Council. First, I took the TRAB exam, which was designed to test medical knowledge and English proficiency. I succeeded on the first trial. After passing the exam and becoming registered, I now had a significant obstacle to overcome. I had to find a job. I applied for senior house officer (SHO) positions meant for new graduates. However, I was 35 years old, graduated 12 years earlier, and I had four young, demanding children. My applications were either ignored or answered with a polite apology; and if I was lucky to be shortlisted for an interview, other younger, childless competitors got the job. Weeks and months went by with no glimmer of hope.

We were on thin ice, spending from our savings, and my monthly salary (100 Iraqi Dinars, which equaled 200 British pounds at the time) was not even covering two-weeks rent. We made a decision to move to another apartment nearby at nearly half the cost, but minimally furnished. After finding a tempting household sale advertisement at a nearby grocery store, we were able to buy what we needed. The sellers, a blind couple with a dog, requested that we not pick up the items we bought until they left for the States the next day. They gave us the door keys and asked us to return them to their neighbors. When we returned the next day, to our shock we discovered that they had rented the place fully furnished, and none of the household items they had sold us were theirs to sell. The experience was a bitter pill to swallow, but as hard as it was, we made ourselves go back out and shop anew.

Mohammed and Afaf in London – 1977

After a long six months, we were filled with joy when an Iraqi doctor, Fadha'a Al-Shanawi, called asking me to take her place as a locum SHO at The Royal London Homeopathic Hospital because she was taking a full-time job somewhere else. The two-week locum in general surgery and OBG was key to my success. The consultant gynecologist was impressed with my performance and gave me an excellent recommendation. Not only that, I received another call for another two-week locum at Charing Cross Hospital in London. Before that locum finished, I had another three-week assignment in Torkey Hospital on my schedule. The seaside city in the south was amazingly attractive, and I couldn't help asking Abdul to bring the children and come for a vacation. The consultant whom I worked there also appreciated my capabilities. With an unbelievable stroke of luck, I got a call from Dunfermline in Scotland for yet another locum. At the time I didn't even know where the place was. The lady on the phone told me that I had to take a two-hour train to London, then another eight-hour ride to get there. I decided to take that locum, too. My lucky day came when the consultant didn't show up to perform the operative list. He called and left instructions regarding the tasks I was to carry out, including performing a "Manchester's Operation"- a major surgery for genital prolapse. All were amazed by the results. Shortly after this last locum, I was contacted for two interviews, one at Norfolk and Norwich Hospital, and the other was in Torkey, where I had worked a few weeks earlier. Both were scheduled ten days apart. I was the lucky candidate to be offered the six-month job of SHO in gynecology at the first interview. At the conclusion of the interview, the head of the department, Mr. Bentall, stood up to shake my hand. He congratulated me for being brave enough to seek higher studies outside my country while being a mother of four youngsters.

Follow Your Heart

The obstetrics and gynecology department at Norfolk and Norwich occupied the second and third floors of a multi-story building; I spent six months on the second floor working for Mr. Bentall and Mr. Carron Brown (in the U.K. physicians in surgical specialties are called Mr. instead of Dr.) as SHO in gynecology. The registrar was an Indian Australian, Mr. Parhar, a cooperative and capable colleague who had recently attained the MRCOG. Carron Brown was a versed surgeon who made his own modifications to many procedures for the benefit of his patients, yet at the same time, he was tough on those under him, demanding perfection in all aspects. He used to have three operative sessions a week. My duties were to clerk patients, prepare them for surgery, and assist in major surgeries, performing minor and occasionally intermediate procedures, as well as doing post-operative care. Work started 30 minutes earlier than normal, and most of the times ended late as well. Most SHOs avoided working with Carron Brown. However, I took advantage of the opportunity to learn from his expertise and discipline and gave my best in return. Soon I gained his confidence. He started giving me more responsibilities and called me "his right arm." While I held that position, my duties were one in two rotas - exhausting but rewarding in terms of experience. I owe him my precision in performance, regarding both operating as well as decision-making. Before finishing my appointment, I had a two-week vacation in Baghdad, a refreshing break to see family and enjoy the relatively warm winter. I was delighted to see the family growing bigger. When we left, my brother Mohammed only had one son, Ahmed. This time there was a second child, so I was able to meet Zeena, too. Amal also had a new little girl, Farah; both were lovely angels. Afterward, my contract was renewed for other six months, again in gynecology.

Blackpool Tower Circus

While we were in Norwich, my brother Dawood arrived with his family, to finish his postgraduate studies in general medicine. His wife was 36 weeks pregnant, her third pregnancy (I wondered how they allowed her on the plane.). Having had two Cesarean sections before, it was necessary to find an obstetrician agreeable to do a Cesarean under the National Health Service. Carron Brown took this on. He asked the senior registrar, Miss Kelly, to perform the operation under his supervision. This was a nice gesture on his part. He really helped us out.

That same year my niece Tina paid us a visit. Joined by three other families, we toured Liverpool, Blackpool, and the Lake District, in the North West. Blackpool is considered the Fun Capital of the U.K. Among the several attractions are: Blackpool Tower, Tramway, Pleasure Beach, the famous Illuminations and North Pier. We witnessed the amazing Illuminations and walked along Pleasure Beach, which is regarded as Britain's number one free tourist attraction. One night we watched the Blackpool Tower Circus. During the show, one of the acrobat's feet slipped from the rope. That was a heart-stopping moment, and the eyes of the whole audience were fixed on her with concern. Then, in a daring, agile maneuver her teammate was able to grab onto to her and save her. Earning a living in that manner is truly not easy. Such performers risk their lives for our entertainment, and they deserve all our gratitude. The next day was spent in the Lake District, England's only truly mountainous region. The area is actually a vast national park that has four mountains over 3,000 feet high, as well as more than 50 lakes and tarns, including England's biggest and deepest.

Bring it on

My next job was as a Senior House Officer acting as registrar at North Gate Hospital in Great Yarmouth, a 30-minute drive from Norwich, on the east coast. Abdul started postgraduate studies at Birmingham University for his Master's degree in community dentistry. I had to cope with the children, the household chores, my studies, and a demanding job. Two children went to the same school, with the other two each going to a different one. I was working from 9 a.m. to 5 p.m. besides being on call for 24-hours every other day. There was no way to pick up the children from school since Abdul had the car with him. That nightmare lasted several weeks until by chance we met the Angel that descended from heaven. Mrs. Adams, a gentle kind-hearted lady, was doing volunteer work giving home help to the elderly. Abdul met her by chance during a doctor's visit for one of our children. She took on the task of picking up the children from school on her bike, bringing them to her house and giving them tea, then bringing them home after I finished work. The children loved her and her teenage daughter. Both mother and daughter assisted them with schoolwork and played games with them. The affection my children had for Mrs. Adams, and the impact she had made remained with them to such an extent that when Mutaz was asked during a job interview at the British embassy in 2004 what he liked about the U.K. he answered: tea time. He meant the times he had spent with Mrs. Adams. Another dear friend who was of great help was Carol Knights, the secretary of my consultant, Mr. Costley. Carol used to take us for a ride or shopping. She even voluntarily helped with housekeeping while I was at work.

Abdul Wahab with our children in Torkey, U.K. 1977

In the middle, Abeer celebrating her 6th birthday. Sutton Coldfield, U.K. 1980

Mohammed, Afaf and Mutaz in Great Yarmouth, U.K. 1978

My parents and niece Tina in Sutton Coldfield, U.K. 1980

Better Safe Than Sorry

Once the six months were over, I received a new job offer at Good Hope Hospital in Sutton Coldfield near Birmingham. It was a big relief for us all that the place was not far from Birmingham University, where Abdul was studying. The four children went to the same school within easy walking distance, and my duties were on a one-in-three Rota.

One of the oddest experiences I had during that assignment occurred when I was faced with a new addition on my theatre list, a pregnancy termination for a lady who was under the care of another team. As is routine, I examined her under anesthesia to detect the uterine size and position, which was 14 weeks in size and retroverted (turned backwards). That meant that there was possible risk of perforating the uterus. The only alternative was to give medications to induce an abortion. Those medications could take several hours or more to work. As a result, I abandoned the idea of surgery, explained the situation to the patient when she recovered from the anesthesia, and arranged her continued care management. The next morning, despite being more senior than I, my colleague, who was in charge of her care, told me that the night before had been chaotic. They had to call the consultant gynecologist, general surgeon, and urologist because, at the patient's insistence, he tried to perform suction curettage and had accidentally perforated the uterus damaging the bowel and urinary bladder. The lesson is: "Better to be safe than sorry." In another incident, a woman in her early fifties had an ovarian cyst for surgical removal. Upon getting her consent for the operation, I explained to her that should the cyst prove to be malignant during surgery, there was a possibility of the need to remove her uterus and both ovaries. The woman got upset and started crying. When the consultant came for his usual pre-op visit, she complained to him about the issue, and he assured her that nothing like that would happen. The cyst was found to be malignant during surgery, and the consultant regretted what he told her earlier. In fact, he did have to carry out the required procedure I had originally discussed.

One of the interesting places we visited on several occasions was Stradford-upon-Avon, the birthplace of the English playwright and poet William

Shakespeare, about 22 miles southeast of Birmingham. There we visited his birthplace house, Ann Hathaway's cottage (his wife's family house), Royal Shakespeare Theatre and Swan Theatre. In Sutton, we had several family gatherings with my brother Dawood, who was working in Peterborough, as well as visits with my sister Najiha, who was studying in Reading, and with other family members visiting from Baghdad.

Having fulfilled the work requirement, two research projects, and the written logbook, I took Part II of the MRCOG exam in 1980. I failed the written part, however. Frankly, I struggled the essay questions. So, it was only in 1981 that I was granted my Royal College membership.

During the summer of 1980, we made a trip to Aviemore in the High Lands of Scotland. Traveling on bus tours, we enjoyed the breathtaking scenery and rich wildlife from the rolling hills of the lowlands to the majestic beauty of Scotland's mountains. In the Cairngorms and highlands, the hilltops were covered with snow in August. We visited a malt distillery and went for a ride in the cable cars at the mountaintop—scary but refreshing. Our accommodation was in a big holiday center, where we enjoyed pony riding, swimming, movies and a beauty contest for dogs. I participated in a running contest for women, but arrived just before the last runner. At an exhibition of modern cars, we liked a new, showcased metallic beige Volvo, and we put in an order for one. Later on, we learned that the color we had chosen was used exclusively for military personnel in Iraq during that time. Our second choice was silver. One of the competitions we entered was name guessing for an exhibited big doll. From a long list of names, Afaf chose the name Dorothy, which happened to be the correct answer. The doll was posted to Afaf a day after the end of our vacation. "Dorothy" never made it to the US. She was left behind. God knows if she survived the three times our home was subjected to looting in Baghdad.

In April 1981, we left Sutton Coldfield for Iraq. That day, during an emotional moment at 5 a.m. in the morning, our next-door neighbor stood outside in the bitter cold weather to bid us farewell while tears filled her eyes. Her sons Richard and Mathew were the best friends of our four kids. Before leaving we sent home furniture from Debenhams with a matching carpet and curtains for the sitting room, a hostess trolley, and bunk beds for the children. The kitchen cabinets were purchased from IKEA. Together with other household goods all was packed and shipped by Pickford Removals to Baghdad.

With friends in Stradford upon Avon- Shakespeare's city

Royal College of Obstetricians and Gynecologists membership – U.K. 1981

Healthcare in the U.K.

During my stay in the U.K. from 1976 to 1981, I was impressed with the high standard of healthcare, scientific approach, and formidable professionalism. The National Health Service (NHS) is a publicly funded healthcare system; it is the largest and oldest single-pay healthcare system in the world. The system provides healthcare to any one legally residing in the U.K. (possessing an NHS number). All can access the full breadth of critical and non-critical care without any out-of-pocket payment of any kind. It is funded by the general taxation system. Private healthcare has continued parallel to the NHS, and it is paid largely through private insurances; it is used by about 8% of the population. The services are the same in both sectors; the only difference is the waiting lists of the cold cases. These cases are not urgent and may take a year or two, or even more, before the needed surgical interventions are performed. Nevertheless, if any change occurs in the patient's condition, it is dealt with accordingly. Urgent cases get immediate care. Primary care can be arranged with the family doctor. Usually it does not take more than a day or two. Specialists see only cases referred by family doctors. They are required to send a report to the referring physician, detailing the condition and any interventions.

Overwhelmed

Heading back home with the children, I took a flight to Baghdad. Abdul had to go to Jordan to bring the car we had bought and shipped, driving from Aqaba to Baghdad. Amal and Farooq greeted us at the airport. Our eyes welled up with tears, and Amal and I shared a long hug. Before leaving the airport, they told me not to be alarmed by the darkness that covered Baghdad. All road lights had been turned off because of the war with Iran, they explained. Also on the way home, they warned me not to be surprised by a marked change in Mom's appearance. For medical reasons, Mom had had all of her teeth extracted. In addition, I had only emerged from the plane, when I sensed a reaction to the extreme heat, and knowing that it was only April made me feel the heat even more. Still, with my dream of earning an advanced degree in the U.K. fulfilled, I was pleased to be home with my beloved family again.

Unfortunately, that joy did not last more than few hours. I started to worry. First, I worried about Abdul and his long drive in the desert. Next, I worried our children's education. They had not studied Arabic formally, and I wondered how they would manage their classwork. Indeed, our whole future became a troublesome concern for me.

How would I describe the times? On the one hand, there was an abundance of goods flooding the market. On the other hand, the infrastructure was just as I remembered it. Moreover, because of the war, all the people I met were far from happy.

As per the requirements following the receipt of advanced degrees, I had to work in a province outside of Baghdad for a period of three years. Fulfilling this requirement was expected of me despite the fact that I had already worked four years outside Baghdad after being awarded my first high postgraduate degree. I submitted a request to be assigned to Hilla. I was informed that since a member of the Royal College of Obstetricians and Gynecologists (MRCOG) already held a position at the hospital, no additional positions were anticipated; although Hilla is a large city. Therefore, my request was rejected. Instead, I was offered a choice of Kut or Ramadi. I chose Kut. Later on, I found out that another colleague holding MRCOG is already assigned there too. Government officials often reserve larger metropolitan areas like Hilla or cities near Baghdad for relatives, friends or party members. The experience was a little bit like a game of hide and seek, only with many unpleasant hidden things waiting for me to discover.

Twinkle, Twinkle little "Najim"...

In late April 1981, we moved to Kut (some 99 miles south east of Baghdad). The children were unaccustomed to the scorching heat and to so many insect bites, and they complained bitterly of the loneliness they experienced because we had no family or friends within 100 miles. Our first residence was a two-bedroom ranch house with a huge back yard. It was one of six houses reserved by the Health Authority for specialist doctors who could rent them at a subsidized cost. The house had been neglected for an extended period of time, and it became tenable only after the painstaking efforts of two handymen. Along with the children's new bunk beds, we brought our old furniture from Baghdad. We had to purchase new appliances in order to settle in. The kindness of our friendly new neighbors eased our alienation; all were doctors with advanced degrees. A few months later, we rented a larger, nicer home. It offered enough room for the children to enjoy; however, no doctors lived in that neighborhood.

One of the most unforgettable incidents that occurred during this period caused us to spend a night in terror. That night, unfamiliar with celebratory gunfire, we became frightened. We thought the enemy had overtaken the city, and we feared even worse possibilities when we heard several bangs on the back door. That door opened out to the narrow corridor that separated our house from that of our neighbors. The banging stopped after several blows, but the shooting of firearms lasted for what seemed to us a very long time.

Abdul made sure to double-check the locks on the doors, and he turned off all the lights. When one of the kids needed to use the bathroom, he slowly, and as silently as possible, accompanied them using a torch to light the way. That night we slept on the bedroom floor in a narrow space. As morning broke, we looked through the windows. Nothing at all seemed wrong. The scene was completely normal. Could we have been dreaming?

Once Abdul opened the front door, our neighbor next door greeted him, and told him with a pleasant smile that yesterday King Hussein of Jordan had visited Iraq. People had always celebrated his several visits during the Iraqi-Iranian war, as he was a supporter to Iraq during that war. Moreover, our neighbor explained that he and his family had wanted to invite us over to their house to share the celebration. He said: "*We knocked on your backdoor several times, but when we did not get an answer, we thought you must be asleep, and decided not to bother you*". Some people trace the practice of firing guns during celebrations back to tribal roots. Back in the day, when a woman was married off to a man from a different tribe, her tribe would fire guns into the air as a symbolic gesture of protection. The shots would be loud to make sure the other tribe would hear them. They would certainly know that the woman was not to be mistreated, and that she had the backing of the entire tribe. The other tribe would fire back. Soon, as a display of pride, they would try to outdo each other.

On one side, our neighbors were a large family consisting of a number of brothers, children, grandchildren and grandparents all living together. The men were truck drivers and the majority of women were housewives. All were grateful for the opportunity to consult with us concerning their medical issues.

Being surrounded by lots of rural and agricultural areas, most locals expressed their gratitude by bringing livestock as gifts. In addition to our two Golden retrievers, Rocky (a female mistakenly given a male name) and Goldy, the "real" male, we had, at some point, five sheep, each named after a certain kind of fruit. Among them were banana – *Moza* and apple –*Tufaha*. We also had two very brave ducks, six turkeys, ten hens and roosters, and a partridge in a pear tree.

In some regions of south Iraq the slang for grandmother is "*Habooba*," a word that means a loving individual. Whenever our neighbor's Habooba was finished baking bread for her family in her neat clay oven, she would gently throw tiny stones on our backdoor to let us know we were in for a treat. She would then hand us several fresh-baked, rounded Iraqi bread – "*Khubuz*" Indeed, she was a woman with a kind heart and extremely delicious home-baked bread.

A particular thorny issue was our children's education. They had studied at British schools, the eldest in grade seven and youngest in second, which meant that they had never studied Arabic formally. Therefore, we had to do something about that. Our neighbors encouraged the children to watch *Iftah Ya Simsim*, the Arabic version of *Sesame Street,* to learn Arabic, but that was not adequate, so we opted for private tutoring in addition to their regular school.

Mr. Najim Qatouf (Arabic for star), a funny and good-hearted teacher, became the private tutor for all four children. He would sometimes watch Egyptian movies while the kids were working on their assignments. Whenever the movie's drama began to heat up, he would get so caught up in the scene that he would suddenly start yelling things like "Ya bint al kelb (you son of a bitch) or "Haramat (What a shame!). God bless his Netflix heart. One time, when he saw a broom leaning against the wall, he grabbed it and started brushing off his muddy trousers caused by a rainstorm outside. Abeer told him that the broom was used for sweeping the floor and wasn't clean, but he didn't seem to mind. Another time, the kids offered him water gum, an aromatic resin chewing gum obtained from trees. It turned out he loved it so much that he took some with him, which left him with a sticky pocket. As much as *Ustad* Najim loved watching Arabic movies, he hated our dog, Goldy. When entering or leaving the house, he would always tell the kids to make sure to hold Goldy nice and tight and to not let go until he was at least a mile away. In his defense, Goldy would go nuts as soon as he caught sight of him at a distance; however, Goldy was just being protective of the children during our absence. By the end of that year the children excelled at their studies. Much of the credit goes to that kind man who gets a gold star for his blessed efforts. Another star goes to the school principal, *sit* Halima Theban, who was like a caring mother and excellent educator to all the school children.

When I started work at Kut Republican Hospital, we were four OBG specialists: Jwan, Saniya, Haithem and me. A few months later Saniya left for the U.K. to accompany her husband, and afterward Haithem was transferred to Baghdad. Jwan and I had to be on call, alternating weekly rotations. We did not have a senior house officer for over a year so we had to perform even the simplest procedures ourselves. I remember once during the Christmas and New Year holidays, Jwan left for Baghdad to celebrate with her family. Because the new senior house officer and intern were also Christians, all three of them left, and I had to carry out all the duties by myself.

The Minister of Health Riyadh Al Haj Hussein had promised to transfer us to Baghdad after we finished three years. Unfortunately, shortly before the end of the third year he was excused from his position. The new minister, Sadiq Alwash, was impressed with the achievements of my department; he had two substitutes take my place before agreeing to transfer us to Baghdad, a process that took nearly two years.

Hanging "Gardens" of Saddam

Saddam Hussein Ibrahim Al-Majeed was born in the village of Al-Oja near Tikrit, in the middle of Iraq. His father died before he was born. From age ten on, his uncle, who lived in Baghdad, took him in and raised him. In 1957, he joined the Ba'ath party, and by the mid-sixties he played an important role in reorganizing the party, in an attempt to recapture power again. On July 17, 1968 the Ba'athists, led by Ahmed Hasan Al Bakir and his relative Saddam, succeeded in carrying out a coup and took power, Al Bakir became president and Saddam vice president.

In April 1969, Al-Bakir tried to persuade the Iraqi religious authority al-Sayid Mohsen Al-Hakim to openly condemn the Shah of Iran because of disagreements between the two over the Shatt al-Arab. When Al-Hakim rejected the request, the government took such radical measures as the deportation of some Iranian students and the arrest of others, shutting down Kuffa University and confiscating its property. Meanwhile, 20,000 Iraqis were expelled and forced across the Iranian border on the pretext of being *Teba'eya* (Iranian descendants). In response, Al-Hakim launched a protest demonstration from Najaf to Baghdad, which was joined by thousands of supporters, sparking government concern. This led to the imprisonment of his son. The arrest ignited a wave of anger, speeches and petitions demanding an end to unfair arrests, deportations, and assassinations. The government responded harshly by arresting religious scholars who participated in the demonstration, and assassinated the religious scholar Abd-al-Aziz Al-Badri, the preacher of Imam Al A'adhum mosque, who endorsed Al- Hakim publically. They also confiscated the endowments of Najaf, prohibited religious processions, closed religious schools and cancelled the reading of the Holy Qur'an from Iraqi Broadcast Stations.

After the death of al-Sayid Mohsen Al-Hakim in 1970, the figure of al-Sayid Mohammed Baker Al-Sadr emerged as one of the founders of the al-Da'awa Party, who was followed by many of Al-Hakim's followers. An assassination attempt targeted at the Deputy Prime Minister Tariq Aziz in 1980, sparked outrage within the government, and a few days later

Al-Sadr and his sister Bintul Huda were taken from their home in Najaf to Baghdad where they were executed. This was the first time in Iraq's history that this happened to a cleric of such high stature. The deportation campaign was resumed and considered "Iranians," 40,000 Shias were deported in 1980 alone.

After the 1979 Islamic Revolution in Iran, Al-Bakir stepped down and Saddam became the president of Iraq, commander in chief of the armed forces and the secretary general of al- Ba'ath Party. Saddam had plans to take the positions as a matter of fact, while many in the party were hoping for a fair transparent election. On July 18, 1979 (only two days after Al-Bakir's resignation) Saddam called members of the Revolutionary Command Council and hundreds of other Ba'ath Party leaders to a meeting, during which he announced that he had uncovered a coup plot. Accordingly, 60 party leaders were then led away and executed. Later, in 1982, Saddam alienated 300 party members for opposing his military plans for the Iraq-Iran war.

The abuse extended to medical professors and to a group of the most efficient medical professionals. In an unprecedented incident that shook the Medical City and College of Medicine-Baghdad University, Saddam, after only four months in office, issued an order to refer 48 senior doctors and professors for retirement. All of them were at the height of their careers and none had reached the retirement age. Many of them were professors who taught me. The first name mentioned was that of my respected professor, Farhan Baqir who was the personal physician of president Al-Bakir. The British medical journal *Hospital Medicine* described the incident as the "massacre of the Medical City."

In 1982, Saddam executed the late Minister of Health, Dr. Riyadh Ibrahim Al-Hajj Hussein, who had been the chair since 1976. According to his daughter, Rayya during a phone interview with *al-Sharq al-Awsat* newspaper, the reason for his execution was unknown to the family, who, after 2003, started digging around for information in order to find a clue to the case. She mentioned that her father was killed on the 10th of November of 1982 after being removed from office in June, shortly followed by his imprisonment in August of the same year. Two committees interrogated the minister – one led by Fadhil Al-Barrack and the other by Sameer Al-Shaikhly; both found him not guilty of all accusations. The case was then transferred to Barzan, Saddam's half-brother, who tortured the minister under Saddam and his guards' direct supervision. From prison, the minister had sent a piece of paper to his wife telling her that he was found innocent, and would be home after meeting with Saddam. However, he did not show up and his family received an order to pick up his corpse. When his brother, accompanied by Dr. Ghazi Al-Habash, received the corpse, they found his head was smashed and covered with dressings; there were several fractures with evidence of gunshot wounds. Dr. Riyadh had been my classmate at the Medical College, class of 1964. He was known for his good manners and wisdom. After graduation, we worked together as residents at al-Jamhoori Teaching Hospital (later on renamed The Medical City) where he gained the respect of our teachers and all the staff. As a minister of health, he was efficient, honest and modest.

In 1985, Professor Dhiya Al-Musawi, the chairman of forensic medicine at Baghdad University Medical School, died in a horrific manner during a university ceremony after drinking a glass of soda offered to him by a dental student. The soda was mixed with cyanide. Rumors abounded that he knew too much about the government's crimes so they had to get rid of him. Through the grapevine, people were talking in whispers about the executions of Dr. Ismail Hassan Al-Tatar, a well-known dermatologist and a close friend to the ruling elite, who was executed on September 28, 1988 along with his friend, the famous pediatrician Dr. Hisham Al-Salman, based on a recorded tape of a joke about Saddam during a private party at a place outside Iraq. Another noted figure in the medical profession was Dr. Raji Al-Tikriti, a well-known military physician, originally from Saddam's own hometown of Tikrit. He was an active professional, and became President of the Iraqi Medical Association after his retirement in 1988. He was executed in 1994; rumors circulated that he was imprisoned and eaten alive by famished dogs.

Another victim was Salwa Al-Bahrani, a university scholar from a renowned family and the daughter of Raouf Al-Bahrani, a minister from the early Iraqi monarchy. She was also the sister of professors Zuhair and Ihsan

Al-Bahrani, recognized medical professors, and the widow of Dr. Salman Tajiddin, a renowned pediatrician. Salwa was taken from her home to the General Security Directorate, to put pressure on the family to hand over her son to the authorities; as he was accused of belonging to the Da'awa Party. She was freed after two days only to die shortly afterward of thallium poisoning which had been put in a glass of yogurt given to her when she was in custody.

The Frog that Turned into a Bull

When the Iraq-Iran war erupted in September 1980, we were still studying in the U.K., and my parents and siblings were visiting. We were torn apart with the bad news, but had hoped that a quick solution would be found. Little did we know at the time that the war would last eight cruel years. Between 1979 and 1980 relations between Iraq and Iran worsened. Then war broke out between the two countries. The attack was preceded by a long history of border disputes.

After World War II and the gradual withdrawal of Britain from the area, a dispute ignited between Iraq and Iran regarding control of the Arab Gulf. In 1937, the British-Iraqi Treaty regulated the relationship between the two countries, putting the border of Shatt-al-Arab on the Iranian side, instead of placing it in the middle of the river; this meant that the whole river was for Iraq. In 1975, this dispute was resolved through the Treaty of Algeria between Saddam Hussein and the Shah of Iran. Accordingly, Iraq gave Iran half of the width of the river in exchange for Iran's abandoning support for the Kurds in northern Iraq against the Iraqi central government.

In 1978, the Shah of Iran requested that the Iraqi government expel Ayatollah Al-Khomeini from Iraq where he had been given asylum in Najaf following his exile from Iran in 1964. The Iraqi government agreed to the request, and Khomeini left for Paris, only to return to Iran a year later to become the President of the Islamic Republic of Iran. Now Saddam was confronted with the man who he had expelled from Iraq just one year earlier. Only this time he had become the Islamic leader in Tehran, one who could gain support from many Iraqis. By the end of September of 1980, Saddam had announced that he was disputing the treaty of 1975 and decided to initiate an offence against Iran on September 21st.

The aim of the war was to weaken the Shiites in the south and the Kurds in northern Iraq. At the same time, Iraq hoped to replace Iran as a dominant state in the Gulf, taking advantage of the conditions of the new revolution. For many years, the war was funded by Saudi Arabia and Kuwait, with a flow of arms from the Soviet Union and the West alike. By the end of the war, Iraq had the fourth largest army in the world, yet Iraq had accumulated huge amounts of debt, without achieving a victory or border security. The price of war was far too high on both sides. The number of Iraqi casualties was half a million, and the material losses were 500 billion U.S. dollars for each of the two countries.

Convoys of martyrs became the norm in the streets of Baghdad and Iraq. Most young men were on the front lines, and large numbers of families had no breadwinners. Children were raised in the absence of their fathers, and there was scarcity of manpower. To solve the problem of manpower, the government brought in a million Egyptian workers, mostly unskilled, (Some references speak of four million.) All this changed the fabric of society and disrupted family ties. One could hardly find a family that escaped losing at least one family member. Some had been killed, others captured or lost, and still more were disabled. The government provided compensation to the families of the martyrs and to some of the very poor that compensation was satisfactory. Some families had devastating stories. One widow had to remarry again. Her first husband, who was presumed dead, was actually still alive, and he returned to her several years later, after being released from captivity. Everywhere there were signs of grieving. Black banners are typically used in Iraq to announce the death of a person. They were scattered everywhere on walls, in public squares, storefronts and yards. In addition, some mourning women wore only black for years to express their grief for a lost loved one. Black fabric and clothes became the color most frequently imported by merchants.

Once while we were on our way from Kut to visit my parents in Baghdad, I noticed a black banner near Beirut Square on Palestine Street mourning the young martyr Ali Abed Saleh. I was shocked. Ali was my cousin. Alas, he never had the opportunity to blow out the candles on his twentieth birthday cake. Since he suffered from rheumatic heart disease, he had been drafted into the army as a noncombatant soldier. However, not even that had saved him from being killed. We went directly to my uncle's house to console the bereaved mother, who had lost her husband just a few months earlier. Another family member, my newlywed cousin Adiba, was widowed only seven days after her marriage. Her husband had joined the battlefront; he did not return and was considered missing.

Postgraduate studies were cancelled for a time at some colleges to allow for a larger number of graduates to join the reserve service. Normally postgraduate students can postpone this service by completing four months of training before going on for advanced studies. Male graduates, who were not pursuing further studies, were drafted into the army for a minimum 18-month period that might be extended for several years. Meanwhile, females joined public hospitals as volunteer nurses for the same period. The wages for both were ridiculously low. Many doctors lost their lives in the war. Most were young, new graduates, though some well-known specialists also died during war-related events. A well-known orthopedic surgeon Dr. Kais Abdul-Majeed, who was a fellow at the British Royal College of Surgeons, moved to Basra Hospital with a team of physicians to treat the wounded there. Along with several others, he was killed by a missile, which fell on the doctors' residence as they were dining.

On August 8, 1988 both Iraq and Iran declared their acceptance of Security Council Resolution 598 to stop military operations. The three-day celebration by all Iraqis cannot be matched by any celebration I have ever seen or heard of since. Millions went out into streets dancing, singing and celebrating. They hugged each other, sounded their car-horns, and provided sweets, refreshments and mutton meat to the needy.

Before the Iraqi-Iranian war, Iraq was one of the safest places to live. It had one of the lowest incidences of AIDS and drug abuse. The country had experienced its most dramatic and successful period of economic growth. Its citizens enjoyed high standards of healthcare, housing, and instruction—easily comparable to those of European countries. Major projects were undertaken including: hospitals, schools, universities, 5-star hotels, tourist cities, and highways, in addition to others. Hundreds of university graduates were offered scholarships to study abroad. Many modern shopping centers had been constructed and stocked with high quality merchandise. In those "Central Markets" goods varied from large machines and appliances to home goods and personal needs; all sold for below-cost prices. Farmers and workers in the most remote villages furnished their homes with modern appliances and drove modern cars.

In-law or Outlaw

Saddam had been married to his cousin, Sajida Khairalla Talfah since 1963. They had two sons and two daughters. In 1986, Saddam married a second wife, Samira Al Shahbender. There were rumors that Kamel Jajju (Saddam's personal guard) was the one who introduced Samira to Saddam, prompting the hatred of Uday, Saddam's son. In 1988, Uday gunned down Jajju at a reception honoring Suzan Mubarak, the then Egyptian president's wife. Saddam ordered a legal trial for Uday but eventually pardoned him. Another prominent figure was Adnan Khairalla Talfah, Sajida's brother and also Saddam's cousin, a companion from his youth and an efficient military commander who served as Defense Minister from 1979 until his death in 1989; he was believed to be opposed to the invasion of Kuwait. And was liked and respected by most military leaders, raising Saddam's concerns. Adnan died in a helicopter crash in 1989.

Hussein Kamel, son-in-law and second cousin of Saddam, rose through the army ranks to become Iraq's Minister of Military Industries, heading the Industrialization Commission and supervising Iraq's weapons development program from 1987. He was married to Saddam's daughter, Raghad. On August 2, 1995 Kamel and his wife defected from Iraq, along with his brother Saddam Kamel and his wife Rana Saddam Hussein. The two Kamel brothers along with their wives were granted asylum in Jordan.

Hussein Kamel began to cooperate with the U.N. Special Commission (UNSCOM), the United States' C.I.A. and the British M16, in addition to providing inspection teams with a wealth of information. In February 1996, after speaking with intermediaries from Saddam Hussein, the brothers were convinced they could return safely to Iraq with their wives, and that all would be forgiven. Reportedly, immediately upon return they were ordered to divorce their wives and were denounced as traitors. Three days after their arrival, they refused to surrender to Saddam's security forces and were killed in a 13-minute exchange of fire at their house.

Saddam Kamel stared as Saddam Hussein in the 1980 movie, *The Long Days*, A 150-minute-long biographical account of Saddam Hussein's life. The film was directed by Terrace Young who also directed 3 James Bond films, and was assigned an unlimited budget, a term not used in Hollywood, even in its most expensive productions such as "*The Ten Commandments* and *Gone with the Wind.* The film was broadcasted frequently on patriotic occasions and national holidays.

Back to the Round City

In April 1986, 22 years after my graduation and several transfer requests, the Minister of Health finally bestowed his gracious blessing by approving our transfer to Baghdad our home city. We had already sent our son Mohammed to live with my parents in Baghdad, to enable him to attend Baghdad College, the best high school in Iraq. A few months later our other children followed him. This forced us to make many miserable trips commuting between Baghdad and Kut over the next several months until we received the transfer order. Finally, we moved into our house in Sulaikh, which we had purchased two years earlier but kept vacant, with the hope of moving soon. It was a traditional two-story home with five spacious bedrooms, two-and a-half bathrooms, and a yard full of fruit trees: citrus, pear, pomegranate, olive, guava, grape, and palm. Now came the time to enjoy the new furniture we had brought back from the U.K. and had kept packed away at my brother's house for five years. Once a local company put together our elegant IKEA kitchen we were all set.

I commenced work at Saddam's Maternity Hospital (al-Habeebiya), where I spent three years working with six other specialists. Abdul was assigned to the medical center on Haifa Street. Shortly after starting work there, I was tasked with heading up the department. The hospital became a teaching center for al-Mustansiriya University medical students, and then postgraduate students. Amidst the whirl of leading the department, I suddenly felt that my world came to a halt. On Jan. 17, 1988, my beloved father passed away. His sudden death was the first blow to shake our foundation. In addition to his compassion, he was the bedrock of our big family; he was wise, impartial and visionary.

In 1988, a new health minister Sameer Al Shaikhly took office. He gave strict instructions, requiring specialists and senior doctors to be available on-site during their on-call duties. While I was on duty one evening, the minister paid an inspection visit to the hospital, which was in order as usual. During the inspection, the minister noticed a trace of cigarette ashes on the floor in the outpatient department. He was furious with the hospital administrator, Zuhair, and dragged him by the collar in front of everyone standing there—a move that intimidated all of us. The minister then asked me if I had any complaints. After witnessing what had just taken place, I was reluctant to openly share my thoughts regarding our needs since I was so unsure of how he might react. I answered no, but he was not satisfied, and he continued by saying he expected a realistic answer. So I told him we were short of nursing staff. He then asked if I had any other requests; I decided to take a chance and asked for an ultrasound machine, which was badly needed by the hospital. The next day his secretary called and asked me to send someone to get the machine from al-Ramadi Hospital, as it was not needed there. I asked Dr. Bashar Omar, who was a radiologist at al Habeebiya Hospital and trained in ultrasound use, to go and pick up the equipment there. He left and took Shobo, the hospital storekeeper, along with him. Later, Shobo told me that Bashar had carried the machine on his lap all the way from Ramadi; eventually he became one of the most well-known ultrasound doctors in Iraq. Al Shaikhly did not last long in office; he was replaced by Abdul Salam Mohammed. The new minster was an engineer who had an advanced degree from the U.K. and was known for accuracy and attention for detail; he made several changes at the ministry of health. He entrusted hospital management to specialists with advanced degrees, instituted the system of units and the system of self-financing in medical institutions. Each institution had to achieve a goal within a certain timeframe.

In April 1989, I attended a course on immunology of pregnancy at Cambridge, U.K. along with a group of Iraqi gynecologists. This gave me a chance to stay with Amal and her family in London for several days. While I was away, my husband called to tell me that the new minister was appointing me as manager at al-Habeebiya Hospital, a position that did not suit my personality or my scientific goals. My colleague Ferdous Al-Saigh was part of the group at Cambridge. A few months earlier, she had asked me to join her team at Saddam College of Medicine, and I had refused at the time, for fear of interference in college affairs from higher officials. At that point I informed Ferdous that I had changed my mind, had decided after all to join her at Saddam College of Medicine, and thus would be submitting my application. Meanwhile, I accepted receipt of the responsibility as a hospital manager because: "It was an order, not an honor." It was a hard job that exhausted both my family and me. In addition, I was a member of several medical committees, including the Consultant Committee to the Minister of Health, the Presidential Office's Special Medical Committee, the Representative Committee of The Royal College of Obstetricians and Gynecologists, and the Examination Committee for the Iraqi Board of Post-Graduate Studies in Obstetrics and Gynecology.

Along with doctors Amal Al- Azzawi and Raja'a Al -Yuzbeki, I was assigned to study the possibility of creating an obstetrics and gynecology section at Ibn al-Baladi Children's Hospital. The hospital manager Dr. Nazar Al-Anbeki was not willing to have an obstetric department under his roof. We conducted several visits and held many meetings, and at last managed to create an outline for the development of a full department, including: labor rooms, operating theater, an obstetric emergency room plus inpatient wards. One of my most significant achievements at al-Habeebiya hospital was the founding of a daycare center for the staff's children. It was heartbreaking to see midwives and nurses perform their duties with one child or more hanging around the work place because the mother had no one to care for her child at home. I searched high and low among the hospital buildings searching for a convenient site to house the daycare. Once I was able to locate a place, I obtained the authorization to use it. I then equipped it, and lastly, appointed a staff of three to be in charge of caring for the children on an 8-hour rotation. The moms most certainly appreciated the daycare.

At a course in Cambridge U.K. with fellow colleagues from Peru and Italy

Our Lady of Mosul

1987 — We decided to spend our summer vacation up in northern Iraq. The journey started with Mosul, also known as the city of two springs due to its pleasant weather most of the year. Mosul is the center of Iraq's Assyrian Christian community, a diverse sect of Middle Eastern Christian sects in the Assyrian-Syriac-Chaldean ethnicity, who still speak and read

Aramaic like back in the days of Jesus. The city is located on the west bank of the Tigris River opposite the ancient city of Nineveh. It has some of the oldest mosques, churches, castles, monasteries and schools. We went by bus with a tourist group including our friends from Hilla, Al- Bairmani family.

One of our stops was at an old church near Mar Matti where rumor that Virgin Mary had appeared in it several times circulated. Some people even claimed that she spoke to them; and that when asked if the war (between Iraq and Iran) would come to an end, she answered: "*Yes, because you are good people.*" Upon arrival, a number of priests were reciting prayers while people gathered around an elegant statue of the Blessed Virgin Mary surrounded by lit candles. As the chanting progressed, bits and pieces of light were gradually reflecting on the wall, like a group of fireflies hovering around. A faint silhouette of what seemed to look like a human figure wearing a head cover formed on the wall. A woman right behind me threw a handkerchief at the wall aiming for the figure. She then asked a man in the front row to hand it back to her so she could keep it as a blessing. Regardless of the what the perceptions were of what happened that day, it was a rich, fulfilling and serene experience to watch devoted worshippers chanting and welcoming people from other faiths inside the church. Outside the church a group of kids were selling the famous *Sajaq* sweet (a sausage shaped gelatin). One year after our trip to Mosul the Iraq-Iran war ended.

Mosul is famous for its pistachio and walnut trees and marble production. While we were there, we got to see *al Hadba*, nicknamed the hunchback for its leaning minaret, the Mosul forests, and downtown *Dawaseh*. The Arabic dialect of Mosul is considered to be much softer in its pronunciation than that of Baghdadi Arabic, bearing considerable resemblance to Levantine dialects, particularly Aleppan Arabic. It is also the closest dialect to that of Iraqi Jews. The letter "R" is pronounced at the top of the throat, the same way it is in French (resembling the sound made when gargling).

People of Mosul are known to be smart. In fact students of Mosul University often rivaled their Baghdadi counterparts and sometimes out-performed them in their studies. Some of the notable Maslawis include: Aseneth Barzani (1590-1670), the daughter of an eminent Kurdish Rabbi,

Samule Halevi Barzani. Her writings demonstrated mastery of Hebrew, Torah, Talmud, Midrash, and Kabbalah, and her letters are both lyrical and erudite. Some scholars considered her the first female Rabbi in Jewish history. My professor Mahmoud Al Jalili was one of the best teachers in medicine as well as the first president of Mosul University, and first dean of its medical school. Al Jalili family served as effective rulers of the city under the Ottoman Empire. They are credited with investing considerable capitol in religious institutions and charitable activities. Kadim Al Sahir, an Iraqi singer, composer, and poet, has been dubbed the *Caesar of Arabic Songs*, and *Iraq's Ambassador to the world.*

They Came to Baghdad

In 1988, our family went to see the play *The Mousetrap — al Masyada* — at al Rashid Theatre, the most modern state of the art theatre in Baghdad, located next to the broadcasting station building. The play is an Agatha Christie murder mystery. It originally opened in the West End of London in 1952, and it had been running continuously since then. It has by far the longest initial run of any play in history. Its 25,000th performance took place on 18 November 2012. It enjoyed the longest running show (of any type) in the modern era.

In the vast theatre hall the light effects and decor were mesmerizing; the background screen displayed an artificial snowfall looking incredibly real. As soon as the red stage curtains opened, the people started applauding. Actress Hana Mohammed "Mollie" was wearing a lovely long maxi and smoking by the piano. She looked much more appealing than when we saw her on T.V. In a nutshell, the story is about a murder that occurs on Culvert Street. Witnesses hear someone whistling the famous nursery rhyme, *Three Blind Mice*, just before the victim screams. Meanwhile, during a severe snowstorm, a group of people gathers at a manor recently converted into a guesthouse and hosted by a young couple. Things get tense when the guests find out that the murderer could be one of them. They start revealing their vile pasts one by one until the murderer's identity is disclosed near the end of the play. Before closing, we were asked not to reveal the identity of the killer to anyone outside the theatre to ensure that the end of the play would not be spoiled for future audiences.

Agatha Christie was an English crime novelist and a mystery writer who was one of the world's top-selling authors with such works as: *Murder on the Orient Express, The Mystery of the Blue Train, and Death on the Nile.* She first visited Baghdad as a tourist in 1927. In fact, her trip to Baghdad was planned at the last minute. Originally, she had purchased tickets to sail to the Caribbean; however, after dining with a couple just back from Iraq, she suddenly changed her plans. Many years later she would become a resident of the City of Enlightenment where she met one of the Middle East's leading novelists, the famous Palestinian author Jabra Ibrahim Jabra who settled in Iraq after the events of 1948.

It was here in Baghdad, while on archaeological digs throughout Iraq with her husband, Sir Max Mallowan, that Agatha Christie wrote some of her most important works. *They Came to Baghdad* is one of her highly successful novels of the spy thriller genre. In this work, Baghdad is the chosen location for a secret superpower summit. But the word is out, and an under-ground organization is plotting to sabotage the talks. Into this on-thin-ice situation stumbles Victoria Jones, a young woman with a longing for adventure, Victoria gets more than she bargained for, when a wounded secret agent dies in her hotel room.

Agatha's 94 books have been translated into 103 languages - 14 more than Shakespeare. She helped her husband with the recovery of intricately carved Assyrian ivory plaques at Nimrud in Northern Iraq. In fact, she put together some of her most popular stories while assisting at digs in Iraq and Syria. She last traveled to Iraq about 20 years after its independence in late 1932. In the U.K. she was honored with the title Dame of the British Empire and died at the age of 85 (1890 - 1976) just three years before Saddam Hussein ascended to power. I sometimes wonder if she would recognize the country and people she was so intrigued by if she were among us today.

The New Nomads

Iraqi authorities launched a campaign to displace Iraqis of Iranian origin, starting with 40,000 Kurd Failis. The number reached 200,000 during the Iraqi-Iranian war. Kurdish Failis were cruelly forced to leave their property, wealth, and belongings. To give an idea on how cruel this was, imagine yourself dragged out of your home along with your entire family without any notice, your food is still cooking on the kitchen stove. Then you are loaded onto large trucks filled with strangers, not knowing where you are being taken or what will happen next; all this happens without you having broken any law in your life. The same happened to many Shiite Arabs, especially wealthy merchants who were taken from their homes or work places. I had witnessed this when it occurred in the Jameela neighborhood in Baghdad and in Kut; moreover, the Kurds were moved from the north of Iraq to far outlying villages in the south while being replaced with Arabs in an attempt to change the demographics of the region.

The family of Farooq, my sister's husband, a well-known Iraqi Arab family from Najaf, also had their share of atrocities. His elder sister Najiyya's husband (a wealthy merchant at Shorja Local market) was deported to Iran. Next, she was ordered to divorce him, or also be deported along with her four children. She chose to follow her husband and left her lavish house and wealth behind. The other sister's husband fled Iraq a few months after their wedding, fleeing from the oppression of the government security. They were only reunited eleven years later when Saddam was toppled. A third sister lost her 16-year-old son, who was taken from their house by security forces; he was never seen or heard from again. While I was working at Kut Hospital, I learned that one of my classmates, Dr. S. A., who was a consultant ophthalmologist in the same hospital and held an advanced degree from the U.K. (FRCS), was deported with his wife for being Faili Kurd. They did not have time to enjoy the new furniture they had just bought for their home.

Death in the Clouds

In March of 1988, the Iraqi army started shelling the Kurdish town of Halabja. Residents detected an odd smell like sweet apples as the tragedy unfolded. It was as if it were an Alfred Hitchcock movie. Sheep and goats were falling in the streets, birds were dropping from the trees, and people were beginning to feel the effects of the chemical weapons — stabbing pain in the eyes, uncontrolled vomiting, tremors and convulsions. Residents attempting to flee, remember seeing smoky clouds of gas, hovering over the ground, and a dusting of white powder. Many of them fell ill and died right there on the streets. The death toll was estimated at 5,000. A lethal mix of mustard gas, Sarin and the nerve agent VX was dropped on the town. Thousands of others died from long-term medical complications. The attacks were unique in history, as in the *Holocaust*, poison gas was used to kill women and children. During those times, households were not allowed to have satellite dishes; the only media sources that people had were the government run TV stations, and newspapers, all of which were strictly censored. I recall once a visit I had from a Kurdish patient at my private clinic. She was offended that I knew nothing about the massacre. Ironically, a short time later, while I was visiting London, I saw poster writings condemning the Halabja massacre at several underground stations as well as on walls in some neighborhoods.

Teach Me a Word and Own Me Forever

I took on the responsibility of being hospital manager for six months, after which my application was approved to join the teaching staff at Saddam College of Medicine and the hospital connected to it on October 29, 1989. The Minister of Health, Abdul Salam Mohammed, was scheduled to visit al-Habeebiya Hospital the next day for the purpose of inaugurating the units-system application. We all participated in preparing for the event; hospital staff as well as my family took part in preparations including a nice dinner. The minister himself did not come, but in his place he sent his deputy Nazar Al-Shahbender, along with the general director of technical matters, Qusay Al-Khayat, and the general director of services, Abdul Jabber Abdul Abbas. They were all pleased with our accomplishments. Nazar said to me: "Your hospital is not matched by any in Iraq except Saddam Hospital in Tikrit," — which was the best at the time. On November 1, 1989, I took up my duties at al-Kadhimiya Teaching Hospital. Two weeks later I received an official letter of acknowledgment from the Minister of Health in appreciation for my efforts in managing al Habeebiya Hospital.

The college I just joined was newly founded and students were in the third year, so we had no teaching duties since obstetrics and gynecology courses begin during year four. The OBG department occupied the second floor of the six-floor modern general hospital; one side served the gynecological patients, and the other was for pre-natal and post-natal patients. A well-equipped special-care neonatal unit was attached to the labor rooms and to the obstetric theaters. There were two major surgical theaters for obstetric cases, three second-stage labor rooms and a six-bed first-stage labor room, a minor theater room and a special-care room for managing critically ill patients. Gynecologic surgeries were performed in the main complex theater on the first floor, and the outpatient clinics were part of the main outpatient department that occupied the ground floor.

Anything But the Heart

During the time period when senior physicians were required to be available on-site during their on-call duties, dentists, too, had to follow the same order. In the summer of 1988, while I was on night duty at al Habeebiya Hospital and Abdul at Haifa's Health Center, he had his first heart attack. He managed to drive himself to al-Kindi Hospital where he was admitted to the intensive care unit. After his recovery, we changed our life-style as much as we could, and he was faithful to taking his diabetic medications. Months later, in spite of these efforts, he had a second attack.

After his third hospital admission, we were advised to go abroad for a consultation and possible cardiac surgery. In Jordan, while we were waiting for a visa to enter the U.K., we met Dr. Na'if Al-Dibs, who performed a cardiac catheterization and discovered a three-vessel occlusion. Dr. Dawood Hananya performed a successful bypass operation, which resulted in having over ten years of a symptom–free active life. Fortunately, I was not alone in caring for Abdul in Jordan, his brother Abdul Kareem came from London on the day of surgery to share in his care and provide moral support. His brother even took it a step further by insisting on paying for all the expenses. Within a month Abdul was feeling better than ever; however, we diligently returned to see the doctors in Jordan at least every year for follow up.

AbdulWahab in the Indian corner of our sitting room - 1994

Here We Go Again Rima

Hatim Alta'ee, a famous 6th Century Arab poet well known for his incredible generosity ironically had an incredibly stingy wife, "Rima." Adding lard to cooking was a staple of Arabic cuisine; overly concerned about the lard, every time Rima was forced to add it, the spoon in her hands trembled. Hatim's guests could always tell how and why Rima's cooking was so tasteless. Growing tired of this problem, Hatim decided to trick his wife. He told her that the most beautiful women in history prevented their hair from turning grey by adding lard to their cooking, the more they add, the more beautiful they become. The trick worked, and Hatim's guests could again tell the difference in Rima's cooking. As the years passed, her hair, like most hair, began to turn grey, only then did she have an "Aha!" moment, and she immediately went back to her "teeny habits"... And so did the Iraqi regime. And here comes the story of a second war:

The Ottomans occupied the northern part of the Arab Gulf, which included Kuwait. Kuwait was part of the Province of Basra until the end of World War I. After the Ottoman Empire collapsed, the British divided the Middle East. In 1914, the British Resident Abroad announced the intention of his country to establish an Independent Principality in Kuwait under British protection. Acting on this decision, the British High Commissioner, Percy Cox, decided to demarcate new borders in the year 1922. The area remained under British control until 1961, when Kuwait was declared an independent state. The issue of Kuwait always stayed in the back of the minds of many Iraqi politicians, even in those of successive governments before 1958; they never forgot the issue. Nouri Al-Said, who was an English supporter, talked about re-annexation of Kuwait shortly before the 1958 July revolution!

Prime Minister Abdul Kareem Qasim declared that Kuwait was part of Basra in 1961. The British responded by sending armed forces to Kuwait, supported by Saudi forces. The Arab countries, encouraged by Egypt, immediately accepted Kuwait into the Arab League, an act which forced Qasim to withdraw from the Arab League, a mistake that lead to Iraq's isolation at that time.

By the end of the Iraq-Iran War in 1988, Iraq's economy was drained; its debts exceeded 100 billion U.S. dollars, half of it owed to Kuwait. Kuwait refused to pardon Iraq of its debts. For 8 years Iraq believed it was defending the Eastern Portal of the Arab homeland and was fighting a traditional enemy of Arabs, Iran. Angry with his Arab brothers for letting him down, Saddam contemplated his next move, another war. As Rima knew well, old habits are hard to break.

The Titanic Has Sailed

At dawn on August 2, 1990, Kuwaitis awoke to the sound of Iraqi tanks, armed vehicles, and artillery attacking their borders. Within seven days the Iraqi government pronounced Kuwait its nineteenth province. One justification given for the attack was: Kuwait and the United Arab Emirates had increased their oil production, and the increase led to a decline in oil prices. That caused Iraq to lose an estimated 14 billion U.S. dollars a year. The Gulf States were not alone in flooding the oil market. Iran and the Soviet Union did so as well. Another justification offered was the Kuwaiti theft of Iraqi oil from the Rumaila super giant oil field. That field is located in southern Iraq, just 20 miles from the Kuwaiti border, and the oil drilling there was worth 4 billion U.S. dollars.

Before initiating the attack, Saddam wanted to test the waters with Iran and with the U.S. His first move was to bribe the Iranians to ensure that they would not support the Kurds against the central government, and so with a stroke of a pen, half of Shatt-al-Arab was given again to Iran. This step ignored the bloodshed of the half a million Iraqis who had lost their lives. Not to mention the millions who were injured, widowed, orphaned, and displaced. Certainly, no small addition, were the privations brought on by the extremely fragile economy caused by the Iraq-Iran war. Now Saddam awaited the Americans' reaction. However, the U.S. reaction to Saddam's intentions was not clear. On July 31, 1990, Assistant Secretary of State John Kerry declared to Congress: "The United States is not obliged to defend Kuwait and has no intentions of defending Kuwait in the event of an Iraqi attack." In Baghdad, a similar message was perceived directly during a July 25, 1990 meeting between April Glaspie, the American representative and Saddam. By that time, Saddam's intentions were evident. Repeatedly, Saddam classified Kuwait as a threat to Iraq's safety. American ambassador April Glaspie informed her Iraqi counterpart that, "Inspired by friendship and not by confrontation, Washington does not have an opinion on an Arab-Arab conflict." At that time Iraq was a modern secular state, with wide religious freedom. The standard of living was high, women enjoyed positions of distinction, and compared to other Arab countries, women enjoyed a high literacy rate.

The United Nations Security Council issued several resolutions demanding that Iraq withdraw its forces and end its claim that Kuwait is an Iraqi territory. Since Iraq did not respond to any of the resolutions, the Council adopted Chapter VII of the U.N. Charter. It established Decision 678, which authorized the liberation of Kuwait by any means. This decision gave the right to 32 countries, including most Arab states, to use force to liberate Kuwait. Think; *Operation Desert Storm*. The alliance launched an air attack beginning on January 17, 1991, followed up with a land attack on February 24th, and concluded with the announcement of the liberation of Kuwait on February 27, 1991. The shelling continued for five weeks on military targets, on infrastructure targets, and strategic places as well as bombing of military units retreating from Kuwait along al-Basra Road. Later, al-Basra Road came to be known by locals as "the death road." To achieve Saddam's goal of raising oil prices, some retreating soldiers burned Kuwaiti oil fields on their way back. When the war was over, Iraq was subjected to instant global economic sanctions, and sometime later, suffered a ban on flying.

Escape to Nowhere

On January 17, 1991, 3:00 a.m., we awoke to the roaring bombards of *Asifat Al Sahra - Operation Desert Storm*. It was, indeed, a storm. I promptly called the girls to come downstairs from their bedrooms, and we all took cover in the family room. Such a bombardment is something you never think you will ever hear in real life. If I had to describe the sounds and vibrations we felt for the first time in our lives, I'd say it was a combination of the worst thunderstorm and earthquake anyone could ever imagine. To have lived to tell the story is nothing short of a miracle. In the aftermath, the boys got the car ready so we could flee. In less than an hour, we packed our stuff and headed to Hilla, where we sought shelter at our friends the Al -Bairmanis. On arrival we found their house already packed with relatives, who also had recently arrived as unexpected guests. We left a short while later for Sacred Karbala (one of the holiest sites in Shia Islam after Mecca and Medina). Sayid Abbas, my brother's father-in-law, owned Hotel Zamzam downtown. Not surprisingly, only two rooms were vacant. The average highway speed was some 100 kilometers/hour; we could only move about 30 because of the swarms of cars on the road. It was something like being caught in a New York subway rush hour on a rainy day ... only worse. Gloomy faces, some people still in their pajamas, others obviously having a bad hair day had already boarded. Roof racks were overloaded with luggage, mattresses and even fuel cylinders. Rumor had it that if war broke out, Bagdad would most likely be the central spot. Some believed that the U.S. would make it a second Hiroshima; others speculated about airdrops. Since the sacred cities down south were usually a red line for the Americans, who logically avoided any provocation with Iran (a Shia theocracy). Consequently, those fleeing considered them safest and set off in their direction.

Sleepless in Karbala

After staying at Hotel Zamzam for two days, I felt torn. Being the senior gynecologist at work that day, I felt, on the one hand, a moral responsibility towards my staff and patients. On the other, however, was another clear responsibility. Deeply, concerned about my safety, the members of my family were pleading with me to sit tight until the situation was more clear. I was the rope in a game of tug-of-war, but not for long. As the Hippocratic oath sounded louder and louder in my ears, the "rope" just evaporated into thin air. I'd face Qibla, say a little prayer, and with my son Mohammed as driver of our 1980, spacious, silver Volvo, off I would go to Baghdad. As we approached the city, cars became fewer and fewer in number. A deserted city, Baghdad looked like a scene from a Wild West shoot out.

Finally, I arrived and began to attend to my duties at Kadhimiya Hospital. I must give tribute to my brave residents, Thikra, Maysoon, Hala, Mohsen, Ma 'ad, and many others, who went above and beyond the call of duty. The moment my eyes met those of my co-workers, a spontaneous smile spread across our faces, translating into the unspoken acknowledgement: "I see you too have the Hippocratic oath echoing in your ears." Some residents and nurses were scattered here and there, but all operating rooms (OR's) were filled with emergency patients around the clock. After getting that sweet rush of job satisfaction, it was time to check on family. I was relieved to see that although shaken, my mother and sisters were all safe. My brother Abu Ahmed was also there with his family. Initially, when the first bombardment occurred, I had urged them to leave the city with us, but they just would not consent. This time, however, I told them that I was not leaving without them. Off we headed to Hotel Zamzam. All agreed that I still had not lost my ability to persuade.

Kawkab, my youngest sister, left without her husband Muwafaq, a school teacher, who was drafted into the army during the Iran War, and who was again drafted for the second time.... and counting! He was no different than many others who got separated from their loved ones. In some unfortunate cases loved ones were separated for good. A few days later, the Eskendarya tractor factory, located not too far from us, was shelled.

Most occupants of the area, including us, took cover in a makeshift shelter, the basement of a hotel. It was dark and damp, and unequipped to house refugees. Dripping water could be heard, finding its source proved impossible. In short, it was a mini-version of the insect scene in the Indiana Jones movie *The Temple of Doom*. The kids coped with seeming ease. After all, to them everything is more exciting than going to school even if the situation is marked by real war replete with real missiles and bullets. However, that was not the only form of entertainment available to them. In an attempt to cripple the regime and thus anger the inhabitants and incite a rebellion, coalition forces had destroyed the power plant. Kids being kids, however, they creatively took advantage of time to play all sorts of games. One such game is called *Mahebis,* a type of parlor game. The children would divide themselves up into two teams and compete with one another. The game is similar to one called *Jenkins,* where players conceal a small coin or ring in the palm of their hand. The rival team has to guess which hand conceals the coin. Traditionally, *Mahebis* is a game played at night during Ramadan (the fasting season). Whenever there was a raid, the sirens would sound alerting everyone to take cover inside the shelter. Thirty minutes later, the sign for all was clear was given and we emerged from the shelter to live yet another hour.

Terror From the Sky

Not much was happening in Karbala in terms of activity. Our group of three families graciously shared stashes of food, dried fruits, meals and Iraqi Standard teatime. Water in the tanks did not reach above the first floor. Therefore, water had to be carried up in buckets from a well in the basement to our rooms, which were located on the fourth floor. Now, walking up and down stairs a dozen times or so a day for water wasn't fun. However, the basement was our sole source of water. Most of our time was spent outdoors, therefore, all female family members were required to wear Abayas as a form of respect and modesty in a conservative city. One of the best treats was frequently performing *Ziyara-* visiting the shrines of Imam Hussein and his half-brother Imam Abbas, which were located within a walking distance of 10 minutes.

In 61 Hijri (680 AD), Imam Hussein, the grandson of the Prophet Mohammed was martyred on the 10th Muharrum, the first month of the Islamic calendar and one of the four sacred months of the year. He was martyred alongside 72 of his followers at the Battle of Karbala. An army of 30,000 carried out that order, which had been commanded by Yezid, the Umayyad Khalif. The shrines are sumptuously ornamented with precious metals and shiny surfaces. In fact, the minarets and domes are covered with pure gold, and on the inside, the tombs are covered with gold, silver and mirrored tiles. The mosaic floors are partly covered with plush Persian carpets. The area around the shrines was an outdoor bazaar with peddlers, roadside venders, merchants, pilgrims and a variety of stores ranging from fabrics, foods, merchandise and a variety of other goods. (You can smell the fresh aromas of spices, and the homemade famous white cheeses.) Flocks of pigeons peacefully hovered around the shrines every time bombings were halted. Their presence gave the people a sense of hope. As dark descended upon the city, people started carrying lanterns or lighted candles. I made a mental note to remind myself to include more carrots in our diet.

Gasoline became very scarce. One day, heavy explosions were heard, but they were not close to the hotel. Earlier my son Mohammed had headed off walking to the gas station to buy fuel and had not yet returned. He was some 30 minutes away still, and I became very concerned: explosions and gasoline are not a good combination. I put on my Abaya and went out into the streets with Mutaz. We had to stop frequently to ask for directions. Midway, we saw a missile heading westward. We could hear it whooshing, and seconds afterward it was out of sight. Then, all of sudden there was a terrible blast. Fearing the worst, I started to walk as fast as I could to catch up to Mohammed. Mutaz was calling out to me to no avail. I kept tripping. I fell twice, and eventually the "Abaya" completely fell off me. More worried than embarrassed, I swiftly carried on. Finally, we were close. A constant stream of people could be seen carrying plastic containers. All in a row, the line seemed endless. I was dusty, out of breath, and my heart was pounding intensely. Most people remained in the line, but after seeing how hurt I was, Mohammed left the line, and we all walked back to the hotel.

Right Direction, Right Time

We had been staying at the hotel for about a month, going back and forth to Baghdad as often as we could, to check on our work and homes. One morning, my brother discovered that the gasoline from his car had been stolen. At this point we were all stressed out. The gypsy-style living had taken its toll on us; however, the capital was still way more dangerous than we wanted to risk. We had a lengthy discussion about the pros and cons of leaving. In the end, the decision was made to return to Baghdad together thinking that if we're going to die, then let it be in our own homes with a little bit of dignity; so that's what we all did. Before the week was over the Hotel Zamzam was leveled to the ground. The 1991 uprising erupted in most of the southern provinces including Karbala and neighboring Najaf. In almost no time at all the authorities managed to crush it severely. People were subjected to torture, and both private and state properties were looted, burnt, shelled and sabotaged. Nothing was left intact, not even the holy shrines and the "Valley of Peace" in Najaf, where the largest cemetery in the world lies, were left untouched. Casualties were in the thousands; fingers were pointing in several directions as to who was responsible for the chaos. Some said Iran played a vital role in the events; others placed blame wholly on the authorities. Nevertheless, regardless of who was responsible for what, in the end, it was innocent Iraqis, as always, who remained the sole losers in the whole equation. My niece, Ayser, who was living with her grandparents, while studying Engineering at Babylon University, was among the large number of people displaced. Many of them fled to the orchards – "*Besateen*", but only for a short while because soon the orchards were all bulldozed and leveled to the ground.

Six Packs at No Cost

For few weeks, it appeared as if Baghdad had no Baghdadi's. We only left the house whenever absolutely necessary. Nothing was back to normal; there was neither potable water, nor electricity, and fuel lines seemed endless. People started cutting down trees from public gardens to use mainly for cooking. Luckily, our house was right by the Tigris River – "Dijlah". Each family member would take a bucket to the river and fill it with water several times a day. Some people would even wash their clothes and dirty dishes by the river. Our diet principally consisted of legumes, canned foods, homemade bread and dried fruits. We had no choice but to become vegetarians for a while. Frozen foods were spoiled so they had to be thrown away. The strenuous work we had to perform worked our muscles so that we chuckled saying it saved us a gym membership. Prices of merchandise skyrocketed, the Iraqi dinar collapsed 45,000 fold below its value, and government employees became the most vulnerable. Prior to this new situation, getting a governmental job was considered a dream job for most university graduates. However, after the rise in inflation, the average monthly salary would be enough to purchase only four dozen eggs. With this ridiculously low wage, people turned towards the private sector and handcraft professions. It became a common occurrence to see a medical doctor or an engineer doing blue collar or menial jobs. Despite the hardships endured, there was a somewhat positive side to this. It rid the community of the "culture of shame," for now it was acceptable within the culture for anyone, regardless of social class or educational level, to work doing whatever they wanted in order to earn a living and provide for their families. Majeed, one of my medical students, who was always top in his class and was once a bright promising physician, became a trader in foreign currency, which was illegal in Iraq. Eventually, he landed in jail and was tortured.

No Valentine's for Iraqis

The Amiriyah tragedy was an aerial attack that burnt, boiled, steamed, suffocated, and incinerated 408 civilians. Almost all of the 408 victims died. Most of them were women or children. Many husbands and fathers left the shelter before nightfall, so their wives would have some measure of privacy. During the Gulf War, the air-raid shelter, Public Shelter No. 25, located in the Amiriyah neighborhood west of Baghdad, was attacked. According to U.S. government sources, the attack was based on electric signals and human intelligence reports suggesting the place was a military command site. The shelter was utilized during the Iraq-Iran war by hundreds of civilians. Two laser-guided bombs, each capable of delivering a 2,000 pound GBU-27 punch were dropped on the shelter. The first "smart" bomb cut through 10 feet of enforced concrete, before a time-delayed fuse exploded. Minutes later the second "not so smart" bomb followed the path cut by the first. People staying on the upper level were incinerated by heat, and boiling water from the shelter's water tank killed those below.

In the years following the tragedy, the shelter has been transformed into a memorial to those who died within it. It features photos of the civilians who were killed at the site. Dignitaries and peace groups are often escorted on a tour of the place where the atrocity took place. They move past twisted steel, scorched walls and floors smudged with melted skin, bone, and bloodstains. This massacre took place on February 13, 1991, at 4:30 a.m. While the rest of the world was getting ready to celebrate Valentine's Day, just a day away, Iraqis were painfully grieving yet another loss.

Enough is Enough

The turmoil began in Basra on March 1, 1991, just one day after the Gulf War ceasefire. A tank soldier fired shells at a portrait of Saddam, and other soldiers applauded, igniting a series of anti-government rebellions in southern Iraq. There was more than one reason to fuel the revolt: the anger and devastation brought by two wars fought in a single decade, the government suppression, and a perception that the power of Saddam Hussein was vulnerable at the time. The United States encouraged the uprising, but ultimately turned its back to it leaving the rebels to face a heinous retaliation by the regime's zealots. The rebels in southern Iraq consisted of demoralized Iraqi Army troops, and banned anti-government parties; in particular, "Al-Da'awa" and the "Supreme Council for the Islamic Revolution." Shortly afterwards, another wave of insurgency broke out in Kurdish-populated northern Iraq. These rebels were crushed by Saddam's loyalist forces, spearheaded by "Haras Jamhoori" – Iraqi Republican Guard, elite troops reporting directly to Saddam. They were known locally as Wasps – "*Zanabeer*", because of their red or maroon berets and their unmatched aggressiveness. Tens of thousands of unarmed civilians were killed and two million Iraqis fled for their lives.

The rebels had killed Ba'athist officials in many southern and northern cities. The fighting continued until October, when an agreement was reached for an Iraqi withdrawal from Iraq's Kurdish-inhabited region. That withdrawal led to the establishment of the Kurdish Regional Government. The allies established Iraq no-fly zones in the aftermath of the uprising. Many casualties were buried in mass graves that contained thousands of bodies and were discovered by 2003. Of the 200 mass graves the Iraqi Human Rights Ministry had registered, the majority were discovered in the South, including one located south of Baghdad, which is believed to contain the remains of 10,000 to 15,000 victims.

Death of Iraqi Venice

The government systematically intensified forcing the relocation of Marsh Arabs, and draining the unique habitat that was once home to millions of birds from 40 species, as well as serving as a stop-over for millions of other birds including flamingos, pelicans and herons traveling from Siberia to Africa. The Iraqi marshlands – *Ahwar* are believed by some biblical scholars to be the site on which ancient stories of the Garden of Eden and the Great Flood are based. The livelihood of the inhabitants depended on fishing, farming, weaving, hunting, and grazing water buffalo. Marsh Arabs are known to be overly generous especially to visitors, who would enjoy the experience of a lifetime when they were invited into a guesthouse – "*Mudhif*". Marsh Arabs are also famous for their strong physique. Among the stories told by the elders are tales of men wrestling and subduing wild boars with their bare hands. The marshes suffered an ecological catastrophe. The scope and range of that loss can be compared to the drying out of the Aral Sea in Central Asia and to the deforestation of the Amazon rainforest, which was caused by the systemized Drying Project in 1991-92. How sad it is to see 5000 years worth of culture and beauty assassinated by a flick of a finger.

A traditional reed house from the inside, Mudhif -Courtesy of Mohammed Al-Dhamat

Eat Masguf and Then We Can Talk

Iraq has 46 freshwater fish species in addition to the marine ones. The most famous are *Shabut* and *Gatan*, from the carp family; the latter is the bigger. It may reach approximately 450 lbs. There is also Barbel–*Bunni* and *Zajr*. In local folklore the *Bunni* fish says: "*If you find a fish tastier than me, then don't eat me.*" The most expensive marine fish is the Pomfret – *Zubaydi*. Some fish are consumed fresh and some are smoked, while others are salted and sun-dried by people in the southern marshlands. The fish is normally first de-salted, and then cooked with rice to prepare a dish called *Masmouta*. Fish from the river Tigris is highly valued by Baghdadis because they believe the best fish come from running cold-water sources with stony riverbeds.

Choosing a good, fresh fish and knowing how to cook and eat it, is a difficult skill that few have achieved. This skill is equal to, if not more important than, knowing how to choose red, sweet watermelons or pomegranates, olive oil or natural honey. Some believe the most delicious fish are caught in September.

Masguf is a traditional Mesopotamian dish, consisting of grilled fish cooked on an open fire. It is by far the national dish of Iraq. The word itself is slang and is derived from the Arabic word "roof," a reference to opening and spreading the fish into a single flat round piece. Masguf is cooked in two stages. First, the fish is exposed to the heat using the fire's flames to sear it, which makes it crisp. After the fish splits open, it is cleaned and seasoned with rock salt and paprika, then placed beside the fire with nine or ten others, all impaled on sticks arranged in a circle around the crackling twigs. It is cooked for one hour, and during the last ten minutes of cooking time, the fish is laid flat on its back right on top of the ashes and embers, which are raked together. *Masguf* is more often than not, a picnic treat, so preparing it requires a certain skill. The key to Masguf is freshness. Traditionally, the fish is killed only when the fire is ready for barbecuing. During Summer, particularly on moonlit nights, picnickers make huge campfires along the banks of the river. The capital, Baghdad, prides itself on making the best *Masguf*, especially on the tree-lined Abu Nu'as Boulevard along the Tigris River. It is believed that if one dreams of live fish in water, it is a sign that they will make more money. So next time you dream of fish, stay tuned for a treat.

Masguf – grilled fish in Betawin, Baghdad – Courtesy of Yasir Muhsen

Snakes and Ladders

The United Nations Special Commission (UNSCOM) was an inspection panel created with the adoption of United Nations Security Council Resolution 687 in April 1991. Its purpose was to oversee Iraq's compliance with the destruction of Iraq's chemical, biological, and missile weapons, and to cooperate with the International Atomic Energy Agency's efforts to eliminate nuclear weapon facilities. In the aftermath of the Gulf War, it also included Iraq's recognition of Kuwait's sovereignty as an independent state, and making up for the losses inflicted on that country.

In 1996, the Iraqi regime agreed to the terms of U.N. Security Council Resolution 986, Oil for Food program. The program allowed Iraq to sell 2 billion U.S. dollars' worth of oil every six months, as a way to purchase supplies for its increasingly impoverished and malnourished population. This agreement also allowed the U.N. to oversee the use and management of oil revenues, insuring that some of the funds went to war reparations and UNSCOM costs in Iraq during that period. The supplies purchased with oil revenues were to be supervised by U.N. inspectors to ensure fair and equal distribution throughout the Iraqi population.

Inspectors withdrew in 1998. The successor of UNSCOM was the United Nations Monitoring, Verification and Inspection Commission. During the Security Council meeting of December 15, 1998, two letters from weapon inspectors were considered. One was from Mohammed al Baradei. That letter stated that Iraq "has provided the necessary level of cooperation to enable...[our] activities to be completed effectively." The other letter, authored by Richard Butler of UNSCOM, deplored "the restriction, lack of disclosure, and concealment." Regardless, *Operation Desert Fox* had already begun at the time of the meeting (just hours after the inspectors had been evacuated). The United States declared that: "Iraq's policy of unremitting defiance and non-compliance necessitated the resort to military force." The United Kingdom stated that the objectives of the action were "to degrade Iraq's capability to build and use weapons of mass destruction and to diminish the military threat Iraq poses to its neighbors. The targets chosen therefore were connected with military capability, weapons of mass destruction, and the ability to threaten neighbors."

The Supreme Art of Teaching

Despite the heavy workload and, at times minimal resources, obstetrics and gynecology was definitely my cup of tea when compared to other disciplines, because results, providing relief and satisfaction, were relatively quick. For example, when a woman arrives in labor, after a few hours she may be stable again, and a new life is welcomed into the world; whereas in some other specialties, it might take days or even weeks to get such a satisfactory result. I also found my groove in teaching medical students. That experience was a real eye opener. It is funny how 17 years of university teaching at al-Nahrain College of Medicine flew by as if it were only 17 days. Mutaz once pointed out that 17 is the number of prostrations – *Raka'as* Muslims perform in daily prayer. Indeed the sanctity of teaching makes me feel as if I'm engaging in a prayer every time I teach a class, for it brings me closer to God. Wouldn't the world be such a better place today if all worshippers, regardless of their faith, not only preached that "work is a form of worship," but actually lived as if that were so. Just imagine the impact!

My students were unique. They were lucky to have many opportunities for hands-on experiences because the number in each group was always small. My family was forever supportive and proud of me. Even while at home, regardless of the time, my residents would call me whenever a procedure needed to be performed, and when they couldn't handle a particular case, the hospital would send an ambulance to my home to pick me up, typically around 2:00 or 3:00 in the morning. If my ride to work was running late or simply not available, Abdul would volunteer to get up and drive me to the hospital instead of staying all warm and cozy in bed. Most of the time he would wait for hours at the nurses' station until I made sure the patient was well so we both could go back home together. Even my children would get involved. Their favorite bedtime story would include a narration of how things had turned out well with patients, without, of course, violating patient privacy. In 1990, Dr. Faisal Al-Sudani, my esteemed professor and friend, joined us. With him present, our team had medical debates that were both useful and entertaining. He was an entertainer by nature, jumping from historical anecdotes to scientific facts as he captivated us with his storytelling. Alas, we lost contact with him amidst the gust of events.

We were starting to teach the fourth year students for the first time and everyone was nervous. The administration took us on a tour to see the equipped auditoriums weeks before starting. We were told that every lecture would be videotaped, something which certainly didn't help to ease our anxiety. Just imagining the scenario of having to scrutinize and evaluate everything from our body language and tone of voice down to where we place our hands. Dr. Kamal Al Samara'ee, known as the godfather of Iraqi gynecologists, inaugurated the first lecture. He was a super star in gynecology, a teaching professor, friend, and neighbor. He published his four-volume memoir titled *Talk of the Eighties,* which refers to his age. He gifted Abdul with a copy of the memoir while visiting Al Samara'ee for one of his Friday gatherings of friends and colleagues. Dr. Samara'ee was a witty person. Once, the deputy dean of the college entered his classroom and addressed the students for few minutes about some new regulation. He then turned to Dr. Samara'ee and asked him: "Do you know who I am?" In the Arabic culture it is distasteful to say "I don't know," so Dr. Kamal, who had no idea who the gentleman was, answered in a calm, diplomatic manner: "Yes, you're my brother," an answer reflecting respect to a fellow "brother" in medicine.

I shouldered the burden of being chairman of the department when Ferdous and Iffat left the college in mid-1992, at a time when Samira, Layla, and I were the only staff members. Our students had advanced to the sixth year, meaning we had to start their training immediately. I asked gynecologists from the Ministry of Health to give us a hand with the clinical teaching, and we had to cancel our summer vacation that year. The first batch of our students graduated in June 1993. External examiners from other universities were impressed by the high quality of our students. Each batch consisted of 50 to 55 students. The first student, Fadi Kaloti, was rewarded with a scholarship to study abroad. Most of my students are presently successful physicians in Iraq, the U.S.A., U.K., Australia,

France, Germany, Sweden, and the Arabic Gulf. In 1994, my respected professor Kais Kubba joined our department, and he kindly accepted to chair the department. I became his deputy until he retired in late 2000, when I resumed the duties of chairman once again. The first batch of postgraduate students in obstetrics and gynecology graduated from our department in June of 1994 with an advanced diploma. There were 10 altogether including the residents from our department.

Serving as head of a department at the university could be quite challenging. One incident that particularly upset me occurred during the final-year exams that sixth-year students take. A student did not show up on the scheduled day of the written and OSCE (medical skills) exams. Her excuse was that her father had an illness. Later on, it appeared that his illness had not been a significant one. Although I could sympathize with the student, I did not let that affect the resolution of the situation. It was felt that it was important to follow the regular protocol for university exams. Otherwise, it would set a precedent for future students. The decision of our department was to let her sit for the exam two months later, taking the exam along with those students who had not received a passing grade on the first try. That decision did not please some colleagues on the College Board, and it cost me their friendship.

Saddam's University president handing me a certificate of appreciation - 1997

Another challenge I faced occurred when the time arrived to work on the final exams for 4th and 5th year students; my deputy and I spent long hours preparing for the written questions paper that included: Multiple choice questions, single-choice questions, long and short essays. She took the drafts with her to type up at home, and then went on a last-minute vacation, thinking that OBG exam would be the last one on the exam schedule. I was shocked when I accidently discovered that the exam schedule had been changed, and I had to hand in the exam question paper that same day. With the help of a colleague, I worked hard to get it done and handed in on time. This was particularly a stressful event.

During the first few years of my career at the university; my clinical duties, teaching, and administrative tasks kept me very busy, not allowing any time for conducting research, apart from supervising small projects for sixth-year medical students. A few years later, I supervised the research projects of Iraqi Board postgraduate students, and later I carried out research projects in collaboration with other colleges. Our research was principally in the areas of: preeclampsia, pre-term labor, ectopic pregnancy, polycystic ovaries syndrome, silent chorioamnionitis (infection of fetal membranes), and adverse pregnancy outcomes. After submitting four published research projects, I was promoted to the position of assistant professor in 1998. The title, professor, was bestowed on me in 2006 (effective June, 2005) after the submission of 10 additional published research projects. The requirements for granting the title, professor, were: six years' service as assistant professor, plus a minimum of six published research projects, one of which must be original.

Having never requested that any of my patients to be admitted to a private hospital, my practice in private hospitals was limited. However, I advocated for public hospitals, where I gave the best care I could. To me public hospitals, at least, in those days in Iraq, were better equipped and had well-trained, supervised resident staff 24/7. Only if the patient requested private care, and insisted on it, would I accede to her wish. The medical system in Iraq gives doctors the opportunity to work in public institutions as well as in ones within the private sector, as long as it does not affect their duties in the public sector.

Grandchildren Ahmed & Ruaa in traditional Arabic
Attire at Baghdad waxworks museum -2002

My granddaughter Shams in traditional Arabic Attire at Baghdad waxworks museum 2002

Fertile July

I traveled abroad several times a year to attend medical conferences and participate in presentations. I had been to Jordan, Syria, Kuwait, Egypt and Lebanon, besides attending most of the conferences, workshops and scientific meetings in Iraq during my 42 years of service.

In the spring of 2000, I attended the European Society of Human Reproduction and Embryology's annual conference (ESHRE) held in Bologna, Italy. There were 12 Iraqi delegates including Professor Hammash, our university president. We witnessed the recent advances in infertility management and assisted conception technology presented by international experts in the field, as well as pre-conference workshops and massive exhibitions of related literature and equipment. Bologna is one of the oldest and most cultured cities in the world where the oldest university in Europe was established in 1088. It was declared the European Culture Capital in the year 2000, and in 2006, it was chosen by the United Nations Educational and Cultural Organization (UNESCO) as the "City of Music. We enjoyed walking under roofed arcades that are typical of the city, stopping by such wonders of art and sculpture, as Fountain of Neptune in Piazza del Nettuno, Piazza Maggiore, and the Basilica of San Petriono. The visit to Rome was even more exciting. Walking around Italy is like touring a big, gorgeous art museum. We were amazed at all the eye-catching sculptures and fountains as well as those impressive archeological sites that date back some 2000 years.

I was thrilled to know that we were going to pay a visit to the Vatican, the Papal residence, and the world's smallest country. It is completely encircled by the city of Rome. Among its most popular attractions are: St. Peter's Basilica, the most important church in the world where magnificent altars and monuments are sights to see. The Basilica has an enormous dome, and it houses the Sistine Chapel. The Vatican museums boast one of the most impressive art collections in the world. We entered Vatican City through the expansive St. Peter's Square, which is elliptical in shape. It is surrounded by two huge colonnades with Doric columns arranged in four rows atop of which stand statues of saints. Hundreds of thousands of guests gather in the square to receive the Pope's blessing or to participate in masses.

We spent a day in Venice enjoying a ride in a gondola through the Grand Canal, and then concluded the day window shopping at the Rialto Bridge, where Dr. Hammash bought a pair of shoes which would be a gift for his wife when he returns to Iraq, He asked me to try on several styles for her and, finally, we found the perfect pair.

On our return flight, we changed planes in Frankfurt, Germany. An Iraqi doctor, who had studied in Germany, was interpreting to the passport officer, and whenever she asked about the birthdate of each of us the answer was always July 1. The woman looked puzzled thinking it was a kind of joke, however, it wasn't. The story goes like this. Prior to 1958, most Iraqis only had the year of birth registered on official documents. After the July Revolution took place on July 14, 1958, a law was passed requiring that all Iraqis add a specific day and month to their official birth record, in addition to the year already recorded. However, in honor of the revolution, the government declared that July 1st would be the day of birth on all identification cards, for those who did not have a specific day and month recorded before. It took more than a few minutes to convince the officer that we were telling the truth. At last, she reluctantly agreed to stamp our passports. Once safely aboard the plane, we laughed at what a fertile month July is in Iraq.

In 2001, I attended the following year's ESHRE conference, only this time it was in Rayon, Switzerland. We were nine Iraqis who attended. I enjoyed the beautiful weather and the amazing charms of nature. The place is filled with peace and tranquility. I walked along the Cornice for hours without feeling fatigued. We met Dr. Alaa Al-Alwan, a well-known Iraqi physician, who was working for the World Health Organization (WHO) in Geneva. He and his wife Dr. Hanan Hamami invited us for dinner at their home. They were so generous and kind that we all felt at home.

My last trip as al Nahrain University employee happened in February 2003, just a month before the Iraq invasion. This time I went to Beirut, Lebanon's capital, accompanied by three colleagues to observe postgraduate family medicine training. I was impressed by the system as well as the medical services in government institutions. The late Rafeeq Al Hariri established the institute we visited paying all the costs out of his own pocket. Students there received supervised hands-on training in all medical specialties as future family doctors. We visited The American University in Beirut and enjoyed a picnic by the sea. Our last day was devoted to visiting Jeita Grotto. Along the way, we noticed a sign for a private wax museum, and we asked a taxi driver to take us there. We found it a sophisticated and impressive museum. On exhibit were statues of many international figures. A motion detector, which sprang into operation as we passed by each statue, signaled the play of an excerpt from a famous speech. Each speech corresponded with the figure we were passing. Finally, we reached Jeita Grotto by boat. We marveled at the wonderful stalactites and stalagmites, a system of two caves made of karstic limestone spanning 18 km in length situated north of Beirut. Jeitta is a finalist in the new seven wonders of nature competition.

Ashes to Ashes

In mid-July of 2002, while having renovation work done to our house, my mother suffered a stroke, she had been hypertensive since her early forties, and was under regular medical care. We all participated in her care, first at Ilwiya private hospital, then later back at her home, but all was in vain. We lost our beloved and loving mother on September 29, 2002, the day my sisters, brothers and I, along with our families, felt ourselves to be real orphans. The huge heart of the woman, who embraced us all, stopped beating. The house where we grew up and which held all our memories, both good and bad, was closed. No more weekend gatherings and no more daily phone conversations with Mom. Her altruism and sacrifice knew no limits. During the last 10-15 years of her life she did not wear any new clothes, despite the fact that each one of us would bring her lots of everything and always the best, she used to give them away to the needy.

END OF THE BEGINNING
2003 AND BEYOND

The Last Wednesday

The months preceding the invasion of Iraq went by painfully slowly for Iraqis. Anticipation, anxiety and fear of the unknown hovered over us like our own shadows. People were reliving the 1991 atrocities. The government was in complete denial, mobilizing the media with flowery speeches, and distasteful sycophantic songs embracing the wise and almighty leadership, instead of addressing international demands and the people's concerns. Many families fled the country or left for nearby cities.

We rented and equipped a house in Baquba, the capital of Diyala province some 31 miles northeast of Baghdad, but because we were tied to the needs and commitments of our work and family, we never left Bagdad. The name Baquba originates from the Aramaic words "Bet" (house) and "Yaqub" (Jacob), meaning "Jacob's house." We "fortified" our house in Baghdad to increase our chances of survival in case it was bombarded. The windows were covered from the outside with a thick waterproof fabric that was pushed aside during daylight hours. Transparent nylon sheets were placed on the inside. Since our spacious living room had two exits, we removed the furnishings to create a sleep space on the carpeted floor. One exit through the main entry way led out to the main street. The other exit was through a side door that led onto a side street. We bought extra water tanks and drilled a well in the garden. It was equipped with a manual pump. Valuables and documents were collected and put in a bag that was kept close at hand.

March 19, 2003, is a date that will certainly not be forgotten, for late on that night, the air strikes began. We were resting on the floor, tightly holding on to the children and muttering prayers. During the subsequent days, the attacks significantly intensified at night; sometimes, they lasted until sunrise. The already scarce electricity was completely cut off. We hooked up our TV to a car battery, and restricted our usage to watching the news, for that was our only way of keeping up with what was going on. Once the battery died, our sole source of information was the BBC channel on Abdul's 30-year-old, large, black Phillips radio. As water became scarce, we started pumping water from the garden well; however, it was good only for cleaning purposes. Cooking took place in the backyard patio – "Tarma", and bread was baked on the stove one loaf at a time. Abeer was mainly with her family at her in-laws' house, but one night, she came over to stay with us at our house. That night, the attack was horrific. Earlier that day, the national TV had broadcast interviews with the first American prisoners of war, who were captured during an ambush of the 507th maintenance company, in the town of Nasiriya, about 225 miles southeast of Baghdad. The clip showed a few young men and one woman, being asked questions by an Iraqi "presenter" who spoke such poor English that the soldiers could not understand most of what they were being asked. It was obvious that the Americans wouldn't think highly of the interview, and only eventually would they respond; however, that response came sooner rather than later. As night fell, draping its darkness all around us, we could hear the sharp sounds of bombshells being dropped followed by the floor shaking underneath. The blows literally felt as if the entire house were being lifted up into the air and thrown back down again on the ground. The curtains tore, the closet doors opened, and their contents were thrown about. With each bombshell blast the doors shook violently. The door to the storeroom, right under the stairs, was blown off. The impact felt incredibly close. That led us to believe the target was Dr. Ammash's residence, which faced Ohud Square and was just about six houses away from us. Dr. Huda Ammash was an American-educated Iraqi scientist, dubbed Mrs. Anthrax and Chemical Sally by the western press, because of her association with the Iraqi biological weapons program. Later, as it

Stove used for cooking and baking, Lantern for lighting during wartime – Courtesy of Ali Bader

turned out, her house was intact. Separated only by river Tigris, the *Istikhbarat,* the central intelligence building on the opposite shore was the actual target of the bombardment.

The next morning, our neighbor Abu Mustafa decided very suddenly to leave the city with his family and to go to Baquba for one day. He uttered something about this day in particular being critically important, without giving a specific, clear explanation why that would be so. With their leaving town to go to "Baquba," the City of Citruses, only two families were still left on the entire block, us and the family from the house across the street. We felt more worried and isolated than ever, but did not leave the capitol, although we had rented that house in Baquba. We finally decided to go to *Zayuna*, a neighborhood southeast of Baghdad, to a then vacant house, which belonged to my sister Najiha's brother-in-law. We spent the entire day preparing the house and finally settled in there with my sister's family. Only minutes after our going to bed, the bombing started again. This time the windows shattered scattering glass all over. This was the second time Abeer joined us for an epic night. Mutaz joked that every time Abeer is with us, she attracts missiles and bombs like a magnate. At sunrise, we got into our cars and headed back home, leaving everything as it was. We found out that night's bombings targeted the Olympic Committee, Saddam's commandos training camp, and the ministry of defense, all of which were located in that neighborhood.

In the afternoon of April 9th, Kawkab and Muwafaq came over to our house; they had seen American trucks pass by the *Qanat al Jaish* - Army Canal in their neighborhood. We all decided to spend the night at Grandpa's house in *Sulaikh*. An hour after we arrived there, a clamor was heard out in the street. Muwafaq went out to see what was going on and neighbors told him that Saddam's rule had fallen. Najiha saw a woman carrying a computer screen passing by along. Soon, we realized that the number of people who were walking by carrying objects was growing by the minute. We knew then that another chapter had begun.

This time it involved looting and sabotaging public and state-owned institutions. The next day, we woke up early to the sounds of U.S. tanks patrolling the neighborhood. We went back into our house feeling completely overwhelmed. Our hearts were filled with a sorrowful sigh, a feeling that was stronger than one of the relief of being rid of tyranny. Its source was the collapse of our beloved homeland. Afaf, Mutaz, and myself simply sat down in the kitchen. All of a sudden, my eyes welled up with tears; slowly those tears began rolling down my cheeks, and I started to weep. Afaf soon followed.

At work, there was a makeshift office on the ground floor of the college. There the dean and hospital manager were stationed. The college administration had made a deal with the neighborhood residents to protect the hospital and college from theft. In return, they received electricity from the hospital generators. The exchange worked well. Nothing was stolen from the college, or from the hospital. Meanwhile, over at the neighboring college of law, literally everything was looted, including toilet seats.

Alif-Ba'a, are not only the first two letters of the Arabic alphabet, but also the name of the most popular local weekly magazine. Established in June 1968, it was distributed every Wednesday. The magazine was read avidly by a vast array of readers. Because of its inclusive reporting, covering everything from politics, culture, arts, community and more, it enjoyed a good reputation both internationally and within the Arab world despite being available only in Arabic. Every week 250 thousand copies were distributed and although the demand was greater, the publishing house was unable to exceed that printing capacity. Following the 1990 economic blockade, the number of issues produced was reduced to 30 thousand copies, and the magazine consisted of only 48 pages instead of its former 80. Regardless, it was still the best. The Alif Ba'a issue for the week of April 9th 2003 was already printed and ready to be distributed when US forces rolled into Baghdad. Unfortunately, copies of that printed issue never made it to marketplace. Instead, they were left at the Al-Hureya publishing house in Wazzireya, Baghdad, which was eventually looted and burnt to the ground. Thirty-five years of eloquent entertainment and education was silenced forever. It was indeed, the last Wednesday edition!

Baghdad is Burning

On April 10, only one day after Iraq's occupation, the religious cleric Abdul Majeed al Khu'e was assassinated in the mosque of Imam Ali in Najaf. The first resistance the coalition forces met was that of Fida'yee Saddam, "Saddam's Sacrificers," and the Ba'athists supporting him. Eliminating them was not that difficult, however, some of mistakes the occupying leaders made led to a crystallization of resistance, and a deepening of violence. At the same time the instability and lack of security control, encouraged terrorists from other countries to enter Iraq and to act against Iraqis and occupiers alike.

The unrest started in Fallujah on April 28, 2003 when the coalition forces opened fire on a large group of demonstrators, killing 15 and injuring others. Fallujah became a center of attraction for terrorists, who were not only against the occupiers, but were also against Iraq's stability and rebuilding. On May 18, the Americans dropped a plan to give authority to a democratically elected government in Iraq. Instead, they proposed another plan to the Security Council, one that gave broad powers to the U.S. and U.K. in Iraq. It authorized rebuilding Iraq as well as providing humanitarian aid and instituting a new government. Passage of this plan allowed them to appoint a national government of their choice called the Governing Council, which was appointed in July 2003.

In July 2003, while we were sleeping on the rooftop, we heard a lot of shooting all around the area. A few bullets struck near where our beds lay, so we ducked down as quickly as we could. Later on we discovered that the shooting was to "celebrate" the killing of Saddam's two sons, Uday and Qusay. In August 2003, the Jordanian embassy was bombed, raising fears of repeat attacks on diplomatic missions in Iraq. On the 20th of that same month, the headquarters for the UN mission was bombed, killing the Special Representative of the U.N. Secretary General, Sergio Vieira de Mello, and wounding 100 others. That incident led to a withdrawal of the U.N. mission from Iraq until July of 2004. Before the end of that same month, during Friday prayer, a car bomb exploded near Imam Ali shrine in

Najaf. The blast killed 80. Among the victims was the well-known religious figure, Mohammed Baqir Al Hakeem.

In June 2004, the Security Council called for the formation of an interim, national government to mark the end of occupation and to lead a new era in Iraq. That newly-elected interim body was headed by Iyad Allawi, the first Prime Minister after Saddam. Allawi's government made several attempts to control the oil infrastructure and restore order in Iraq's main cities. Continued resistance, coupled with the poor condition of the army and a challenged security, foiled those attempts. At the same time, groups of former Ba'athists, as well as Al Mehdi fighters (affiliated with Muqtada Al Sadr) engaged in acts of violence and opposition. Therefore, the government decided to crush the resistance with the help of the Americans. At one point Al-Sadr and his followers in the Al-Mehdi Army controlled the streets of Baghdad, so the coalition forces tried to put him on trial for murder, but he fled to Najaf. Many confrontations took place in and around the city during June and July of 2004, ending with a siege of the mosque. Finally, the fighting stopped. but only after a successful mediation on the part of Ayatollah Al Sistani. As a result, Al Mehdi fighters were incorporated into the official army marking a turning point in the Iraqi scene.

On November 2, 2004, Iraqi and American armies broke into Fallujah beginning a fight that lasted two weeks. It was one of the bloodiest battles in which the American army was engaged. During the battle, 6,000 Iraqis were killed; another 200,000 fled the besieged city. Humanitarian organizations were not allowed to assist the townspeople. In that same month, a battle to stop the resistance took place in Mosul. It lasted eight days. Waves of violence continued in Mosul for well over the next four years. This violence targeted, in particular, religious minorities, and it led to the displacement of numerous Christians, who fled to the Nineveh plains east of Mosul. Early in 2004, significant violations against Iraqi prisoners surfaced, and that news spread quickly to the general public. The abuses at Abu Ghraib prison included horrifying treatment of prisoners. Some prisoners were beaten, others were burned, still others were exposed to dog bites, sexually assaulted, forced to remove their clothing and then humiliated. The prison was under American supervision at the time when these offenses occurred. The discovery of what was happening at the detention center sparked international outrage. The global community considered the prisoner treatment a vast violation of human rights and strongly denounced those acts. As a result of the international clamor, the officials involved were tried, convicted, and punished.

Open Sesame

Theft and vandalism at the National Iraqi Museum and Iraqi archeological sites started immediately after the occupation of Iraq on April 9, 2003. Hundreds of people attacked the museum, stealing artifacts and dragging them through the streets in wheelbarrows and wagons. The museum was a reservoir of enormous wealth containing artifacts from Mesopotamia including the Sumer, Akkad, Babylon, Assyria and Chaldea civilizations. It also included artifacts from the Persian, Greek and Roman Empires, as well as various Arab civilizations. It contained clay tablets of Hammurabi's Code, the first legislative system in the world. It held poetic epics; records of historical events; and achievements in the mathematical sciences. It also contained a library of tablets whose contents were not yet explored. Not only Iraq suffered the loss of these ancient and historical treasures, they were lost to all humanity as well.

The Museum closed in 1991 after the Gulf War, and it was reopened to the public only a few months during the year until the 2003 occupation. Several global organizations, including the British Museum, had asked for its protection before the war and gave advanced warning of the pending disaster. The International Council of Museums based in France, organized a meeting in May 2003 to make a red list of the most important relics and artifacts at risk of theft, enlisting Interpol's cooperation in order to locate the stolen items and retrieve them. The list was issued in Arabic, English and French. An estimated 15,000 artifacts were stolen and less than half were recovered.

The treasure of Nimrud, which remained immortal for 2,800 years, was found in a dark underground room covered with water, after the bombardment of the Central Bank of Iraq by the American forces. The treasure is made up of 613 pieces of gold jewelry, precious stones, and ornaments dating back to the Assyrian civilization. Experts estimated that the looting and destruction was the worst since the devastation of Baghdad by Genghis Khan in the thirteenth century.

An American team headed by Bogdanos, the author of *Baghdad Thieves*, took up the task of searching for the stolen artifacts and efforts to retrieve them. They found signs of three thefts from the museum between the 8th and 12th of April in 2003. Forty carefully selected items were stolen from the display shelves and from the restoration and rehabilitation rooms, indicating that the thieves had prior knowledge of their importance. This included the al-Warka mask, which was later found through the efforts of American forces and Iraqi police. The same holds true for the Bull Lyre of Ur, which is considered the earliest musical instrument. Effects from the royal tombs at Ur were also stolen from underground storage locations at the museum. Interestingly, the team discovered that the steel doors of the reservoirs had not been damaged. That indicated that the thieves possessed the correct keys with which to enter. Content catalogues and all electronic records were destroyed. The exceptional effort of the team resulted in the recovery of thousands of items.

Lyre of Ur- Courtesy of www.lyre-of-ur.com

An Iraqi Jewish Archive was found soaked with water inside the building of the secret police. American soldiers removed it and it was sent to

Washington for repair based on the promise to return it. Together with other social and economic documents in Hebrew, Arabic and English, the archive held a copy of the Torah written in1586.

In 2003, The National Library in Baghdad suffered two major fires, one on April 10th and another on the 12th. Approximately one quarter of the total book collection, including rare books and newspapers, was looted or destroyed. Fire consumed as much as 60% of the Ottoman and Hashemite documents, and nearly all government archives. Virtually the whole collection of photographs and maps was destroyed. It contained an illuminated copy of the Quran and rare Islamic manuscripts with ash and soot damage to much of what remained of the collection. Baghdad's other major libraries suffered as well, besides museums and libraries in other provinces.

Looters also damaged some of Iraq's most beautiful buildings and old city neighborhoods such as: the 12th-century Abbasid palace, the 14th-century al-Mustansiriya School, the 16th-century Saray Mosque, the Souq al-Saray, a covered marketplace where old books are sold, and the 19th-century Saray administrative complex.

Souq al Saray, Baghdad – Courtesy of Belal Dhafer Saleh

A Graveyard of Buried Hopes

With electricity still scarce and telephone lines completely damaged, the mobile phone arrived on the scene in Iraq for the first time courtesy of the private sector. The phones could be used for overseas calls; however, they were made available only on a very limited basis by individual vendors on Palestine Street, East of Baghdad. Having heard about the phones, we went to the location only to find scores of people waiting their turn to make a call. When it was finally our turn, we called Mohammed in Australia. It was a very short conversation, yet a huge relief for him. The call went like this, "We are all alive...Well, don't worry about us. We'll stay in touch. Bye!"

By now it was the daily norm to see American soldiers and tanks moving about throughout the neighborhood. Every time they passed by they would greet people by raising their arms into the air. At first, the exchanges between the two were friendly in nature, some people offered them homemade foods, and in return the soldiers would share their REMS (ready-to-eat meals). They also shared magazines and candy, played with the children and chitchatted with the adults. Additionally, they were cooperative and responsive to minor local incidents. Some soldiers even managed to touch the hearts of Iraqis, but no one could have predicted how dramatically this image would change.

In early May, we resumed our duties at the college and hospital. Saddam College of Medicine was the first one to resume regular studies. At the first board meeting we discussed changing the name of the college, and it is amazing how history repeats itself. The Royal College of Medicine was renamed "The Iraqi College of Medicine" in 1958, now Saddam University was renamed Al-Nahrain University, with our college becoming its medical school. We started making up for all missed classes. Students were dedicated and cooperated well. The final-year exams were conducted and carried out in record time and the Board of the college designated this group of students as "The Batch of the New Iraq."

The first administrative change was to appoint a new hospital manager. Dr. Aqeel, one of our first batch graduates in 1993, filled the position. He had limited authority, especially in the area of finances. I remember his response regarding my request to finish the final touches on the Infertility and IVF Center. The building frame was already completed before the war, and much of the expensive, advanced equipment was already there. He told me that the Americans did not agree to complete or generate new projects, only to restore existing old ones. Aqeel did not last long as the hospital manager, because the hospital became affiliated with the Ministry of Health, instead of being under the Presidential Office together with Saddam College of Medicine.

Dr. Kais Al-Bustani, who was appointed by the Ministry of Health, replaced Aqeel. The university became affiliated with the Ministry of Higher Education. The new manager was sincere and treated all with respect, but sadly, his staff was lacking his good manners. In late 2004, a huge sum of money was dedicated to restore hospitals; nevertheless, the renovations at Kadhimiya Hospital were superficial. The only work done involved painting all the walls with bright colors along with some other minor changes in the emergency department, but the main problem of clogged plumbing was never addressed.

The issue of security still remained fragile, so we commuted to work as a group. Our neighbor Dr. Subuh and her daughter would join Afaf and me, or we would go with Dr. Liqaa and her husband. In spite of these measures, we were still harassed on several occasions by people we had not seen before in Baghdad. These strangers looked and behaved in an odd manner. Plainly, they didn't belong to the Baghdadi community. Still, we had to keep telling ourselves that tomorrow is a new day..

Going.... Going .... Gone

The destruction in Iraq was not limited to buildings, infrastructure, and the disbanding of the Iraqi army and police. The most significant damage rendered was to the human soul; it crippled it. In one brief moment in time, centuries of ethics and values, and a whole civilization, the legacy of an entire nation, was simply wiped away.

The first few days gave witness to the "*Hawasim,*" which in Arabic means "The Decisive War," a name given it by Saddam himself to counter what the U.S. dubbed Operation Iraqi Freedom. The general public tended to use the later name to describe those who plundered the government's institutions, presidential palaces, and museums. Even the Baghdad zoo was left with only 35 of the 650 animals it had housed. Baghdad became a neglected, ugly, and dangerous city where liquor was openly sold on street corners, especially in New Baghdad and al-Nasr Square. Thugs engaged in unethical and offensive behavior especially toward women. I had heard of a shameful incident in which a devout 60-year-old woman, wearing the Hijab was sexually assaulted by two former inmates in the marketplace, during the daytime. The men were armed and determined. A few months before the war, Saddam had granted amnesty to all prisoners excluding political ones. Soon the Baghdad streets had become infested with all sorts of criminals, and militias from some of the political parties, which were emerging within the Iraqi arena. Laws and ethics were ignored. Many of these persons and groups lived by their own rules, freely doing whatever they wanted. Abduction became as routine a part of the rhythm of daily life as did cars strapped with bombs and improvised explosive devices. No district in Baghdad was spared those horrible acts, although it was worse some districts than others. Anyone who ventured outside the house exposed him or herself to possible danger. Even within the house the fear of harm very real.

On one occasion, a car exploded some 20 meters from our house, followed within minutes by another blast just beyond our backyard. The explosions shattered the glass from our windows all over the place, and many of our China porcelain plates were broken. However, the genuine tragedy was the loss of three members of a poor family, who were renters in a building nearby. One of the explosions caused a building to catch fire. A peddler who was sitting on the sidewalk selling Qaymer-Iraqi cream lost her life. That same day, I was readying myself to be discharged from Ibn Al-Bitar Hospital after having suffered a heart attack. I spent two days on the cardiac inpatient unit with Mutaz at my bedside. The explosions occurred an hour before discharge, so we were forced to wait another four hours for the area to be cleared. The next day, on the same inpatient unit where I had been a patient only the day before, unknown individuals raided the unit and abducted three physicians.

At home, having tea for our evening supper in the garden became too risky. We stopped allowing the children to go out into the garden without supervision. Worse yet, when the power was out at night, we were frightened to go out to turn on the generator in an effort to avoid any danger that might be lurking around the four sides of the garden. I went back to practicing in the clinic, but only for an hour or two each day. We traveled during daylight hours in a neighborhood taxi as opposed to using our car, to avoid abduction. Once we got into a random taxi, and the driver burst into an angry rant. He went on and on, shouting and cursing about government corruption while driving recklessly. It was a huge relief to finally arrive two blocks from our destination and get out of that taxi.

Another horrible incident occurred nearby my clinic. Two brothers, a dentist and an ophthalmologist, got into an argument that escalated to the point where the dentist shot his brother dead in cold blood. The next day, I was shocked to see a banner hanging on their house wall mourning the man as if he had been the victim of an accidental death! God, how things change! I began to wonder if this was the same country where the Babylonian Hammurabi wrote the very first codes of law recorded in history back in 1754 BC.

Back with the Wind

Death snuck its way in and around every corner and alley. At work animosities and feuds erupted on a large scale for the first time. Before, all hospital staff had been living and working in harmony. Hostilities were followed by threats and then by assassinations. The dean received a threatening letter with a bullet inside the envelope. Thugs attacked the university president at a gas station. When he voluntarily offered them the car keys, he was told that they wanted him, not his car! One of the fifth-year students was assassinated few feet from the college gate without anyone knowing who or why. An ENT specialist was abducted from the hospital parking lot in front of the guards who stood there indifferent to his plight. To this date, nothing about his fate has been heard. A plastic surgeon at Kadhimiya Hospital was shot dead while driving his car. A medical assistant on the intensive care unit was also assassinated near the hospital gates. My colleague Dr. S. H. was abducted in the driveway of her home and forced into the car trunk. She was not freed until her husband paid the whole of the life savings they had accumulated during 20 years of hard work. A neurosurgeon from Baghdad Medical College was abducted and beaten; luckily, following a ransom payment, a co-worker found him alive in a garbage dumpster.

The episodes at the hospital pretty much summed up the ugly transformation throughout the entire country. In a nut shell, you wouldn't be subjected to death unless you were: Shia, Sunni, Christian or some other minority, rich or poor, highly educated or illiterate, a Baathist or someone with no party affiliation, carrying a weapon or unarmed, a woman wearing the Hijab or one who wasn't, a man perceived as pro-American just because he wore shorts or had a "marine" haircut or was simply an unlucky bystander. Still, it was believed that Iraqi scientists and well-to-do people were being systemically assassinated or forced to migrate.

Abdul's first cousin Saad was abducted. His family paid the demanded ransom, but he was never returned to the warm embrace of his family. Months later, a family friend was at a morgue filled with corpses in Najaf. He recognized Saad from the photo ID. Munir, the 20-year-old son of two chemistry professor colleagues of mine and a friend of Mutaz, was abducted. Friends, relatives and colleagues were going in and out of their home in an effort to support the family. From the moment his mother received the news, the only thing she would do was read the Quran around the clock. The abductors set him free after receiving a ransom. When Munir was freed, he had a scruffy beard. As he walked into his parent's home filled with acquaintances, he said only one thing: "*Asalam Alaikum*," which is a formal Islamic greeting that literally means "Peace be upon you." After uttering those words, Munir just walked directly to his room. It was a very awkward and uncomfortable scene. Everyone held their breath, thinking he must have lost his mind. Later, Munir told Mutaz that it was an awkward moment for him as well. He simply didn't know what to say. He shared with us some of the horrific experiences he suffered while in captivity. He was blindfolded the whole time, left sitting on the floor with the rest of the captives. The abductors repeatedly told him that his father was a good man, but now it was time to leave the country for good because now the country belonged to them. Not surprisingly, the abductors cursed and abused their captives. A person sitting next to Munir was shot dead in the head and his blood splashed Munir's face. Another captive, whom Munir identified as Egyptian from his dialect, was tortured awhile when the abductors started joking about his snoring and wetting his pants. They didn't realize that the angel of death had come to take him away.

The disappearance of a way of life is a central theme in the movie *Gone with the Wind*. The characters are faced with the horrors of war and it's aftermath. Violence, death and destruction surround. A new reality slowly takes shape, one that is difficult to comprehend and take in. This is what Iraq was like. One day, out of nowhere, someone like Munir is gone with the wind. Then suddenly, the wind brings him back. We were fortunate that Munir returned unharmed, unlike many who did not. One feels helpless, unable to turn the tide. All I could do was just stand there and witness all that Iraq once was gradually disappear.

Like millions of others, we were a peaceful family. Abdul refused to even possess a gun at home during the worse times of chaos. We were not affiliated with any political party and did not enjoy any privileges. Our mission was to raise our children and grandchildren to be respectful men and women. We served 42 years in the medical field, always keeping our patients' interests and humanitarian service as our priority. After 2003, we were robbed and threatened. It was only by some miracle that we managed to escape abduction twice. At work, I was subjected to harassment by the General Director of Health, who along with many others, considered professionals in high positions as part of the previous regime. In November 2004, we attended a medical conference in Aleppo, Syria where I participated in an oral presentation. On the way back, we encountered a gang of armed robbers whose faces where covered over by hooded masks. They stopped our car as well as the one ahead of us. My husband and I along with two female colleagues were riding in one car, and in the other were two male and two female doctors. They scared us and stole everything light and expensive that we possessed.

An incident that really rattled me was finding a doll in our back yard. The doll was mutilated with stabs marks on its chest, an arm and leg were missing, its eyes were poked out, and a rope hung around its neck. I pretended to be calm so not to alarm my husband and children. I commented that it probably belonged to the neighbor's daughter, and it must have fallen into our garden while she was playing. We all knew that it was highly unlikely that, at her age, the teenage girl next door would play with dolls, yet no one said anything. Our silence said it all. The next morning, I suffered a heart attack and was admitted to the intensive care unit. Within a month I suffered another attack and so, upon my doctors' advice, we had to leave immediately for Jordan. Mutaz accompanied me on the flight to Jordan while the rest of the family left the next day for Syria where an extended family member who was married to a Syrian welcomed them. Finally, we were altogether again and settled in Jordan since Abdul's doctors as well as mine were there. Once my health improved, I felt nostalgic for my work and my home, and I returned to Baghdad, accompanied by Abdul and Mutaz.

One Way Ticket

During a board meeting at the college, less than three weeks after my return to Baghdad, I suffered a new heart attack. This time, as soon as I was discharged from the hospital, we mobilized ourselves in order to leave as soon as possible. The biggest turning point in our lives came around the middle of September of 2005. We were leaving our beloved country, our precious home, our loving family, and a dedicated humanitarian profession. We were leaving a life full of work, splendor, and luxury for one that would be totally unknown, a life of humiliation and austerity. Although I am grateful for my family's safety, still to this very day, I have been unable to find a way to alleviate the profound sadness and pain that continues to penetrate and fill my heart as I struggle to accept this reality. Forty-two years of struggling to build a future and a career is hard to dismiss. I know we were not the only ones forced to make this difficult choice. To save their lives, millions of Iraqis also made this same decision.

Others, who were unable or unwilling to leave, chose a different path, one that may not have been any less painful.

We left during the early hours of the morning. The darkness seemed to fuel our sorrow. My eyes drowned in tears and my lips silently uttered good-byes to all the gloomy streets and supermarkets as we drove by them, one by one. Among them was Omar Bin Abdul Aziz Street. For 45 years, it had been my route back and forth. We passed the al-Ana'am, al-Waha, al-Jazeera and al-Rayyah food markets, whose establishment and flourishing I had witnessed over the years. As we passed 14th Ramadan Street, I wondered if I would ever again see al-Sa'aa Restaurant, al-Asal Sweets, Abu Riyadh Food Supply and Syed a-Haleeb. Gazing at each one, my eyes and heart felt an unbearable weight of memories and grief. Up to this point, we had had no intention of leaving Iraq for good. Our house was built to accommodate our four children and their future families. With that very purpose in mind, we had built and furnished a new extension to our house in 2002. A thousand questions raced through my mind, moving faster than water over Niagara Falls. How could I survive without Iraq? Was it over? Was I going to leave everything behind? Where were we going to end up? Would we make it? What was all of this for?

Left (Standing) Mutaz, Afaf, AbdulWahab, Mohammed (Sitting) Malka and Abeer – 1993

Once Upon a Thyme

Amman, the capital of Jordan, is a beautiful modern city, initially built on seven hills. Now it spans over 19 hills, combining 27 districts. It is considered one of the most liberal and westernized cities in the Arab world. Most buildings were constructed during the Iraq-Iran War, from the 1980s and onward. Getting around is easy and affordable. There is a public transportation system as well as taxi service. There are several malls that sell mainly imported goods. Electricity and Internet facilities were excellent and affordable in 2005, though those prices were higher than in Iraq. The lifestyle of Jordanians has been greatly influenced by America. In the area of medicine, they have acquired modern equipment and followed recent advances. This is the city we chose as our destination after we left Iraq. We had to start over from scratch. We furnished an empty apartment with everything we needed. We spent three long days going from store to store searching for furniture and household items, but we had to be frugal since we were on a tight budget. The children had to start school immediately. Their tuition fees, transportation, uniforms, and stationary needs were all added to the long expenditure list. In Iraq, they had gone to one of the best schools for free. Books and stationery were free, too. We used to drive them to and from school, stopping to buy their favorite snacks on the way.

To my disappointment many Jordanians did not have as friendly an attitude towards Iraqis as they had had in the eighties and early nineties. Neighbors and taxi drivers alike made us feel unwelcome. At school, the kids were called "terrorists" several times. Given that Saddam used to give Jordan Iraqi oil for free, it's not surprising that many Jordanians openly blamed Iraqis for toppling Saddam Hussein. Nevertheless, the good always outweighed the bad. Drs. Sameer Haddadin and his wife Alia Dababneh treated us with such warm-heartedness and generosity that they made us feel more like family than friends. Dr. Sameer had studied dentistry in Baghdad and had been Abdul's mate from college. Later on Rani Haddadin followed in his father's footsteps. He studied at the same college in 1993.

After two months, Afaf was lucky to find an administrative job at an Iraqi company. Shortly afterward, Mutaz, too, found a job, working as a hotel front desk clerk for an Iraqi businessman. Not only could Iraqis not get work permits in Jordan, but even Iraqi businessmen were allowed to hire only a very limited number of Iraqis. I applied to the Jordanian Ministry of Health for an appointment at a newly-opened public hospital that was in need of a gynecologist with an advanced degree, but I was rejected because of my age. Fortunately, few months later, Mutaz was hired at the Le Royal Hotel, and soon promoted to a training manager position. Accordingly, he was granted a work permit and legal resident status, which could be renewed annually.

Thyme – "*Za'atar*" is a herb that grows wild in Jordan and is commonly eaten with pita bread dipped in olive oil. It is one of many popular Jordanian health foods. Available in the U.S. in Arabic stores, it is something I recommend you try.

Too Many Walls, Not Enough Bridges

Having to leave home and country can lead you to dwell on memories. Al-Kadhimiya is an enchanting town in northwest Baghdad. It is regarded as a sacred destination for Muslims, particularly for Shia Muslims. The name is derived from two Imams buried there, who were descendants of the Prophet Mohammed. One was Imam Musa al-Kadhum, who was said to be an extremely gentle, pious, and tolerant man. He was called al-Kadhum because he forgave people and never became angry, even if cursed. The second Imam was his grandson, Mohammed al-Jawad, which means generous. The town hosts their shrines and a mosque; therefore, understandably most of its inhabitants are Shia. Shia Muslims carry their dead to greet the Imams for the last time before taking them to Najaf for burial. Rather than visit sacred shrines as they embark on their new life together, a newly engaged couple typically visit the town's gold market to buy the dowry – *Nishan*. After all, the town is known for having the best jewelry shops in Baghdad, and there, gold is mostly 21 carat. The groom also visits the site on his wedding day to pray for blessings. How interesting that life and death intersect at this corner of the earth.

The hustle and bustle of people and the golden domes can take you back in time. Think of the story *1001 Nights*. Once, I remember I was about to leave to go to Kadhimiya market with my sister Najiha, when my youngest daughter Abeer said: "Mama, bring back some gold for me." She spoke as if she were asking for candy. Initially, we weren't planning on swinging by the gold market, but what woman could resist the temptation of at least going window-shopping. We did end up going, and we bought two bracelets, one for Abeer and another for Afaf. While we were in one of the shops, a young man was introducing his fiancé to the goldsmith. The man had brought along his mother and older sister as well, since the entire family were loyal customers. We noticed that every time the poor fiancé saw something she liked, the goldsmith would suggest a different piece. Apparently, the bride-to-be didn't notice how the groom's sister would look at the goldsmith in a certain way so as to make him understand that they didn't have much money to spend. In the Kadhimiya neighborhood, and especially on the perimeter of the shrines, women were expected to wear the Abaya, and laymen were to behave in a respectful manner while out on the streets. One day, I witnessed one young child say something foul to another child, and a stranger reprimanded him, saying: "Watch your manners. You're in the presence of the Imam!"

On the northeastern end of Baghdad sits the town of Adhamiya, which houses the Shrine of Imam Abu Hanifa, also known as the Great Imam. He was of Persian origin and was the founder of the Hannafi Sunni School. Hence the majority of inhabitants were Sunni. The scent of history in this part of the city is evident in every corner constantly reminding the viewer of the glorious ages. Turkish pilgrims traveling to Mecca by land would often visit both towns in order to pray and to ask for blessings. My once peaceful neighborhood was in Adhamiya, where I had lived and opened my private clinic. My work was at the hospital and college in Kadhimiya. These two gems of Baghdad were as near and dear to my heart as my aorta and pulmonary artery.

Since our departure to Jordan happened practically overnight. Abdul, Mutaz and myself decided to return briefly to Iraq to close up the house and determine what we should take back with us. Unfortunately, my health interfered with our plans, and we were unable to accomplish much in the end. However, while we were back in Iraq a horrendous incident took place. It was in August of 2005, when the tragedy of "Jisr al-Aeimma" Imams Bridge occurred. The bridge lies north of Baghdad, between Adhamiya and Kadhimiya on the Tigris River. Hundreds of thousands were crossing the bridge on foot from various Baghdad districts, passing through Adhamiya, destined for Kadhimiya, as part of the Shia observance of commemorating the martyrdom of Imam Musa Al Kadhum. A malicious rumor was started by an al Qaida affiliate about the presence of suicide bombers on the bridge. The rumor spread among the pedestrians. It caused them to panic and to stampede over one another. Hundreds of people fell into the river and drowned; others were trampled to death during the stampede. The incident took the life of over 1000 innocent Iraqis. A 19-year-old Sunni hero from Adhamiya named Othman Al-Obaidi took action. That courageous young man managed to rescue seven people, who had fallen into the river. As he attempted to save an eighth person, he fell victim to exhaustion and he drowned. The whole of Iraq observed three days of mourning in honor of the victims of the tragedy. The bridge was not re-opened until November of 2008. The Imams' bridge was not used only as a means of transport. It was also a symbol of harmony and a place of solidarity. If the bridge could talk, I imagine it saying: "Remember what Imam Ali said: "If a man is not your brother in religion; he is your brother in humanity." Enough of walls and barricades, my heart longs for millions of bridges that bring people together.

Shrine of Imam Mousa Al Kadhum – Courtesy of AuthorHouse

Gallant Tiger

In a humble house, which lies in a small alley in Safina, Adhamiya, Um Othman was making tea for her only son Othman as he was studying for his finals. Othman was a well-behaved student in the electrical program at one of the vocational schools. He was loved and respected by everyone in his neighborhood – *Mahala*. The 19-year-old adolescent was an avid, well-built, and strong wrestler. He used to practice his hobby at the Adhamiya Sports Club in Antar Square, a five-minute drive from our house. In addition, he was a skilled swimmer. His paternal uncle Nabil first taught Othman to swim in the river when he was three years old. People criticized the uncle for not training him in a safe swimming pool instead of the river. Nabil always answered that he wanted Othman to grow up being a fearless hero.

On the day of the bridge tragedy, calls went out from the loud speakers at the mosque of Imam A'adham's and other nearby local ones requesting help. People came from both ends of Adhamiya and Kadhimiya and dived into the river trying to help those who were drowning. The scene was frightful. Hundreds of women and children fell 30 meters from the bridge into the Tigris River, and desperate cries for help could be heard. Most of the casualties were the weakest members in the crowd, women, elders and children. Some people died instantly as they fell and hit the concrete base; others died from drowning.

Othman rushed to the site. Without hesitation, he stripped off his clothes and dove into the river. He wrestled the waves, racing to reach and rescue the people. As he jumped into the water, a young boy had fallen close by him. First, Othman saved the boy; then he returned to save his brothers and sisters. Although exhausted, he was able to save seven people. The eighth person was an old woman, who in her panic grabbed onto him, causing both of them to sink and drown. Meanwhile Um Othman was helping provide water, food, and basic first aid to the injured at her house. The houses in the area turned into makeshift hospitals treating the pilgrims – *Zuwwar*. A man came to her house and said, "*Othman died.*" The mother's legs gave out from under her, no longer able to stand, she fell on the ground feeling as if she were going to die. She was remembering every single milestone in her son's life. One of the people around her shouted: "*He died after saving seven people; he's a martyr.*" Filled with tears, Um Othman stood up in pain, and with great pride, said, "*Inna Lillah Wa inna Ilaihi raji'oon*" – "*We belong to God and to him we shall return.*" This is a Quranic phrase that Muslims recite in the face of tragedy. Othman Abdul Hafiz Al-Obaidi dreamed that Iraq would be unified once again, free from ethnic or religious turmoil. Rest in peace, tiger of the Tigris, for the story of your heroism lighted a million candles of hope at al Aeimma Bridge.

Ladies and Gentlemen... We Got Him

On February 26, 2006, the two shrines of Imams Ali al-Hadi and Hassan al-Askari in Samarra were bombed, causing the destruction of major sections of the shrines. The next day, an al-Arabiya news channel correspondent, Atwar Bahjet, was assassinated on her way back to Baghdad from the scene. In June 2007, the two 36-meter high minarets at the same location were bombed. Then, bloody sectarian fighting broke out that lasted two and a half years, resulting in hundreds of casualties and millions of displaced persons. The shrine has a golden dome, which is 36 meters high, 68 meters wide and covered by 72.000 golden pieces. It is believed to be the biggest dome in Islamic world. One of the planners and perpetrators, a Tunisian, was arrested, followed by the arrest of 10 others. They were hanged in November of 2011. The violence peaked in 2006, yet continued until after mid-2008, mostly because of sectarian hostilities.

The International Organization for Migration (IOM) reported in 2009 that, "More than 1.6 million Iraqis were displaced internally as a result of the violence that followed the bombing of the al-Askari Shrine. Three years later, those displaced continue to suffer from scarcity of food, lack of shelter, health services, and security as well as uneployment. Their future is still unknown while humanitarian aid is scarce."

In mid-2006, Iraqis started to gradually take over responsibility for the country from the multinational forces in Basra, Amara, Mosul, Nasiriya and Najaf. Abu Ghraib prison was also handed over to them in September 2006. In June 2006, the al-Qaida leader of Jordanian origin, Abu Musa'ab al-Zarqawi, was killed. He was responsible for the explosion of two major hotels in the middle of Amman, the Jordanian capital, as well as thousands of casualties and extensive damage in Iraq. Finally, after being captured and later tried and convicted by the Supreme Court for the killing of 148 Iraqis in Dujail during the early eighties, the former Iraqi President, Saddam Hussein, was hanged on December 30, 2006.

Before 2006 came to a close, a number of Iraqi tribes, headed by Abdul-Sattar Abu Risha, formed the *Sahwat al-Anbar* (al-Anbar - Awakening). This tribal alliance revolted against the terrorist organizations in Anbar, west of Iraq. The men of the Sahwa continued their fight against terrorism. Aided by Iraqi tribes, the Americans were able to bring some security to Anbar and the surrounding areas. President Bush visited Iraq and congratulated Abu Risha and other tribes for their achievements. A bomb killed Abu Risha in September of 2007.

Heaven Sent and Heaven Stole

In the spring of 2006, Abdul's health deteriorated and after two hospitalizations, his big, loving heart stopped beating. Words cannot express our great loss. Abdul Wahab was everything in our lives. In times of crisis, he was salve for our wounds. On June 29, 2006, we lost the beloved mentor, protector, and supporter of the entire family. He showed such great kindness and respect to all around him. He respected women and believed in their capabilities. He was thoughtful of relatives and friends alike, wherever they were, and lent a hand whenever needed. He was laid to rest in Sahab Cemetery near Amman. That is why we cherish Amman above all other cities. The poor security conditions prevented us from carrying out his desire to be buried in Basra near his parents.

The four years we spent in Jordan were not easy ones. Apart from Mutaz, we were all illegal residents, so we could not go anywhere outside Jordan and were unable to work. In late 2006, I was granted an annual residence permit as Mutaz's widowed mother. Since the children could attend only private school, we always faced difficulties and delays at the start of each school year as registration time came around. All illegal residents in Jordan have to pay one Jordanian dinar (1.3 U.S. dollars) a day for each family member. Otherwise, they would not be allowed to reenter in the country, and no exceptions were made for us. Medical care could be obtained only through the private sector. Abdul Wahab and I had long lists of medications we needed to take daily for life at prices not easily affordable. On top of that, Afaf's postgraduate studies also needed to be paid. Along with occasional support from my son Mohammed, we used our life savings to cover most of our expenses. In 2006, after the president of al-Sulaimaniya University, in Iraq, reviewed my resume, I was invited to meet with him. I had to fly from Jordan and spend a week there, at my own expense, to be able to meet with him. He requested a written approval of transfer from al-Nahrain University. When I explained to him that I had already retired from that position, and that I had come only because of his request, he offered a response that failed to demonstrate respect for, or an acknowledgment of, my credentials. He literally told me, "*This is your problem, not mine.*" Another disappointment I encountered was the language barrier. I couldn't find a word of Arabic throughout this lovely city in northern Iraq, not in government offices, nor in any other establishments, nor even on shop signs. This convinced me that the north of Iraq was not for all Iraqis; although Iraq has been and always will be for all Iraqis.

A short time later, I went for another job interview in Amman, organized by a private company, for jobs in the Gulf. The place was crowded with dozens of highly qualified Iraqi doctors, from all medical specialties. I was offered an OBG consultant job in Dubai. They took my passport and original certificates to process a visa. Afterward, it appeared that the offer was a hoax, a big lie, but the worse part was that they didn't give me back certificates, as they did in the case of many other applicants. A few months later, while I was visiting my daughter in Dubai, the same scenario repeated itself when a businessman, who owned a medical center, promised me a job. He took my certificates (certified copies this time) to process the work permit. I was not granted the job, nor were my certificates returned.

Purely by chance, I happen to see an ad on the Internet, in April 2007. I applied, and was offered a job at the Asian Institute of Medicine, Science and Technology (AIMST) at the university in Malaysia. The university board president and owner, was also a federal government minister. He was a modest and worthy man who, over the phone, requested that I start work as soon as possible. He did that without even asking to see my degrees.

Grandchildren Ahmed, Shams, Ruaa and Abdullah - Amman, Jordan 2007

Car Bombs Alarm Clock

On April 12th of 2007, a car bomb blew up al-Sarafiya Bridge, resulting in approximately 800 killed and over 320 injured. Most of the bridge was destroyed and several cars fell into the river. The bridge connects al-Utaifiya to Sarafiya north of Baghdad. It was the highest and most beautiful of the twelve bridges in Baghdad. It had been built by a British company in 1946, was parallel to the railroad tracks and had a special walkway for pedestrians. One of the most exciting features of Baghdad was crossing the river by train via the bridge. This was not the first time an important bridge in Baghdad was damaged. In 1991, the suspension bridge collapsed due to bombardment by aircraft during the Gulf War. Built in

1964, that bridge was the first of its kind in the Middle East. Iraqis built a two-story bridge on top of its ashes in 1992.

In May of 2007, a bomb placed in a van near the al-Gailani Shrine exploded causing damage to the mosque. Sheikh Abdul Kadir al-Gailani was a Sufi scholar who founded Qadiriya Way. Forty-two casualties resulted from the bombing, including 20 deaths. A witness mentioned seeing five mutilated bodies, including one of a pregnant woman. Another said he saw people burning in their cars, while an injured traffic policeman was asking for help. Over 20 cars were damaged, including two burnt public transportation buses and several parked trailers. Another witness stated that his home was completely demolished while he was outside.

In March of 2008, the Christian cleric Archbishop Paulus Faraj Rahho was assassinated. He was believed to be the highest-ranking cleric from the Catholic Church from among those killed since 2003. On October of the same year, a bomb was detonated at Sayidat al-Najat Church in Karrada, which is south of Baghdad, killing 50 innocent worshipers. A hundred hostages were also taken and the Islamic State of Iraq claimed responsibility for the act.

The American-Iraqi Treaty was signed in August 2008. Accordingly, an agreement was reached for the departure of combat brigades from Iraqi cities by June 2009 and the complete withdrawal of troops by the end of 2011. On January 2009, President Barak Obama took office in the White House. He had promised in his election campaign to end the war in Iraq and to bring the fighting troops back home to the U.S. On August 7, he made his first visit to Iraq as Commander and Chief of U.S. forces.

Sarafiya Bridge in Baghdad – Courtesy of Mazin Jawad

Heart to Heart

I would like to share these words written by my son Mutaz about Baghdad:

Yesterday, I had such a bizarre dream ... a serene moment that took me high to the seventh sky ....
I went to Baghdad, to visit our house one last time; right by the Biblical Tigris River-Dijlah... Our 30 year-old palm tree embraced me with a motherly hug... The bricks of the walls of the house were eager to listen to my stories...A flashback took me to that moment, back in the old good days, when people were still human...
The Tigris smiled at me and said: "Hello stranger, I remember you, long time no see...I knew you would be back one day ... because whoever drinks from my abundance will always come back for more." Come sanctify your tired body in my waves."
I spread my father's praying mat on the green lavish lawn to begin noon prayer - Dhuhur one last time under the most beautiful sky ... I look up and rub my eyes hard as I see a flying stork heading west and carrying a huge baby in a cloth bundle... as it gets closer the baby became thousands of babies, but they were not ordinary ones; they were the scientists, doctors and artists. They were the Iraqi elite.

Without knowing why, I start shedding tears of olive oil, our humongous olive tree that we used to call aunty, wipes away the tears and says: "I raised you well, son". Suddenly, it vanishes into thin air.

I feel a flame of sorrow pouring into my heart, and decide to go inside... but then, it starts snowing... snowflakes in souring July - Tamouz, in Iraq? Does all this make sense?

A beautiful, but strong woman descends agilely from the sky and lands in the garden. She says: "I am Ishtar, the goddess of love and war,

I give you this apple from the Garden of Eden. Divide it among your family members and together you shall eat it"... "Never forget your roots. You are a Sumerian king on a mission to bring happiness and prosperity to all creatures around you." She too, crumbles and vanishes into thin air, leaving me in astonishment.

I then go inside the house that was once full of guests... I remember to enter with my right foot first for blessings. The laughs of my baby nephews and nieces echoing in a beautiful symphony played on the strings of the Gold Lyre of Ur.

How could this be possible, Big Ben in our living room? What on earth is happening? The magnificent clock struck zero ... the sound hit me like a brick on my head. As the moment came to an end, I knew it was time!

I swallowed all my pride and pain, and said: "Farewell my beloved, please forgive me for leaving the warmth of your eyes in search of my freedom." It hurts so bad. I wish Grandma was around to make me her famous Chai Arayis tea ... the wind was whistling like the spirits of a thousand ancestors telling me, "Its ok, we will be with you".

I bid farewell to the Tigris River, to my heart, right over here... right now.

I run as fast as I can like a ship's flag amidst the gust.

No destination in mind ...No exile to welcome me...

No home like home...

A tired stranger carrying his homeland in his backpack.

Oh Baghdad! What is all humanity worth without you!

Tell me, what I should tell the butterflies who abandoned the roses once I told them about your lips!

Ironically, Baghdad now is no longer for only Baghdadis.

It has become the embodiment of all life and death, peace and war, enlightenment and darkness...

It is, every love story, every stranger, Every Martyr,

Every church, masjid, synagogue and temple...

Every grieving soul that breathes pain.
Every disappointment, excitement and achievement, every sip of cardamomed tea, every dream and nightmare... Every mother that always forgives our ungratefulness and chronic stubbornness.
Baghdad ... is every "phoenix" inside us waiting to be reborn!
Written with the daunting loneliness of my long shivering nights,
The old songs that flow into my blood cells like a waterfall of light and glory. The poems, pictures and golden ages.
This piece is but a humble tribute to the city that falls asleep every day between my eyelashes...
Dedicated to the bitter-sweet
Mother of all symbols
Her Majesty ...Baghdad!

Malaysia Truly Asia

My flight to Kuala Lumpur was on Emirates Airlines. From there I took a domestic flight to Penang. The university driver picked me up and took me to Singai Petani, where the old university building is located. After passing over a wide 30-km long bridge, we arrived at the modern university complex in Semeling, where my apartment was located inside the teaching staff headquarters.

AIMST was a recently established private university in Kedah State, situated in the northwest of Malaysia. It is located at Semeling complex and includes colleges of medicine, dentistry, pharmacy, nursing, engineering and others. It is equipped with all modern facilities including accommodation, entertainment, and shopping. My residence was in one of the two 8-story buildings dedicated to the teaching staff. I had a three-bedroom apartment with a spectacular view and new hard furniture, all provided free. A short time later, my son Mohammed came to visit from Australia and bought me some appliances and other necessities. I couldn't wait to start teaching, and to my delight, a few days later, I was asked to give two lectures and correct the third-year medical students' exams. My non-mastery of the computer was quickly overcome by instructions from my fellow colleagues.

The students were impressed with me and thanked the dean for making such a successful choice.

I headed the OBG department; lecturing for 3rd, 4th, and 5th year students, besides tutorial, seminar, problem-based teaching, and clinical sessions. The achievements the university had made were a source of pride. Besides graduating two batches of well-trained students a year, during my tenure at the university, it had arranged for over a dozen scientific activities which included courses, workshops and seminars for the teaching staff. I supervised a research project for a postgraduate student and planned for a Women's Health Conference.

Malaysia is a federal constitutional monarchy in South East Asia consisting of 13 states and three federal territories. It became subject to the British Empire in the 18th century and achieved its independence on August 31, 1957. The country is multi-ethnic and multi-cultural. The main ethnic groups are Malays, Chinese, and Indians. The economy recovered from the 1997 Asian financial crisis faster than its neighboring countries.

I visited the capital Kuala Lumpur, a sophisticated, modern city, distinguished by its twin Petronas Towers. The towers were the highest in the world between 1998 and 2004, with a height of 1,483 feet. A bridge measuring 58 meters connects the twin 88-story towers. In 2004, the Taipei Tower established in Taiwan surpassed it measuring 1,667 feet in height. Currently, the tallest is the Khalifa Tower in Dubai, which was completed in 2010 and has a height of 2,716 feet.

I had been in Penang twice. It is an island blessed with many eye-catching vistas; it is truly a tropical paradise. One can go from the sandy shores to the vast open sea, and then from Penang Hill to the botanical gardens and the butterfly farm. Penang has its own twin towers, modern hotels, and several universities, as well as modern shopping malls. Accompanied by my Indian friend, Shakila and her daughter, I spent a day in Langkawi, one of Malaysia's beauties. In a two-hour trip up river from Alor Star, we arrived in "the Jewel of Kedah," as they call it. It is one of the most enchanting islands on earth. I could not help saying to Shakila: *"If only my family could see this!"* We hired a taxi for about 35 U.S. dollars and drove the whole day, traveling about the city. The place I found most exciting was "Under Water Life," the biggest aquarium in Malaysia. It is inhabited by 1,000 crocodiles on a 20-acre lot. Afterward, we visited the bird garden, followed by a visit to a museum that houses the belongings of Malaysia's former Prime Minister, Mahathir bin Mohamed. He served between 1981 and 2003.

In July 2008, I had the opportunity to participate in a three-day visit to Malacca with a group of teachers and our students. Malacca is a small friendly city, described as a living museum because it possesses many attractions. In fact, the city is a mix of old and new. The most interesting landmarks we visited were: Stadthuys, the oldest surviving Dutch building, Fort A'Famosa, which housed the Portuguese administration during their tenure in Malaysia, the beautiful Christ Church, and the oldest Buddhist temple in the country, the Malacca River, and Junker Street night market. We went up the rotating tower and enjoyed a ride on a horse-drawn cart decorated with colorful flowers. Malacca lies 148 km from Kuala Lumpur, half way between Kuala Lumpur and Singapore. On our way back, we took a side road to visit a huge Indian temple, "Batu Cave Murugan Temple" rests on top of a high mountain. It is a Hindu shrine and tourist attraction near Kuala Lumpur. The statue of Murugan is 50 feet tall. It is the highest statue in Malaysia; its ladder has 272 steps. Most students and a number of the teachers ascended the stairs and entered the Temple. I went with Nigaraja to inspect the smaller surrounding temples, as well as other attractions in the area. The area attracts thousands of visitors yearly. Among the many friends I made there and with whom I have remained in contact are Judith from Scotland, and Veena from India. In addition, I have stayed in touch with Giriga, Nigaraja, and Shakila who were the best colleagues and friends anyone could have.

Nigaraja and Malka in Malacca, Malaysia - 2008

Murugan Temple, near Kuala Lampur - Malaysia 2008

The Land of Opportunities

At the end of the summer in 2008, I went back to Amman for a six-week vacation with the family. Mutaz had already arranged an appointment for me to meet with the International Organization of Migration (IOM) officials regarding re-settlement. A few days later, Afaf received a date in three weeks' time to leave for the United States with her children, but Mutaz linked his case to mine. While the normal asylum process was still far from finished, my six weeks came to an end. I felt very torn. My job was vital to me, yet my family was my number one priority. I chose my family over my job, and so with a heavy heart I wrote my resignation. I had to call Judith and ask her to dispose of my belongings and to send me a few chosen items and I mailed her my key. That was the end of my long career in medicine.

After Afaf's departure, we spent nine more months in Jordan, during which I had three interviews at the IOM. I received an orientation course and had to have several medical tests done. On May 30, 2009, we were informed that we would be leaving for the States on June 23, 2009. Three weeks was not long enough to organize and resolve all our domestic and financial issues; however, we were forced to just leave most things as they were. The most heartbreaking task that we did was visiting the cemetery where Abdul was buried in order to bid farewell to our beloved.

An IOM officer greeted us when we arrived at Amman Airport. The officer gave each of us a carrier bag containing all the required documents. Then, he facilitated our departure, and wished us a safe journey. The 14-hour flight to New York seemed longer than one might imagine. My feelings surfaced anew as if I was leaving home for the first time. Mutaz was trying to comfort me, but it wasn't much help, as I could perceive a hint of sadness in his voice and eyes. We reached JFK airport before noon and spent two hours completing all the official transactions. On the way to Philadelphia, the picturesque view of nature was comforting and relaxing. Gradually I felt more at ease and started thinking of the future.

Mickey Mouse Has a House

Following a three-hour drive from JFK Airport, we finally reached Philadelphia. The picturesque landscapes interspersed with clear blue lakes vanished as we approached the city. Afaf was living in a second floor apartment in a row house. An Iraqi family occupied the first floor. Each apartment had its own entrance besides the main door. I found the steps to the apartment very narrow and steep, not like what we were used to in Iraq. The small eat-in kitchen opened out into the sitting room, which was a good size; it was bright with sunlight from two windows. A narrow, dark corridor led to two bedrooms. I shared the larger room with Afaf and her two children, and Mutaz took the smaller room that was filled with the pieces of luggage. The place was old and a perfect habitat for mice. The carpets resisted cleaning despite our diligent efforts. The mattresses were old and rested on the floor without a frame except mine. As Afaf knows well, I am terrified of mice. The only new household items were the curtains and sheets I brought with us from Malaysia. To be honest, I didn't expect things to really be any better after all we were refugees now, and had to start over again from scratch, leaving luxury behind. Our first dinner was kebab provided by the Iraqi neighbors downstairs, who according to the tradition, are required to welcome new neighbors. At night, we ate Dolma (stuffed grape leaves), that Afaf had prepared for us.

The next morning, we woke up early and went with Afaf to the Nationalities Service Center (NSC) to complete the formal paperwork. The next few days were spent getting medical care and vaccinations at a local hospital as scheduled. We lived in that apartment for a whole year, of course after obtaining the owner's approval. By the time we arrived, the children were well settled in at school and could communicate fairly well. Within two months though, I had a heart attack and was admitted to Jeans Hospital, where I received excellent medical care.

We had several relatives and friends scattered throughout the United States, but we had made up our minds not to contact any of them until we were settled and had jobs, which was exactly what we did. After Mutaz started working, the first person I called was Dr. Cecile Ibrahim, the widow of

Abdul's cousin who lives in Rhode Island. I had never met her before, since she had left Iraq with her husband, Dr. Ismail al-Jasim, around the mid-1960s. They never had the chance to enjoy their newly built home in the prestigious Mansour district. From the way in which Abdul praised and loved his cousin, I always felt very close to her though we had never met face to face. That has changed now and we are very close friends. Her parents and siblings were among the few Jews who managed to stay in Iraq until 1977, when they left for Britain. Next, I contacted my second cousins, Maythem, Rasa'il and Hamid in California. Three months after Afaf arrived in the States, Mohammed made his first visit and bought her a 1995 Nissan. Gradually, we got to know a few Iraqi families. I met Dr. Tahseen Al-Saleem's wife during an outing for the ladies. When she told her family about me, her son-in-law, Dr. Firas al Saidi, who had been one of my students at al-Nahrain University, jumped out of his seat in excitement. He immediately called and came to visit me the next day along with his wife and daughters.

I didn't forget my passion for practicing medicine, so I went to the headquarters of the Education Commission for Foreign Medical Graduates (ECFMG) on Market Street. I reported that I passed the exam in 1967, but had no documents with me. Within a short period of time, the official came out to tell me that they found my marks and date of my exam. What an amazing documentation system! She gave me my examination number and said that I can give it to an institution willing to hire me. She also told me that the exam system had changed in recent years and was carried out in three steps (basic sciences, medical knowledge and medical skills) and that I might possibly be exempt from one or two. By that time, we had already moved to a new house and ten days later, I fell on the stairs and broke my ankle; hence, my dream of going back to work just faded away.

In mid-2010, Mutaz got to meet Janice Kelsey online through the List Project. She and her family throw a potluck party every year to celebrate 4th of July. The celebration ends with fireworks in the evening. We were generously invited, though none of us had met Janice before. Mutaz had to work that day, but after much hesitation, I ended up going with Afaf and the children. Janice and Dave gave us such a warm welcome and made us feel as if we were among family. The number of guests at the 2010 party was nearly 100. At that gathering, we met several Iraqis. One of the guests gave me a big hug after finding out who I was, thanking me for teaching her son Dr. Laith Riyadh, who was one of my former medical students. We were more than lucky to meet Madeleine Segall-Marx (Maddy), a sculptor and philanthropist from New York. Within a few days, Maddy introduced me to Dr. Mazin Mohsen, another former student of mine. He was born by cesarean section, one that I performed over 30 years ago. Mazin introduced me to Liz Henry from New Jersey, another philanthropist. Maddy is the recipient of over 40 awards for sculpture, and has recently completed a ten-year art project titled "The Singing Bowl: Voices of the Enemy," it features 25 anti-war artworks from nations in conflict. We got to see her amazing art collection at her home in upstate New York.

In 2011, I received a phone call from Baghdad informing me that burglars had broken into our house and stole our belonging. Other incidents followed this one; we even found out that the 25 year-old King Sago palm tree in our garden was uprooted and stolen. My heart was heavy with sadness when I learned that our personal photo albums and frames were also stolen. Even today, I don't dare to ask whether my two most treasured paintings of downtown Norwich are still there or not. They were gifted to us by my consultant at Norfolk and Norwich Hospital, Mr. Bentall. He chose them from a collection he had drawn, when Abdul and I visited him at his home to wish him well in 1977.

Our Chinese chest, the only possession we could ship to the U.S. from Baghdad in 2015

Memories From My Zooleya

Iraqis have a special affinity for Persian handmade carpets. It doesn't matter whether they are the heavy ones made of wool, or the light ones made of silk. We also love their beautiful manifold designs. They're considered the world's most superior carpets and often take their name from the area where they are made, for example: Hamadan, Mashhad, Kerman, Kashan, Shiraz and Bidjar. I had a few valuable Persian rugs, but one in particular I will never forget was a "Tabriz". My parents gave it to me as a wedding gift. It was a large 10 by 14 foot carpet. Red dominated the background, then designs full of ornate curving featuring intertwined floral and vine figures distributed throughout the backdrop, along with a finer design encircling the borders. The Iraqi embassy in Washington, D.C. has a larger, yet similar one in its waiting area; however, it is in a different color. Every time I go there, I take a good long look at it and sigh with longing. My

"Iraq" memories are like my unforgettable and colorful "Zooleya". They are both forever engraved in my heart. I want to say goodbye one last time... hoping to have closure once and for all.

Farewell my spacious three story villa with its balconies looking out onto the magnificent Tigris River. Farewell my dear Kadhimiya Hospital, the second floor offices, my co-workers, brilliant students, patients, residents and nursing staff. Farewell dear family, neighbors and friends. All of you were landmarks in my life. Farewell, Imam Kadhum and Abu Hanifa shrines. Farewell, *Ilwiya* recreation club and *Alif-Baa* magazine. Farewell to you my Alice in Wonderland Garden, my gardenias, jasmine and roses. Farewell to you stone garden where my son Mohammed spent every penny he saved as a teen. He invested so much time and money to buy and plant the most exotic cactuses and succulents. Farewell to the persistent cleaner who swept the neighborhood streets at 6 a.m. in the morning, to the 1000 varieties of fresh dates tasting sweeter than honey, to the freshly baked bread from the *Tannor,* and to the pigeons that sung lullabies to my grandchildren. Farewell my olive and citrus trees. No more homemade pickled olives and no more fresh homemade juice on Friday morning. Farewell my favorite collection of Abba albums, my cutlery and jewelry, my "*Brother*" sewing machine, my Indian handmade engraved wooden dining room and reception room sets, our photo albums that captured all the happy and weird moments. Farewell al Rashid hotel, the moonlight night-sleeps on the rooftop, farewell to the Baghdad wax works museum, and to the wide roads inlaid with giant Eucalyptus trees. I will forever carry you in the blood that runs through my veins.

Oriental hand knotted carpets –Courtesy of AuthorHouse

Pains and Gains

My four children who grew up to be fine men and women are the apple of my eye. When trudging through hard times, their achievements give me the strength to go on. The creative writing instructor, Robert McKee, once said, "Storytelling is the most powerful way to put ideas into the world today". Therefore, I asked each of my children to share their stories. The reminiscences of Mohammed, Afaf, Mutaz and Abeer are arranged according to their birth order:

Mohammed, Managing Director and Owner of a consulting firm in Sydney, Australia:

"The beginning of my story is no different to any other 6-year-old child; however, I got to know my parents work first hand, when, for the first time, I waited on a busy street for nearly an hour without being picked up. It was in fact my last day of school in Babylon during a golden era in Iraq; an era that I would never experience again. My parents were late picking me from school, because my mother, a gynecologist, had to perform an urgent operation at the hospital. This would later become the norm and something to which I grew accustomed. My mother filled up with tears when she pulled up and saw me standing all alone, waiting and a bit scared. I came to understand firsthand what it meant for both my parents to be doctors. It was a lifetime of on-calls, emergency surgeries and midnight call outs, but the next chapter in my life would transform my thinking as a child. That last day of school in Babylon ushered in an era of mobility, of new adventures and new challenges.

The next chapter of my life started in London. My parents were international students studying in the United Kingdom. With four children, social, financial and educational challenges ahead of them, I grew up quickly and diligently. I put on a brave face and looked after my sisters and brother. I learned a social and homemaking system that would serve me well in later years. The challenge for me in the U.K. was to be part of the school hierarchy, and this was hard. This was an elusive goal that I never fully achieved. I was in many aspects the outsider, the kid with the older bicycle and the less cool parents, the one who was picked up in an old red Volkswagen beetle. But those years were as rewarding as they were challenging. I enjoyed every minute of childhood, and I learned to be happy (and stayed that way) around any person in almost any circumstance.

Just as my days in primary school came to an end, and secondary school was about to become reality, our family moved back to Iraq. The real challenges began there. We moved to a small town with a less cosmopolitan population than I had previously experienced during the last six years of my life, and to a nation at war. Everything was different, but the irony for me was that I was not a stranger in the country where I was born. I could not read or write Arabic. School became a precursor to creativity, bravery and social skills as I had to navigate my way through a complex social system that was tough and masculine, and that demanded connections; strong connections. I had none of these pre-requisites for a stable secondary school life. By some miracle, hard work, and luck, or a combination of all three, I completed secondary school and moved on to high school. At that point, I excelled in both Arabic and English, had a cool bicycle and could drive a car. I was in..

My parents' work would cause us to move during my second year of high school, so the settling in was short lived. I had the "privilege" of being accepted into the best school in the country, Baghdad College. The game was different there. The stakes were higher and the players far more challenging. This was the school for the elite. Politicians, business people, influential figures, and their sons dotted the school. I had never before seen more Mercedes SEC560's in my life. I never really felt settled in at Baghdad College. I had one real friend, Marwan, who was a simple and down to earth guy, with whom I bonded. However, as I gained more social skills, I learned how to negotiate and how to maintain both low and high profiles.

After finishing high school, I had hoped to be able to have an easier transition this time by attending a nearby university; however, it was not to be. I was accepted at the regional university, 800 kilometers from Baghdad, where I was a stranger once again. I lived in a small hotel a few hundred meters from the university. Here is where I learned to cook, using the simplest of utensils and ingredients. Here I made more friends, learned how to manage a tight budget and how to succeed in class. In fact, I did so well that I was able to transfer back to the larger, more prominent Baghdad University at the end of that first year.

Back in Baghdad, driving a Volvo, living in my parents' large house and doing what I did well (studying, communicating, and negotiating), I had what was arguably the best time of my life. For the three remaining years of university, I achieved one exceptional result after another, made more friends and overall, became a better person. However, the next phase of my life was just around the corner, and I was proud of having attained the second highest grade in the entire college, an accomplishment that would help me later on in life.

Mohammed -Sydney, Australia

In 1991, graduates in Iraq were required to do two years of military service, which normally extended to five years or more. One of my best friends, Ghassan, urged me to fail the final exams to allow me to delay having to enter the service, in the hope that Iraq would be more stable a year later. I declined because I wanted to face the challenge the exams offered, and so I moved on to the next phase of my life. My decision proved to be a challenge to my friendship with Ghassan, which sadly ended.

Military service made the prior challenges seem like a walk in the park. Training started at 5:00 a.m. and was grueling. This phase lead most trainees to war within six months after finishing the training. I elected to stay at my parents' house and drive 1.5 hours each morning to arrive at the training site by 5:00 a.m. The physical and mental challenges were significant, but this phase of my life lasted for less than four months. In their true style of care, foresight, and generosity, my parents enrolled me in a Master's Degree program in Jordan that was scheduled to start a couple of months later. That enrollment, along with the high marks I received in the undergraduate program, allowed me to leave the army and continue my postgraduate studies; thus, I was on my way to Jordan.

In Jordan, the feelings of being an outsider, in addition to the angst at having to face the challenges of a new system returned. I used all my energy to learn new skills and to have the physical strength to manage. Two years later, I completed a Master's Degree with distinction faster than anyone else had ever completed one in the history of the university. This led to my earning a scholarship to study for a Ph.D. in Germany. Later on, that led me to migrate to Australia, a place I love and the place where I currently reside. Australia is also my country of citizenship. The challenges faced in Germany, and later in Australia, were interesting and familiar. I had now mastered the art of moving and starting from scratch. Today, I am where I am. I am happy, settled and living in the most beautiful city in the world, Sydney, where I run a consulting firm for boutique management. I owe all this to my parents, Malka and Abdul Wahab. They not only enriched my life, taught me, and looked after me, they also provided me with the emotional strength to make this wonderful journey that I call my life up to this point."

My daughter, Afaf, went through the same scenario as her elder brother in terms of jumping from one school to another. She was accepted at Mustansiriya University and became a superstar student. She attained a bachelor degree in electrical engineering and worked as an instructor at the same school. She later married a man who lived with his parents a few blocks away from our house. He was from a well-known family with a good reputation. The family always seemed friendly and polite, but often the darkest of secrets are well hidden out of sight in the most unlikely of places. Afaf had two adorable children from her marriage, Ahmed and Ruaa. She would always say that she accepted her fate of having a bad husband, but could never tolerate his being a bad father. She eventually filed for divorce after four years of marriage, a painful, yet courageous decision. She took her two kids and came back to live with us. Being the independent person that she is, Afaf joined me at the same school at al Nahrain University, where she excelled as a member of the Information Technology Department. A few years later, she obtained her Master's degree in software engineering from Liverpool University, U.K. Today, Afaf is a software developer at a large company based in Pennsylvania. While being a full time mother, software developer, and homemaker, she was generous enough to share these bits of her story in between her breaks.

Afaf, software engineer at a large company in Pennsylvania, U.S.A.:

Father named me after his mother "Afifa," who passed away shortly after I was born. The name "Afaf" has several meanings in Arabic. Among them are: chaste, virtuous, decent, and pure. My parents, being doctors, were away from the home more often than not. Since I was the older of two girls, I felt it was my duty to take on my mother's responsibilities while she was away. I used a small stool to be able to reach our kitchen sink to wash the dishes, and I learned to cook when I was 11-years-old. My favorite show was a local cooking show called "*Leki Ya Seyideti-For you, my lady.*" It was broadcast on Iraqi TV, on channel 1. I followed the recipes as accurately as I could, and sure enough, the result was many delicious dishes and even cheese! When all else failed, I had an amazing source for recipes, my lovely grandmother, *Bebe Salima*. She was always so warm and welcoming. Whenever I would call her, to ask how to make a certain dish for which I had the ingredients, she would explain it to me in detail, then, tell me to call her if I got stuck.

Grandma was my mentor, not only in cooking, but also for all household chores and life lessons. Whenever I went to visit her, I would sit in her kitchen and closely watch how she made different dishes with her agile hands. She took great pride in her cooking and worked with food like an artist creating a work of art. They say cooking is "*Nefes,*" meaning if you are a caring, generous and loving person, your food will taste as good as your deeds, and vice versa. Never in life have I tasted food as delicious as Grandma's. A particular recipe I loved learning was called *Kubbat Haleb*, a rice dumpling stuffed with ground beef, onions and spices, then deep-fried to a golden yellow color. The trick is to cook the rice to just the right texture and add only enough stuffing to make the dumpling firm enough so that it won't fall apart when frying. I watched my grandmother countless times, longing to make them myself one day. At last, the moment came, while Grandma was making *Kubba,* with me observing as usual, she stopped suddenly, looked at me and said, "*Take some rice and show me whether you can make a dumpling.*" Without hesitation, I quickly took some rice and kneaded it into a beautiful firm dumpling. She took the dumpling and examined it. After making sure I had gotten it right, she said I could continue to make more. At that point, there was not much left to make, but I worked fast and made the most of the remaining rice. From that day forward, I learned to make all sorts of dishes. Today, despite the fast pace of life in the U.S., I still manage to provide homemade goodies to my family and guests. After a feast - *Uzoomeh,* I often hear the line, "Seriously, you should start your own food business." The best thing about food is that it brings people together. When I'm able to lift people's spirits by making a meal they really enjoy, I am the happiest person on the planet. I call it "Kubba power."

I never imagined my life without a husband and father for Ahmed and Ruaa. In fact, I would never have guessed, even for a fraction of a second, that I would file for divorce and become a single mom. The love and support my family has for me and my children are endless. However, that didn't stop me from needing to learn to do everything with my own hands, whether the task be renovating the house, light construction work, assembling furniture, or fixing my own car."

Afaf and Ahmed – Niagara Falls, Ontario, Canada

Mutaz, Arabic medical interpreter and medical terminology trainer in a large hospital in Philadelphia:

"I was born in *Ibn Sina-Avicenna* Hospital, in the upscale neighborhood of *Karadet Maryam* close to the presidential palaces in Baghdad. I like to think that my place of birth somehow explains the affinity I developed for medical terminology. The name Avicenna has strong significance since he was one of the most famous thinkers and writers of the Islamic golden age. He wrote 40 works on the topic of medicine. His most famous books are *The Book of Healing* and *The Canon of Medicine,* the latter became a standard medical text at medieval universities, and it remained in use well into 1650. It was reprinted in New York in 1973.

By age three, we were living in the U.K. I am the only one among my siblings who has curly hair. The others all have beautiful straight hair. I didn't mind though as people loved my curls - especially women - and I often got pats on the head. My best friend at White House Common Elementary School was Stuart Yates. Stuart was a white boy with red hair and freckles. We shared a passion for animals, and both of us wanted to be zookeepers when we grew up. When the decision was made to move back to Iraq, our parents, who seemed little bit nervous, sat us down and tried to explain what that meant. I remember the only question I asked Dad was: "*Are there any animals in Iraq*?" The question drew a bright smile on his face as he said: "*Yes, there are all kinds of birds, insects, fish, turtles, lizards, and frogs.*" Yippee! I'm going to have my own live Kermit, I thought. At that moment, I felt like Mowgli and I couldn't wait to tell Stuart.

In Iraq, the first notable encounter I had at school was with the life sciences teacher *sit* Sadiya. She was a strict old woman, who always wore black in memory of her brother, who was martyred in the Iran war. She was a little bit taller than the average height of a pupil. At that time, I understood more Arabic than I could speak. Actually, I had only a few words on which I could rely in order to get by. When Sadiya asked me a question, and I did not know how to express myself, I just stood silently in front of her waiting to see what would happen next. Thinking that I was being disrespectful, she approached and slapped me on the face - a popular form of discipline surpassed only by hitting the open hands with a ruler. Suddenly, the girl next to me confidently said: "*sit, hada ingilizi*" - "*Miss, he's English.*" The teacher replied in astonishment: "Ya*! Sowdah bwijhi*" - Heavens, oh my! After class, the worried teacher rushed to the school principal thinking that she had jeopardized the strong international ties between Iraq and the U.K. for hitting a "British" student. We found this out because the principal was one of mom's patients and she told her the story at her first opportunity. I loved science so much though that in no time this "British" student had become one of Sadiya's favorites. I also remember my grammar teacher *sit* Jenneh insisting that I use my right hand to write with, in spite of being left- handed. This is a cultural preference toward largely using the right hand.

As far back as I can remember, Afaf, who was the smartest of the four of us, was my math teacher, well through my early college days. She would teach me diligently for hours although she had her own homework to have fun with. As kids, Mohammed would often sneak in when we were studying, and he would start saying and doing funny things to distract me. I couldn't help myself, so I joined in with him for a good laugh. Meanwhile, poor

Afoo would get frustrated and boiling mad at him for getting me off track. The amazing part was that Mohammed always got away with it, and Afaf had to go back to square one and start all over with me. At the end of school year, when it was time to turn in our old books, the bookkeeper, after checking my math book, would give me a satisfactory look of praise for having studied so hard. Little did he know that all the wear and tear on the book was just a result of the frequent blows Afoo inflicted on my head.

In high school, I followed my brother's footsteps by enrolling at Baghdad College and keeping a low profile. Ibrahim Izzat (son of Saddam's vice president, Izzat Al Douri) was in my class. He had a skinny physique just like his father. His personal bodyguard would park Ibrahim's shiny red Mercedes right by the entrance to classroom. The two sons of Sabawi Al Tikriti, Saddam's half-brother, were in a different class. During one of the national celebrations, they brought a number of Arabian horses to the football field. Those majestic creatures so took my breath away that I couldn't resist approaching and patting one of them on the back. Senior year coincided with the 1991 war. Later that year, the exams had been leaked. Therefore, I was unable to fairly compete and be admitted to the college of dentistry as my father had been. Instead, I was accepted at the college of agriculture located on the outskirts of Baghdad. When I went to visit the college, I observed all the framed insects elegantly placed in glass boxes and showcased on the department walls and I was thrilled. At first, I thought they were fake because of their incredible variety of shapes and colors. Then I saw how detailed they were. At that moment, I was convinced that this department, Plant Pathology, was the field that I wanted to study and to make my major. After first taking an exam in chemistry, which was not one of my favorite sciences, I was accepted.

I finished my Bachelor degree in agricultural engineering and started working at the Iraqi Federation of Industries (IFOI) in central Baghdad, a syndicate for plant owners and businessmen. My job was to inspect the machinery of food plants. Should a plant owner apply for a bank loan or approach the court with a legal issue, I would provide a detailed report, and then offer an estimate to be used in determining eligibility. I worked there for eight years until the 2003 war broke out. Afterwards, corruption and violence escalated among the board members, so despite being promoted to office manager to the secretary general, I opted to leave. In 2000, while still working for the federation, I joined al *Shabab-Youth T.V.* as a translator, mainly for movies. After finishing for the day at my engineering job at 2 p.m., I would cross the Sinek Bridge over the Tigris River and head to the station building at Salheya. Uday Saddam Hussein oversaw the facility, and he ran it like a military camp. If he was displeased with someone, disciplinary actions ranged from food and sleep deprivation to breaking bones, or other forms of torture. The lightest of the punishments he doled out was having your head completely shaved and having your feet beaten with a large wooden baton with the words "So we don't forget" written on the side. Two of my co-workers, Haider and Basim were sent to a disciplinary camp in Basmaya. The camp was located on the border between Iran and Iraq, and it was a place where spies were executed. They were subject to all kinds of torture because of a trivial argument between the two. Rumors circulated, that while in detention, Basim suffered a nervous breakdown and was seen in the corner chewing on a bar of soap. However, I knew Basim too well. He overcame those dark times to become a Fulbright graduate and later moved to the U.K. for further studies. I lost that job in 2003 when Paul Bremer, the interim civil governor of Iraq, dismantled the Iraqi media represented by the ministry of mass information, which included my department. The facility was not only leveled to the ground, but the TV and Radio library was burnt down erasing the history of one of the first stations in the Arab world.

There is one scary night in 2005 I will never forget. It happened when my mom began to show signs of a heart attack earlier that evening. It was April and the power had been off for days. I wanted to drive her to the hospital, but neighbors said the main roads were all blocked and it was impossible to get through by car. I called 911 and the dispatcher told me that all of the ambulances were packed carrying the injured from car bombs and explosions. Then, I went outside and ran as fast as I could towards the police station one block away. I saw two policemen in a police car. They yelled at me demanding that I identify myself. From a distance I shouted to them, "*I live close by, my mother ... she's having a heart attack and I need your help right now.*" I was panting, my mouth and lips completely dry.

When I finally reached them, the one sitting in the passenger seat pointed to another police car in the distance and said, "*Quick, run to that car, they will help you.*" So I ran towards the vehicle, to the point where I could almost reach out and touch the car, when the driver took off without saying a word. There was no time to waste. I ran back home and dialed 911 again. The same dispatcher answered, and I told him "*Listen, if it takes me the entire night I will keep calling until you send someone, I will not lose my mother.*" I don't know whether the guy felt sorry for me and decided to help or if something else happened; all I know is that an ambulance was dispatched, and my Mom was taken to the safest place for treatment.

I first set foot on U.S. soil at John F. Kennedy Airport, New York, in mid-June of 2009. My friend, Dave Mingey, was waiting for us at the airport and he wanted to drive us to Philadelphia where we would be staying. He handed me an envelope that held a heartfelt welcome letter and several hundred dollars. Dave was the communications advisor where I worked at the Iraqi Reconstruction Management Office (IRMO). It was there that I had my first experience of simultaneous interpreting. One day, he asked my manager if he could borrow me for a few hours. My manager agreed. It turned out the assignment was simultaneous interpreting in a booth at a conference to discuss the "Reconstruction of the Iraqi army." I wasn't familiar with the sound system, and I was all by myself. This goes against the rule that interpreters work in pairs with each interpreter working for only 30 minutes before their partner takes over for the next 30 minutes, continuing the rotation until finished. My voice began trembling for the first five minutes, but soon my sentences were flowing like butter on bread.

In Philly, many people told me that with my diverse background, I would easily find a job. That turned out to be far from the truth. During the day, I would literally go door to door applying for all kinds of jobs, and from evening until dawn, I would apply for jobs online. Three months later, I was able to find work seven days a week, an average of 50 hours, spread over three part time jobs. I worked as an annotator at the University of Pennsylvania, a receptionist at the Richel D' Ambra Spa, located downtown at the Ritz Carlton Hotel, and in produce department at the Fresh Grocer on North Broad Street. I also volunteered to interpret at the refugee clinic at Thomas Jefferson University Hospital every Wednesday. Today, I'm a nationally certified medical interpreter, a licensed medical terminology trainer, certified ESL tutor, Arabic teacher, a contract interpreter listed on the formal roster of the State Department. I am pursuing a Master's degree in Global and International Education from Drexel University. I currently work full time at one of the best nationwide hospitals in the U.S., Children's Hospital of Philadelphia (C.H.O.P.), where I serve in the fields of language interpretation, cultural support, safety coaching, and education. Yet, in the midst of all this, I still feel I have plenty of room to keep growing and learning.

I've worked at many other renowned hospitals before, but it's more than that with C.H.O.P. To start with, it doesn't even smell or look like a hospital. It is like a huge playground, with colorful floors, walls and ceilings. Once you enter one of the elevators in the main hospital building, you will be welcomed by a recorded child's voice informing you of the floor where you have just arrived. Here, you are greeted with a genuine smile. Like the U.S., C.H.O.P. is a unique place that truly celebrates diversity and I adore it simply because: Hope Lives Here".

Mutaz at Madame Tussuads-New York

Our youngest child, Abeer was, as they say in Arabic, *Akhr alangood*, the last berry of the grape cluster. She has had her share of the hardship just like everyone else. She and her two kids waited for a year in Jordan, until Ammar, her husband, could secure a place for them in the United Arab Emirates. When my dear Abdul was taking his last breaths, she surprisingly stayed firmly by his head reciting the *Shahadetain* as a declaration of faith and reading verses from the Quran. This same person, who is afraid of flies and horror movies, got it together and did what needed be done. My hope is that one day, fate will allow us once again to meet and perhaps be permanently reunited.

Abeer, a Science teacher at an international school in Dubai, UAE:

"I was born in the province of Hilla, and my name means: "Scent of flowers." My childhood centered on fun times. I remember the four of us siblings would sit together or with friends and play monopoly, cards, hide and seek, snakes and ladders, and "grandmother's footsteps." Dad called me *Nemlet ilbeit*, the house ant, because every time he hid sweets in the house hoping to surprise us with them later, I would go on a secret mission to find and devour the treat. Luckily, I still have the whitest teeth among the members of my family. I guess it's in my genes. My happiest moments occurred when I could buy clothes and shoes- lots of them. I also had a passion for Arabic drama series, and during the summer holidays I always watched two soap operas, *Khalti Gmasha* and *To mom and dad with regards.* Both programs were among the most famous Kuwaiti productions, and both mesmerized Arabic audiences for years. The second show addressed family issues in a purposeful, educational, and sometimes comic manner.

I received my bachelor degree in Chemical Science from al Mustansiriya University. As an intern, I practiced at *Al Maghreb* lab, which was located next to my parents' private clinic. There I was working on stool, urine, and blood samples. Despite having a career, my nature was such that I was a family-oriented person to the bone. So, I made the decision that if and when, I ever had a husband and children of my own, would dedicate all my time to them. I first met my husband-to-be, *Ammar Mahdi Dawood*, at a college boat-party months before my graduation. Although we had never met or spoken to each other prior to meeting on that boat, we immediately clicked. The next time I saw him was at our house a few weeks later. He was reading the *Fatihah* with Dad to invoke blessings, as part of the engagement ceremony. We were married shortly after graduation. Ammar was a recent civil engineering graduate at the University of Technology. We lived with my in-laws at their house, and, as time went by, we had a daughter "*Shams*," Sun, and then a son "*Abdullah*."

As the security chaos escalated so did my blood pressure, until it became impossible for us to live in fear around the clock. In late 2004, with a heavy heart, we left our beloved Iraq and moved to *Ash-Sham*, Damascus, Syria. The warm hearted welcome the people gave us, created a sense of optimism. *Dimeshq*, or as the Arabs call it, the city of Jasmine, was a true place of abundance. It had atmospheric *Souks,* Roman ruins, amazingly healthy food, free schools and health care even for non-Syrians; not to mention having very affordable transportation. Unfortunately, jobs were very scarce especially for us. Ammar worked as a salesman for a local weekly newspaper. We lived very frugally there for about a year, until finally, we were able to purchase an apartment in Amman, Jordan. It was situated among the lovely hills of *Um Al Sumac*, but we still had hard luck trying to secure a job.

In 2006, we moved to the United Arab Emirates and have been living there ever since. We live in the charming emirate of Ajman, located along the gulf coast. Today, Ammar is working as a senior engineer at one of Dubai's construction companies. Although he had to start from scratch dozens of times, Ammar never gave up or hesitated, even if it meant doing menial labor to pay the bills. I went into the field of education and now I work as schoolteacher at *Al Zuhour International School* - funny the name means flowers. Although I lost my country forever, I found solace in building a career in which I have tremendous pride. I am investing in the lives of countless students, young boys and girls who carry within them the potential of doing wonderful good for their communities and the world around them.

The values I was raised with and share with my family, allow us to flourish in a place as diverse as the Emirates. I could go on and on about this, but instead, I will just highlight a few of my most fulfilling experiences. Once a year, we spend family time at *Global Village Dubailand*; one of the world's largest tourism, leisure, and entertainment projects. It is the perfect destination to celebrate our differences as human beings. It is a place where our five senses come together to create unforgettable memories. While there, I could enjoy sipping Iraqi cardamom tea in a Baghdadi style *Qahwa*-cafe, admire the red square in the heart of frozen Moscow, smell the aroma of flowers' from Amsterdam and find lots of "wow" moments while shopping.

The New Year's Eve celebrations here are like nothing I have ever seen before in my life. I read somewhere that, of the events to welcome in 2016, *Burj Khalifa* attracted more viewers than the popular Times Square New Year's Eve fireworks. A big applause goes to all the brave, hard workers from around the world, who helped build this mega tall skyscraper; yet the idea itself is more important. All the people gather together in the evening as the year draws to a close, looking up into the sky at the same time, wishing for fresh starts and a brighter future. I couldn't help but think of Abba's famous lyrics, *May we all have a vision now and then, of a world where every neighbor is a friend.*" My heart goes out to my fellow human beings, in all the troubled spots around the globe. I pray that someday, we will all look up at the sky and enjoy the fireworks, wishing that everyone finds their "fresh start," just as I have found mine in the land of Emirates."

The City That Loves You Back

I am no longer able to quench my thirst from the Tigris River. I know in my heart though, that God has a reason for allowing things to happen, and that he has better plan for us. Today I can enjoy the scenery of the Delaware River. I can fill my lungs with the fresh breath of freedom and allow myself to go with the flow. As with Baghdad, it is easy to fall in love with Philadelphia, with its historic, cultural, intellectual, and religious richness.

Once the capital city of the United States (1790-1800), this metropolis has an interesting list of "firsts in the nation." Some examples are: The first zoo, first hospital for children (Children's Hospital of Philadelphia 1855) where Mutaz works, first university (University of Pennsylvania in 1740), the first art school and art museum (Pennsylvania Academy of the Fine Arts in 1805), first daily newspaper (published on Sept. 21st 1784) and the first American flag made by Betsy Ross.

Philadelphia is the largest city in the Commonwealth of Pennsylvania and the second largest city on the East Coast of the United States. It witnessed the independence of the American colonies from Britain in the 18th century. It is also famous for such honored universities as The University of Pennsylvania, Drexel, Temple, LaSalle, Villanova, Arcadia, Villanova and the University of the Sciences.

The Liberty Bell is one of Philadelphia's proud symbols. It was cast in London and sent to the building currently known as Independence Hall, and moved in 1753 to the Pennsylvania State House. Presently, the Liberty Bell is housed at Liberty Bell Center in Independence National Park. Some say that the Liberty Bell cracked for the first time when it was tested upon arrival. It has been recast twice, once adding more copper to make it less brittle and later by adding silver to improve its tone. Part of the Biblical verse inscribed on the top reads: "*Proclaim Liberty throughout all the Land unto the Inhabitants thereof.*"

Philadelphia was originally home to the Quakers (the Church of Friendship - a group of 17th century dissidents from the Church of England, who believe in equality and peace. William Penn, a Quaker himself, was a young lawyer, who believed that Quakers should leave England to live in peace. He requested from King Charles II of Britain a safe home in North America. In exchange for the forgiving of a monetary debt that he owed to Penn's father, the King agreed. William Penn became the founder and administrator of the colony, which was named after him, Pennsylvania (Penn's woods). He wanted it to be a place where everyone would be accepting of others, and where everyone would be free to worship the religion of their choice, without persecution. Many migrated there from Germany, Holland, Switzerland, Scotland and Ireland, to enjoy religious freedom, moderate weather and to take advantage of the fertile soil. The colony expanded, rapidly becoming the third largest and wealthiest British colony in America. Penn built the best-organized city, with wide streets and parks well coordinated around a central town square. He called it "Philadelphia," from the Greek "philos," meaning love, and "adelphos," meaning "brother." Hence, it is called "The City of Brotherly Love."

Penn planned to maintain good relations with Native Americans. He wrote to officials in Delaware, saying that he hoped they would continue as good neighbors and friends. He didn't believe in taking others' land forcibly, rather, he believed in purchasing it at a fair price. In this way, he avoided the violence that took place in other colonies between the indigenous populations and settlers.

An American journalist visited us in 2011. She had spent some time in Jordan and speaks some Arabic. We had several friendly conversations about Arabic and American cultures. She asked me which country I regard as home. I told her: "Iraq is my birthplace. I grew up there, and, as a result of its riches, I became what I am. America honored me with what my Arab brothers failed to offer, a fair chance to live a decent life, in a safe environment, and for this I feel a heartfelt fidelity."

One of the most exciting visits I made was to the University of Pennsylvania Museum of Archeology and Anthropology. Upon entering the museum, I saw the last thing I ever expected to see in my new home, artifacts from ancient Iraq. All of a sudden I had a strange feeling, one I had never experienced before; I simultaneously felt very proud of being Iraqi and American. It was here where two great civilizations embraced each other, where east met west.

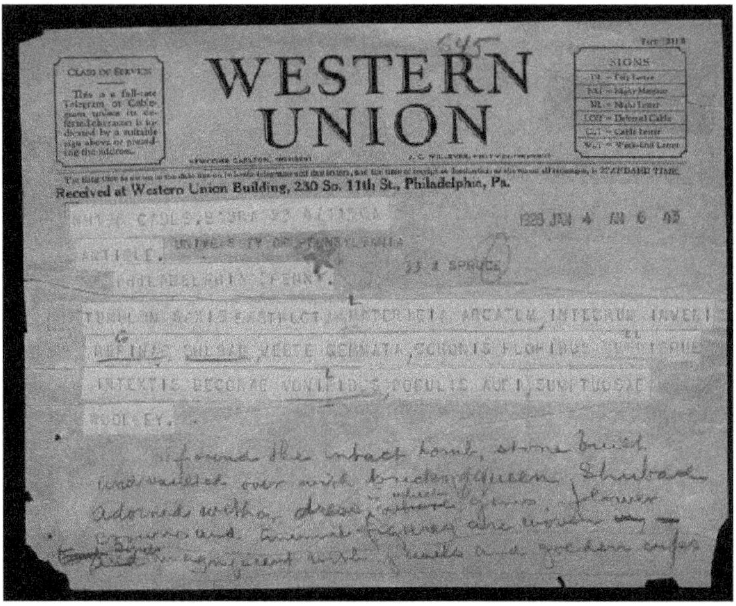
WESTERN UNION
Received at Western Union Building, 230 So. 11th St., Philadelphia, Pa.
1928 JAN 4 AM 6 43

Telegram sent by Archeologist Woolley after finding the tomb of the Sumerian Queen Paubi (Shubad) in Ur, Courtesy of Penn Museum

The iconic Liberty Bell, Independence National Historical Park, Philadelphia, Pennsylvania

Bibliography

- Charles Tripp. A History of Iraq, New Edition 2002. Cambridge University Press. ISBN 0-521-52900-X
- Marion Von Alderstein. The Penguin Book of Etiquette, First edition 2002. Viking, Penguin Books Australia. ISBN 0 670 87757 3
- Joseph Tragert. The Complete Idiots guide to Understanding Iraq, Second Edition 2004. Alpha, the Penguin Group (USA) ISBN 1-59257-357-6
- Gilles Munier. Iraq an Illustrated History and Guide, First American Edition 2004. Interlink Books. ISBN 1-56656-513-8 (pbk)
- http://www.d-maps.com/carte.php?num_car=15300&lang=en

CPSIA information can be obtained
at www.ICGtesting.com
Printed in the USA
BVHW031815120519
548076BV00001B/16/P

9 781524 619701